MUSIC: FOR BEGINNERS

7 Manuscripts in 1 Book, Including: Music Theory, How to Read Music, How to Play Guitar, How to Play Piano, How to Play Ukulele, How to Play Chords and How to Play Scales

Preston Hoffman

More by Preston Hoffman

Discover all books from the Music Best Seller Series by Preston Hoffman at:

bit.ly/preston-hoffman

Book 1: *Music Theory*

Book 2: *How to Read Music*

Book 3: *How to Play Guitar*

Book 4: *How to Play Ukulele*

Book 5: *How to Play Piano*

Book 6: *How to Play Chords*

Book 7: *How to Play Scales*

Themed book bundles available at discounted prices:

bit.ly/preston-hoffman

Table of Contents

3

MUSIC
THEORY
FOR BEGINNERS
The Only 7 Exercises You Need to Learn
Music Fundamentals and the Elements
of Written Music Today
PRESTON HOFFMAN

BOOK 1

MUSIC THEORY: FOR BEGINNERS

The Only 7 Exercises You Need to Learn Music Fundamentals and the Elements of Written Music Today

Preston Hoffman

Table of Contents

Introduction

Thank you and congratulations on purchasing this book, *"Music Theory: For Beginners"* I have written this book to provide you with the steps that you need to take to understand the fundamentals of music theory from a beginner's standpoint.

One of the most common problems that many people face when it comes to music theory is the inability to get a good book that sticks to the fundamental aspects. Music theory is not exactly a topic that will get your heart pounding, so most people want content that will explain music fundamentals in a clear and concise manner. Most music theory books either bore the reader with long, drawn-out explanations, or they toss in some complex concepts that leave you totally confused.

However, this is where this book is different. This book provides you with the only seven exercises that you need as a beginner to master the fundamental elements of written music. These interactive exercises are all based on seven topics that form the basis of every good music theory course. The exercises are spread throughout the book so that once you finish reading each chapter, you can test yourself. I have taken the time to make the questions as challenging as possible yet simple enough for any beginner to understand. In any case, the answers have been provided at the end of the book.

You will not find yourself struggling with complex theories here. I have written this book with the beginner in mind, so every chapter covers a single aspect of music theory. This is to ensure that you move step-by-step, mastering one foundational topic before you move onto the next one. You will learn the common notation system, scales, clefs, key signatures, intervals, chords, and much more.

I have tried to make sure that the topics move sequentially in terms of the level of difficulty. My goal is to take your hand and walk you through every topic and exercise so that you feel comfortable with the content. From my experience with reading and writing music, I know that if you get the first step right, then the next one will automatically fall into place.

By the time you finish reading this book, you will be much more confident in reading and even writing your own music. Yes, it's true! The exercises you will go through in this book will test you and help you grow your musical abilities. I can promise you that with this book, you will finally get to learn all you ever wanted to know about music theory in a fun and interactive way. This is a personal guarantee!

Are you ready? Let's go!

Chapter One: Understanding Music Theory

In this chapter, you will learn about what music theory is all about and why it is important for beginners to have a firm theoretical foundation. You will also go through a brief and painless history of written music. Finally, you will get to discover the seven exercises that are fundamental to the learning of music.

What is Music Theory?

The simplest way to define music theory is this: It is the language that enables you to read, understand, and play any kind of music that has been composed. Music theory is made up of rules and concepts that are designed to govern the way music is written and performed.

Another way to look at it is that music is a language that consists of many various parts. Each part is then divided into smaller sections. If you want to learn how to speak the whole language, you must start by learning the smaller sections first and how to combine them to form the larger parts. Then you must learn how to put together those large parts to communicate whatever message you have through that language.

We learn music theory so that we know how to put the elements together to compose music. That is music theory in a nutshell.

As a beginner, it is easy to fall into the trap of feeling overwhelmed when you hear the words "music theory," but there is really nothing to worry about. The critical thing to keep in mind when learning about music theory is that the music preceded the theory. The art of making musical sounds dates back thousands of years, and at that time, our ancestors didn't have any kind of theory to rely on. They just pounded on their drums and played it by ear. If you are already playing an instrument, then you most likely have a rough idea about music theory. The only issue is that you haven't learned the terms and technicalities yet.

Like I said before, music theory is a language that allows musicians to read and perform compositions the way the composer intended. However, it is important to also note that there are some musicians who are not able to read or write music, yet they can still make awesome melodies and sounds. There are some people who can hear and speak English but cannot read or write it. Therefore, some people view learning music theory as boring and unnecessary.

On the other hand, I believe that a student can progress much further in learning a new language by training himself/herself to read and write it. It is the same with music theory. If you want to master new techniques, gain more confidence, and perform new styles, you need to learn music theory.

Now let's go back a bit into history to unearth the beginnings of music theory.

Musical Beginnings

According to historians, complex musical instruments were already being used as far back as 7000 B.C. Archaeologists have found bone flutes that can still be used to create short performances for modern listeners to hear.

There are pictographs from 3500 B.C. that depict the ancient Egyptians playing clarinets, harps, and lyres. By the year 1500 B.C., the people in Northern Syria had modified the Egyptian harp and created the first ever two-stringed guitar. The instrument even had tuning pegs and a hollow soundboard for amplifying sounds.

So why am I telling you all this?

If you look at the history of ancient music, you will realize that distinct cultures spread out all over the world were able to create music with very similar tonal qualities. How was this possible? It is believed that certain patterns of musical notes just sound right while others do not. If this is the case, then music theory is simply the search for why and how certain notes sound right or wrong. To put it more plainly, music theory is important because it helps us understand *why* an object sounds a particular way and *how* we can reproduce that exact sound.

Ancient Greece is believed to be the origin of music theory. The Greeks even built schools that taught the science and philosophy of analysing music. It was Pythagoras who went as far as creating the 12-pitch octave scale that resembles the one we currently use today. Pythagoras achieved this using a device known as the Circle of Fifths, which you will learn about later in this book.

A lot of the musical theory you are about to learn is based on the works of the ancient Greeks. But unlike the Greek language, this book is much simpler to read and understand.

The Significance of Theory in Your Music

It is easy to think that making great music is as simple as sitting down, playing whatever note you want, going in any direction you see fit, and even stopping at any stage of the performance. That is often the view of most aspiring musicians who would love to play an instrument.

However, such kind of performances, if they do exist, would cause confusion and sound annoying to the listeners. Only those musicians who have thoroughly mastered how to stack notes and chords adjacent to each other can manage to perform a spontaneous jam that listeners would love. In other words, since music is a language that communicates a message, you must learn how to connect with your listeners at all times.

Learning musical theory can also inspire you a great deal, as you will soon find out after you finish reading this book. It is a tremendously great feeling when you discover that you can put together a chord progression and create an awesome song out of it. How would you feel if you could look at a piece of classical music and know that you can play it for the first time?

What about being confident enough to call up your friends and ask them to come over and jam with you? You wouldn't be able to do that without learning music theory since you need a way to communicate with other musicians. You use music theory to talk to one another as you play your various instruments.

The truth is that music theory will broaden your horizons as a musician. If you see yourself as a potential rock guitarist, you will be able to know which notes to play in which key. If it's classical music you are interested in, you will know how to sight-read and maintain a consistent beat. Music is fun but it also requires a prominent level of discipline. At the end of it all, it is worth it!

The Seven Fundamental Exercises

There are a lot of elements that you will have to learn to become an accomplished musician. Of course, we all wish that we could somehow sit down with an instrument and start playing beautiful music without going through the hassle of any formal training. But the reality is that you need structured exercises that will prepare you for your future as a music maestro.

In the next few chapters, we are going to cover music theory fundamentals that will help you get started. There are seven elements that you will have to master to learn these elements effectively. They are:

1. Learning the staff and music alphabet

2. Common notation

3. Basic elements of music (rhythm, melody, harmony, etc)

4. Mastering the scales

5. Building intervals

6. Understanding key signatures

7. Forming chords

Every single one of these elements is critical to your progress as a beginner. They will teach you the individual elements of music and how they are put together to create a solid foundation for reading, playing, and studying music.

Chapter Summary

Here is a summary of the key points of this chapter:

- Music theory is the rules and concepts that enable us to read, understand, and play any kind of musical composition.
- It is possible to play music without learning music theory, but if you want to go further in learning new techniques and performing new styles, you must learn music theory.
- Though complex musical instruments date back as far as 7000 B.C., the ancient Greeks are the ones credited with establishing schools for analysing the elements of music.
- Learning musical theory will enable you to communicate more effectively with listeners and fellow musicians, while also inspiring confidence in your own musical abilities.
- There are seven key exercises that will help you learn the fundamentals of music theory.

In the next chapter, you will learn about the staff and how we use the music alphabet to write music. It isn't a difficult topic, but since the rest of the book will be based on what you learn in the next chapter, you need to make sure that you go through it thoroughly.

Chapter Two: Learning the Staff

In this chapter, you will learn about the staff. It is important to start by learning the main way that we write music. You will learn what the staff looks like, the several types of clefs, and how to arrange notes when writing your music. There will also an exercise at the end of the chapter to test what you have learned.

Human beings started making music way before writing was invented. Even to this day, some musicians choose to play "by ear," which means they don't rely on written music. However, it is important to write music so that it can be shared and studied. This means that we must have system to represent music, hence the need for a music alphabet.

What is the Music Alphabet?

The musical alphabet is an arrangement of letters that enables us to write the sounds that we want to play. Every time you sit down to play music with others, the first thing you do is talk about what you plan on playing. By talking I don't mean just telling each other stories or describing your music verbally. The language of communication should be specific to music, and that is where the music alphabet comes in. The alphabet is the means of representing your music.

Before we go into the musical notes themselves, let's start by learning about the most widespread way of writing music. This is the staff.

The Staff

Now that you have learned about the music alphabet, it's time to tackle a very important component of music. All instruments that play specific pitches are written on the staff, which is comprised of five horizontal parallel lines. Music notes are usually placed either on the lines or in the spaces between the lines. The music on a staff is read from left to right.

In the image below, you will notice some short lines that are above or below the staff. These are known as **ledger lines**. These are used to show a note that is too low or too high to be placed on the staff.

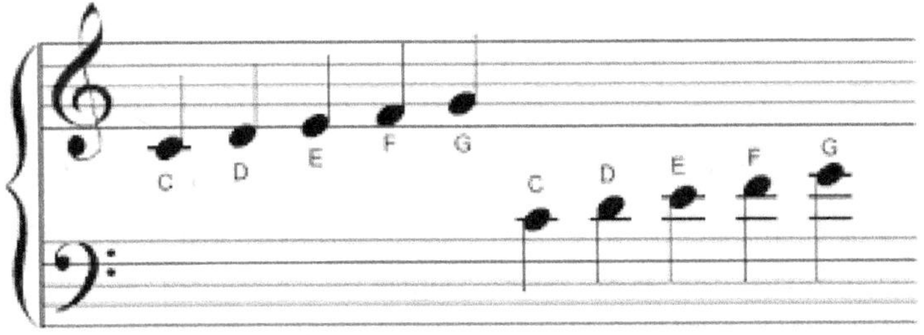

Figure 2.1

To make reading music much easier, vertical lines are used to split the staff into sections. These lines are known as ***bar lines***. Each section that is formed on the staff is then called a ***measure*** or ***bar***. At the end of every staff, there are two lines that mark the end of a section of music or song. These are known as ***double bar lines***. A heavy double bar line indicates that you have reached the end of the song. A light double bar line means the end of a section of music.

Figure 2.2

You may be wondering what some of the symbols and shapes are on the staff above. These will be discussed later in this chapter.

Clefs

In figure 2.2, you notice a symbol that is placed at the beginning of the staff. This is the ***Clef symbol***. It tells you the type of note that is found on every line and space of the staff. There are two kinds of clefs; the treble clef (or G clef) and the bass clef (or F clef).

The reason why it's called a G clef is that its body curls around the line that represents the G note. For the F clef, the symbol curls around the line representing the F note. The notes in the staff are always arranged in ascending order from top to bottom, but they are positioned differently depending on the type of clef being used. The reason why we use different clefs is to cover as many notes within the human voice range as possible, as well as most of the instruments used. People and instruments with high voice ranges use the treble clef while those with lower ranges use bass clef.

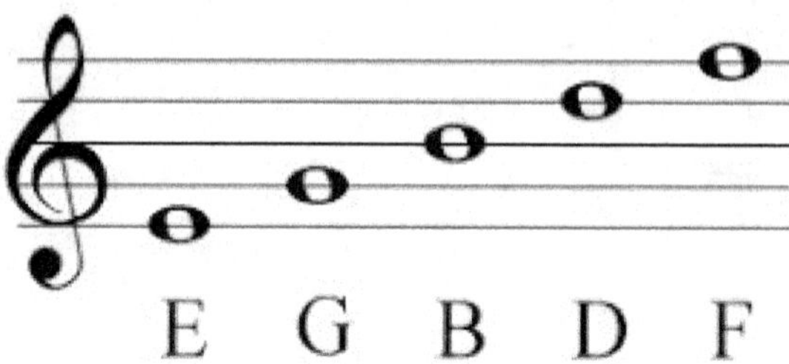

Figure 2.3

Figure 2.4

Exercise 1

1. Draw the staff on a piece of paper and practice writing the two clef symbols on the staff. Draw as many as you can until you learn it perfectly.

2. Draw the staff with treble and name all the spaces on the staff.

3. Draw the staff with bass clef and name the lines in it.

4. On a staff with a treble clef, name the ledger lines and spaces above the staff.

5. On a staff with a bass clef, name the lines and spaces below the staff.

Chapter Summary

Here are some key points you need to remember:

- The musical alphabet is an arrangement of letters that enable us to write the sounds that we want to play.
- The notes on the staff are placed either on the lines or in the spaces between the lines.
- Notes on the staff are arranged in ascending order.
- Ledger lines are used when showing notes that are too high or too low to appear on the staff.
- A bar line splits the staff into sections called measures or bars.
- A heavy double bar line indicates the end of a song.
- A light double bar line indicates the end of a section of music.
- There are two types of clef symbols – the treble clef and the bass clef.

In the next chapter, you will learn about music notation. These are considered the building blocks of music and are necessary when writing your music.

Chapter Three: Understanding Common Notation

In this chapter, you will learn the A-B-C's of the musical language. We will talk about the building blocks that form the foundation of musical theory. These include notes, pitch, octave, beats, and time signature. There will also an exercise at the end of the chapter to test what you have learned.

Common notation simply refers to the standard system that we use to represent music notes. It is more widely used than other types of music notation that have been invented, for example, tablature. You have already learned about one part of common notation in the previous chapter. Now let's talk about notes and pitches.

Notes

Every piece of music you will encounter consists of notes. They are the building blocks of music. A note is simply a letter of the musical alphabet that represents the *pitch* made by a musical instrument.

The pitch of a note refers to how low or high it sounds. Pitch is dependent on the frequency and wavelength of the sound wave of a note. If the frequency of the sound wave is high, and the wavelength is short, the pitch will be high. Since very few musicians are keen on such kind of physics terminologies, they use letters to represent different pitches.

There are seven letters that form the music alphabet. These are:

A B C D E F G A

or:

C D E F G A B C

These seven letters are used to name the white keys on a keyboard. As you can see above, you start with the letter A and proceed to the letter G. After G, instead of going to H, we go back and start counting from A. In music, each set of seven letters (A – G or C - B) is referred to as an **octave**. The moment you reach the eighth note, you begin the next octave.

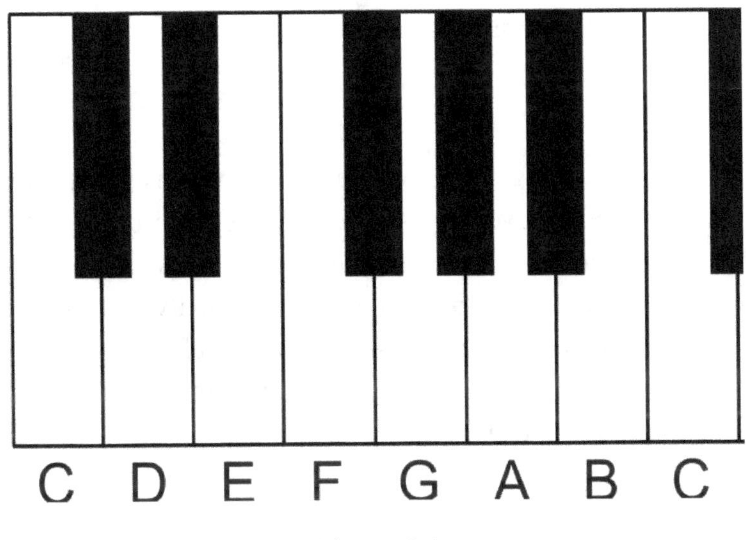

Figure 3.1

But there's one thing that you need to be keenly aware of here. As you move toward the right side, or *up the alphabet*, you realize that you will meet a note with the same letter name as another one before. However, this next note will be at a higher octave than the previous one.

In figure 3.1 above, the second C note has a pitch that is at a higher octave than the first. If you were to move up the alphabet, the third C note would be a higher pitch than the second one, and so on. You can also move in the opposite direction, and this is referred to as going *down the alphabet*.

Sharps and Flats

Though there are only seven letters in the music alphabet, there are more than seven notes. The seven letters from A to G represent *natural* notes. Natural simply means it is a regular note. However, there are five other notes that are usually placed in-between these natural notes. This brings the total number of notes in the music alphabet to 12. These five other notes are represented as ***sharp notes*** (♯) and ***flat notes*** (♭).

A sharp note is a note that is higher in pitch than its natural letter. For example, G♯ (pronounced G sharp) is higher than G. On the other hand, a flat note is a note lower than its natural letter, so A♭ (pronounced A flat) is lower in pitch than A. These sharp and flat notes are used to represent the black keys on a keyboard.

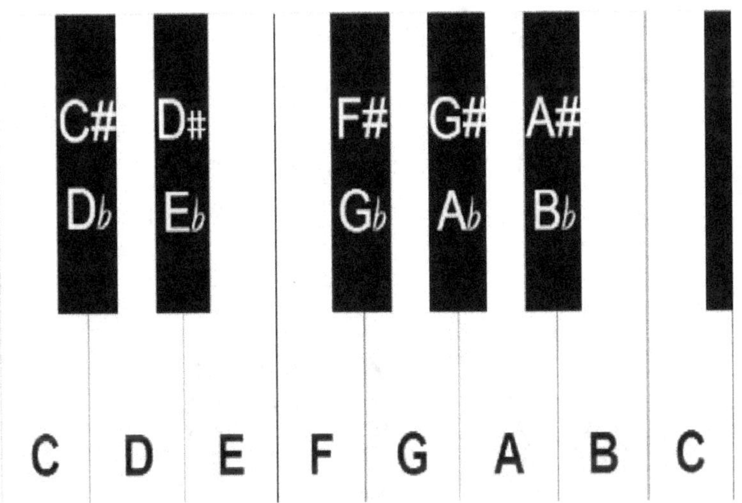

Figure 3.2

From the image above, you can see that in some instances, the sharps and flats occupy the same key. This means that they refer to the same note but are given different names depending on where they are used. This is what is known as **enharmonics**. In other words, F♯ is the same note as Gb, and C♯ is the same note as Db, and so on.

If you are keen, you may have noticed that there are some notes that do not have any sharps or flats between them. This happens between the E-F notes and B-C notes. This shouldn't be taken to mean that there is no E♯ or Cb. We simply refer to them as F or B. So, when you raise an E by one note you get an F. Also, when you lower a C note you get a B.

The sharp symbol usually indicates that the particular note is one half-step higher than its natural equivalent. For example, G♯ is one half-step higher than G. In the same way, the flat symbol indicates that the note is one half-step lower than its natural equivalent. So, A♭ is one half-step lower than A.

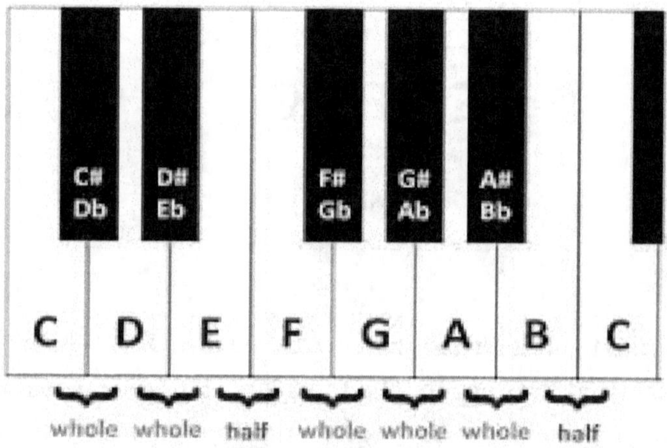

Figure 3.3

In other words, the distance between the G note and the A note is *one whole step*. When you see two adjacent notes having a sharp or a flat note between them, then that means that they are a whole step apart. Therefore, from figure 3.3, it is clear to see that most of the notes on the keyboard are one whole step apart except the E-F notes and B-C notes. These are only one half-step apart.

Parts of a Note

In common notation, sounds are written in form of notes. The two most critical pieces of information that written music should convey to a musician are the pitch to be played and its duration. A note that is placed high on the staff should be played at a higher sound.

To determine the pitch of a note, look at the clef, key signature, and the line or space the note is placed. To determine the duration of a note (how long it lasts), you look at the shape of the note, its tempo, and time signature.

There are three specific parts of a note. There is the head, the stem, and the flag.

- **The Head** (3) – This is the rounded section of a note. The head can be shaded or hollow. Every note must have a head.

- **The Stem** (2) – This is the vertical straight line that is linked to the head. Quavers, crotchets and minims all contain stems. Stems can point either up or down depending on the position of the note on the staff. Notes on or above the centre line have stems pointing down. Notes below the centre line have stems pointing up.

- **The Flag** (1) – This is the line that sticks out from the top or bottom of the stem. Only quavers and shorter notes carry flags.

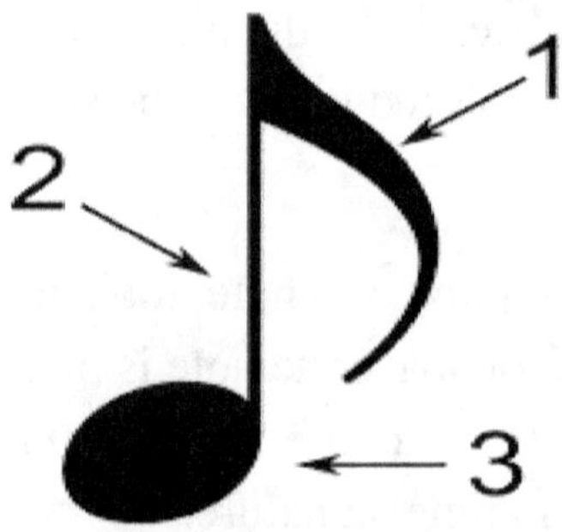

Figure 3.4

The pitch of a note is determined by the position of the head of the note, not the entire body. The head, the stem and the flag are all factors that must be considered when deciding how much time a note is given.

Note Duration and Values

Note duration is defined as the amount of time that a note is played. Each note usually has its own value, and these include the semibreve, minim, crotchet, quaver, and semiquaver. They are shown in this exact order in the image below.

Figure 3.5

The Whole (Semibreve) Note

This note is represented by a hollow oval and has no stem. It is the longest note in modern music and lasts for a full four beats.

This means that for four entire beats, all you must do is play and hold that one note.

The Half (Minim) Note

This is half the value of a semibreve and is held for half as long as the whole note. Two minims occupy the same length of time as a semibreve. It is represented by a hollow oval with a stem.

The Quarter (Crotchet) Note

This is a quarter of a semibreve. Four crotchets occupy the same length of time as a semibreve, which means a crotchet is one beat long. It is represented by a shaded oval with a stem.

The Eighth (Quaver) Note

This is half the length of time as a crotchet. It is represented by a shaded oval with a stem and a flag. The flag cuts the value of a note by half.

The Sixteenth (Semiquaver) Note

Two semiquavers occupy the same length of time as one quaver. It is represented by a shaded oval with a stem and two flags.

If two notes that have flags are next to each other, they are sometimes connected using a ***beam***. This makes it possible to group flagged notes so that the music is easier and faster to read. The same principle also applies to semiquavers. A note must have the same number of beams as it does flags.

Figure 3.6: Semiquaver with beam

Dotted Notes

By now you know that a minim is half the length of a semibreve; a crotchet is half of a minim, and so on. But what do you do if you want a note length that is not half of another note? That's where the dotted note comes in. A dotted note is 1 ½ times the length of the same note. So, you end up with the original note length and half of that note length. For example, a dotted minim would have a duration that is as long as a minim plus a crotchet; or three crotchets.

If a note has two dots, it simply means that each dot adds half the length of the previous note. This is shown in figure 3.7 below.

Figure 3.7

Time Signatures

These are usually indicated at the front end of the staff and are placed after the clef symbol and key signature. The time signature doesn't appear on every staff. It is used only when there is a change in the meter. *Meter* refers to the basic rhythm of the music. Time signature represents the meter and tells you how you should write it.

A fraction represents time signatures. The number at the top indicates the number of beats per measure while the number at the bottom indicates the type of note that will be used to carry the beat. The next section explains this more clearly.

Figure 3.7

Beats

There are many ways to organize music, and one of them is by splitting the time into small periods known as ***beats***. Most of the actions that go with a piece of music occur at the start of the beat. For example, when you tap your foot or clap your hands, you are making those sounds or movements at the start of the beat. This is usually referred to as being "on the downbeat" since it corresponds to the moment when the conductor's baton reaches the bottom of its path.

The downbeat is the most substantial section of a beat, though some are stronger than the rest. Beats form a pattern such as strong-weak-weak-strong-weak-weak. Therefore, beats are further grouped into measures or bars. For example, a beat such as strong-weak-weak-strong-weak-weak would be written as 1-2-3-1-2-3, which means that each measure must contain three beats.

We already talked about how time signature indicates the number of beats per measure and the kind of note that carries a beat. For example, figure 3.7 has a time signature that requires three quarter (crotchet) notes in all the measures on that particular staff. In other words, every measure will have three crotchets. We usually say that such a piece is in "three four" time.

Don't forget what we learned earlier. A crotchet (quarter) note is one beat long. In other words, every measure on the staff should have the equivalent of three beats. These can still be represented as one minim and a crotchet, or six quavers per measure.

Exercise 2

1. Complete the following series of natural notes: A B _ _ E F _ _

2. Provide an alternative name for the following:

    a. A♯

    b. D♭

    c. G♭

    d. E♭

Fill in the blanks:

3. 1 semibreve = _____________ quavers

4. 1 minim = _____________ quarters

5. 1 minim = 1 quarter + _____________ eighths

6. Draw two staves with a treble clef symbol and time signatures showing *two four-time, three eight time,* and *six four time*. Fill in each measure with a different combination of note lengths. Use at least one dotted note in each staff.

Chapter Summary

Here are some of the key points you need to remember:

- A note is a letter that represents the pitch made by a musical instrument.
- An octave is a set of notes from one letter to the next pitch by the same letter name.
- The symbol ♯ represents sharp notes.
- Flat notes are represented by the symbol ♭.
- Enharmonics are two notes that have equal pitches but are known by different names.
- There are five note values - semibreve, minim, quarter, quaver, and semiquaver. Each note lasts half the beat of the previous one.
- Music is divided into short time periods called beats.
- The time signature is shown using a fraction. The number at the top indicates the number of beats per measure. The number at the bottom indicates the type of note that will be used to carry the beat.

In the next chapter, you will learn about the building blocks of music. These are the basic elements of every musical piece, and they include aspects like rhythm, harmony, melody, timbre, and dynamics.

Chapter Four: The Basic Elements Music

In this chapter, you will learn about the essential elements that make music what it really is. These are aspects that even non-musicians can understand. As long as you have an appreciation for good music, you should be able to pick out these musical building blocks.

We are going to cover a number of these basic elements here. It is also important to note that musical theory experts hold differing opinions as to the total number of the elements of music. Some claim that there are as few as four while others say that there are as many as 10. Here we shall be covering rhythm, harmony, melody, timbre, texture, and dynamics.

Creating Rhythm

The primary reason why we study music theory is to be able to describe different musical pieces regarding how similar or different they are about the above six elements. Rhythm is considered one of the most basic components of any kind of music. Some types of music don't have harmony or melody, but every piece of music must have rhythm.

So, what exactly is rhythm?

Rhythm can be defined as the pattern of sounds repeated throughout the music. We can also say that rhythm is the arrangement of note lengths in music. Music and time go hand in hand, which means that rhythm has to be heard over a period of time. Rhythm is usually shaped by the meter and incorporates other elements such as *tempo* and *beat*.

Tempo is the speed at which you play a particular piece of music. When creating a composition, you indicate the tempo using an Italian word. For example, if you look at the starting point of a score, you may see words like *Largo* (slow pace), *Moderato* (moderate pace), or *Presto* (very fast pace). Here are some common tempo markings and their translations:

- Adagio – slow

- Vivo – lively and brisk

- Lento – slow

- Molto – a lot

- Mosso – motion or movement

- Piu – more

- Allegro – fast

- (un) poco – a little

- Meno – less

Harmony

Harmony is the result of having more than one pitch being heard at the same time. When you hear two or more notes being played at one time, you are listening to harmony. Harmony provides support for the melody and gives it texture. Harmony is usually described as being diminished, augmented, major, and minor.

Melody

Melody can be described as the general tune that is created when you play a succession of notes. It is influenced by your rhythm and pitch. A musical piece can have just one melody running through it, or it may have several melodies stacked in a verse-chorus form.

Timbre

Timbre is the quality of a sound that differentiates one musical instrument or voice from another. It is also called *tone color*. Timbre has nothing to do with the volume, length, or pitch of a sound.

For example, if you play a specific note on a clarinet and then on an oboe for five seconds at a specific volume, a listener can easily know that the notes are different. This is because the timbre of a clarinet is different from that of an oboe.

Texture

This refers to the type and number of layers that are used in a musical composition. Texture can be a single melodic line (monophonic), several melodic lines (polyphonic), or the main melody together with chords (homophonic).

Dynamics

This is the intensity that a musical piece is performed. In written music, dynamics are represented by symbols or abbreviations that indicate the volume that a note should be sung or played. Just like tempo, dynamics are derived from Italian words. For example, *fortissimo* indicates an extremely loud passage while *pianissimo* indicates an extremely soft section of music.

Here are some typical dynamic markings:

- mf mezzo forte   = medium loud

- f   forte   = loud

- ff fortissimo = very loud

- fff fortississimo = very, very loud

- p piano = soft

- pp pianissimo = very soft

- mp mezzo piano = medium soft

Exercise 3

1. Test yourself and see whether you can interpret what these Italian tempo markings mean:

   - Poco pin mosso

   - Piu vivo

   - Un poco allegro

   - Molto adagio

2. Write these dynamics in order from the quietest to the loudest: f, p, mf, ff, pp, and mp

Chapter Summary

Here are some of the key points you need to remember:

- Rhythm is the pattern of sounds repeated throughout the music.
- Rhythm depends on the tempo and beat of the music
- Tempo refers to the pace of the music and is usually indicated by Italian words.
- Harmony is created when more than one pitch is played at the same time.
- Melody is the general tune created when a succession of notes is played. A musical piece can have one or more melodies.
- Timbre is what tells us the difference between sounds made by different instruments.
- Texture is the number and type of layers in a musical composition. It can be monophonic, polyphonic, or homophonic.
- Dynamics is the intensity that music is played, and its markings are derived from Italian words.

In the next chapter, you will learn more about the different types of music scales. These are considered to be subsets of the notes you learned in Chapter 3.

Chapter Five: Forming Music Scales

In this chapter, you will learn how to create the different types of music scales. You will start with the simplest one, which is the major scale, and then proceed onto the more complex minor scale.

Music scales can be described as a set of notes arranged in sequential order, chosen to be used for a particular song. Why do we choose those notes? Simply because they sound great together! Though different cultures have adopted a variety of scales, the most common one is the major scale.

In order to create a scale, you need to go through the music alphabet (remember the seven letters from A to G?) and pick out notes that go well together. The notes chosen must achieve a particular sound. In most cases, you can do this by combining whole steps and half steps.

Tonal Centre

Every scale begins with the note that it is named after. That particular note is referred to as the ***tonal centre*** of that scale, and it is where the music in that scale feels "at rest."

For example, in most cases, music in the C major scale always ends on a C major chord. The music will begin on the C note, return to the C note repeatedly, and the melody will be based on the C note so much that listeners be able to identify where the tonal centre of that piece of music is.

Major Scales

If you have ever heard a song that sounds cheerful, uplifting, and fun, then it was probably written in a major key. Music that is written using a particular key only uses some of the many notes available. This sequence of notes then forms what we call a scale. Major keys are used to build major chords to then form a major scale.

It is important to know that different songs can use different scales, and different parts of a song can also make use of different scales. Scales are normally written in a sequential order from one note to the next note of the same letter. For example, we can have a scale that ranges from note C to the next note C, as shown below.

C D E F G A B C

As we already learned, each set of seven letters of the music alphabet forms an octave. Therefore, we can say that the above scale is a one-octave scale. To create a two-octave scale, you simply continue the same sequence until you land on the next note with the same letter name.

C D E F G A B C D E F G A B C

The range of notes from C to C is what forms the scale for C major. None of the notes in this particular scale has a sharp or a flat. On the other hand, the D major scale has two sharps. These are F sharp and C sharp.

D E F♯ G A B C♯ D

So, the question you are probably asking is: How are we supposed to know which notes should be sharpened and which ones should be flattened? The first method involves the use of a chart. However, this can be a cumbersome way since you have to keep referring all the time. You may even be forced to cram all that information into your head. The better alternative is to learn how to use whole and half steps.

Whole Steps and Half Steps

We talked about how the pitch of a sound represents how high or low the sound is. In music, we usually say that one note is either much higher or lower than another. This distance between two pitches is known as a half step. If you look at figure 5.1 below, you will be able to understand this better. This method of counting up whole and half steps can be used to form music scales from scratch.

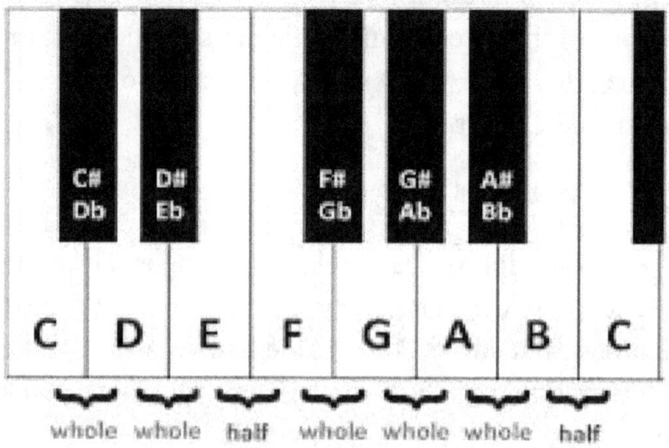

Figure 5.1

For example, we know that the distance from A to A♯ is a half step. The distance between B and B♭ is a half step. In other words, two consecutive half steps form a whole step. The format of any major scale usually follows this kind of sequence:

whole whole half whole whole whole half

This can also be written as:

w w h w w w h

This sequence means that there is a whole step between the first and second note, the second and third note, the fourth and fifth note, the fifth and sixth note, and the sixth and seventh note. There is a half step between the third and fourth note and the seventh and eighth note.

Please memorize this pattern because every major scale you encounter from here onwards will use this same sequence.

So, if we want to form the C major scale, we can write it as:

C w D w E h F w G w A w B h C

Figure 5.2

However, if we want to form the D major scale, we can write it as:

D w E w F♯ h G w A w B w C♯ h D

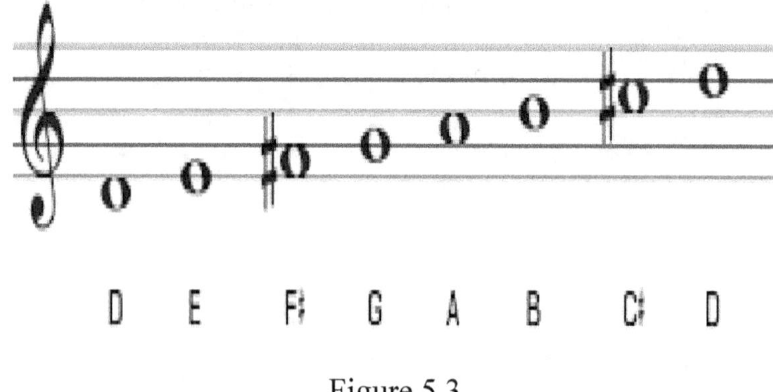

Figure 5.3

Minor Scales

Most people think of minor scales as confusing. This is because many music students usually start learning about the major scale first and end up focusing on it more than the minor scale. This situation isn't helped by the fact that there are a number of different types of minor scales that are often confused with one another. However, we will only focus on the most common minor scale in this book.

It is important to note that a piece of music in a particular major scale will sound the same as music in another major scale. For example, music that is in C major will sound somewhat similar to music in D major.

However, music in D major will sound very different from that in D minor because the notes in a minor scale are arranged in a very different pattern. Music written using a minor key has a sad, ominous, or mysterious sound than that written using a major key.

Natural Minor Scale

A natural minor scale is a scale where every note is played in a minor key signature. A natural minor scale is formed by starting at the tonal centre and moving upward using the following step pattern:

Whole half whole whole half whole whole

w h w w h w w

For example, music written in D minor scale will look like this:

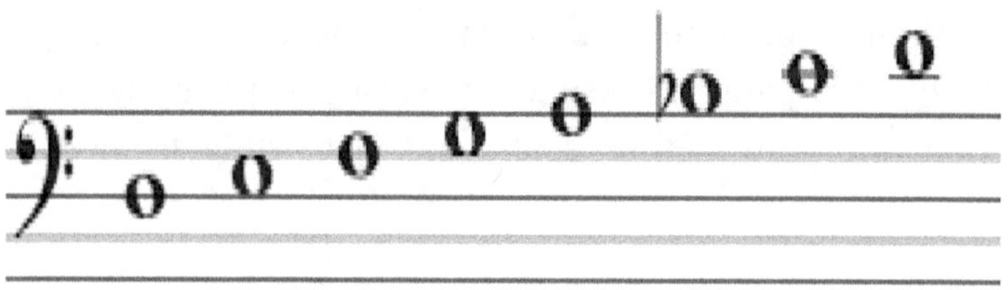

Figure 5.4

Exercise 4

1. Draw a staff with a treble clef. Write down the notes of the A major scale.

2. Draw a staff with a bass clef. Write down the notes of the G flat major scale.

3. Draw a staff with a treble clef. Write down the notes of the F minor scale.

4. Draw a staff with a treble clef. Write down the notes of the A flat minor scale.

Chapter Summary

Here are the key points to remember from this chapter:

- A music scale is a set of notes that sound good together, arranged in sequential order, within a particular piece of music.
- The tonal centre is the first note in a scale and is used to name that particular scale.
- To remember the sequence of notes in a major scale, follow the pattern *w w h w w w h.*
- A natural minor scale is written in a minor key and follows the pattern *w h w w h w w.*

In the next chapter, you will learn about the different types of intervals and how they are built.

Chapter Six: Building Intervals

In this chapter, you will learn about the different types of intervals and how to name them. Intervals are a very important concept in music. In fact, you cannot learn about scales or chords without making some reference to intervals. As a serious student of music theory, you must take the time to learn intervals and how to identify them.

Defining Intervals

An interval can be defined as the distance or space between two notes or pitches. Intervals are described using whole steps and half steps, which we have already covered in the previous chapters. The uncomplicated way to describe an interval would be to say, "E natural is one-half step below F natural," or "A flat is one step and a half away from F."

However, these are small distances. What about when we need to describe longer intervals in a major or minor scale?

How to Name Intervals

The primary factor you have to consider when naming an interval is the distance between the two notes. You need to look at how the notes are presented and then count the spaces and lines between the notes in the staff. Make sure that you include the spaces or lines that the notes are positioned on.

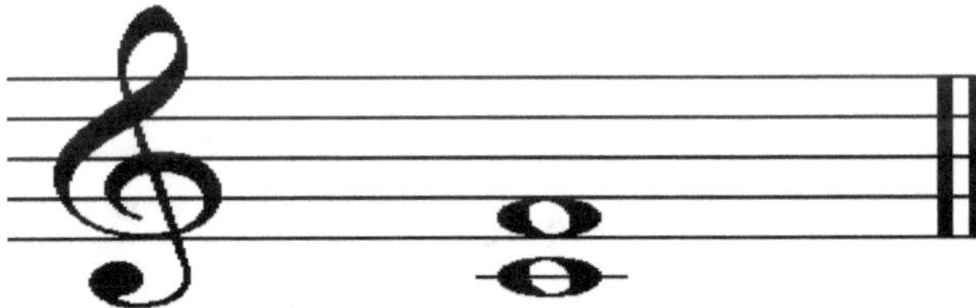

Figure 6.1

Figure 6.2

In figure 6.1 above, the interval between the C and F notes is four. We refer to this *a fourth.* In figure 6.2, the interval count between C and E is a third. At this point, the type of clef, key signature, and accidental (flats and sharps) don't matter.

If the interval between the notes is less or equal to one octave, it is referred to as a **simple interval** *(fig 6.3)*. If the interval is greater than one octave, it is called a **compound interval** *(fig 6.4)*.

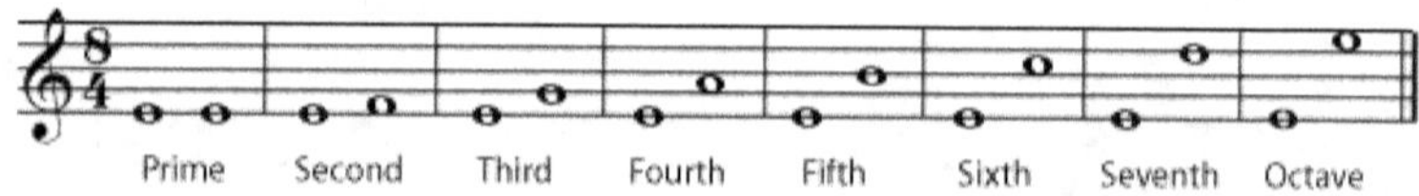

Figure 6.3

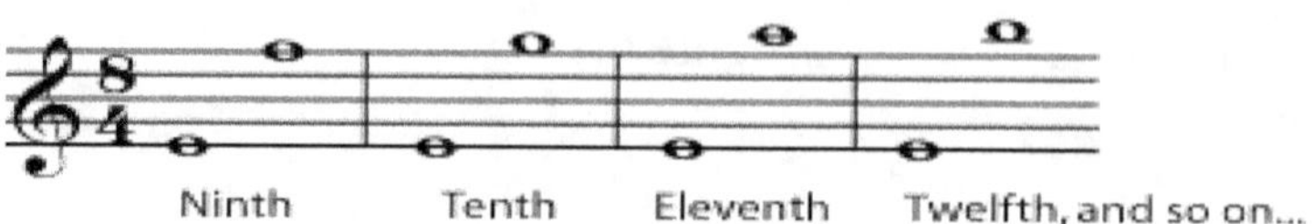

Figure 6.4

Now in the next phase of identifying an interval, we will consider the clef, key signature, and accidentals.

Perfect Intervals

Certain intervals are considered to be perfect intervals. They include primes, fourths, fifths, and octaves. They are called perfect because their sound waves are related very closely to one another. This makes these intervals sound good together.

Another name for a perfect prime is *unison,* which represents two notes that produce the same pitch. A perfect fourth has 5 half steps and a perfect fifth has 7 half steps. A perfect octave is where two notes are eight intervals apart, that is, 12 half steps apart. It is important that you understand how these steps are counted. You can go back and refresh your knowledge from the previous chapter on scales.

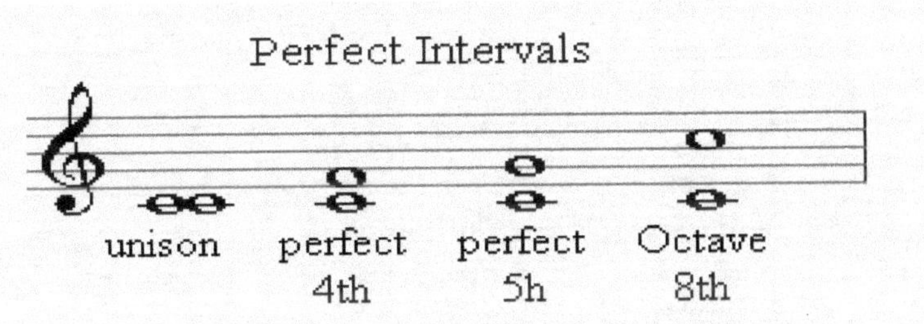

Figure 6.5

Major and Minor Intervals

The rest of the simple intervals form the major and minor intervals. These include seconds, thirds, sixths, and sevenths. A minor interval is one half-step smaller than a major one. They are described as follows:

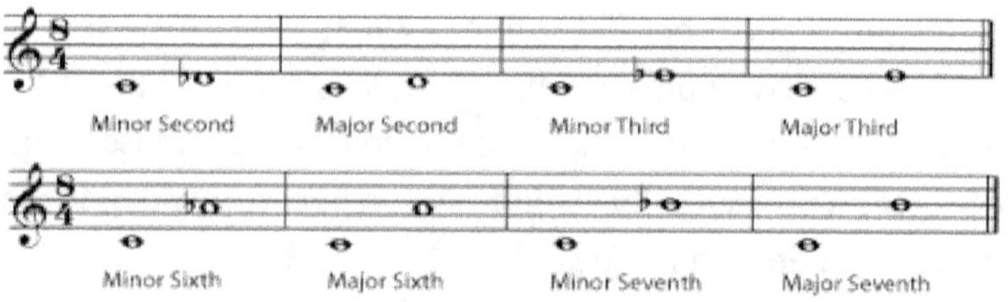

Figure 6.6

- Minor second – 1 half step

- Major second – 2 half steps

- Minor third – 3 half steps

- Major third – 4 half steps

- Minor sixth – 8 half steps

- Major sixth – 9 half steps

- Minor seventh – 10 half steps

- Major seventh – 11 half steps

Exercise 5

1. Give the complete name of the intervals.

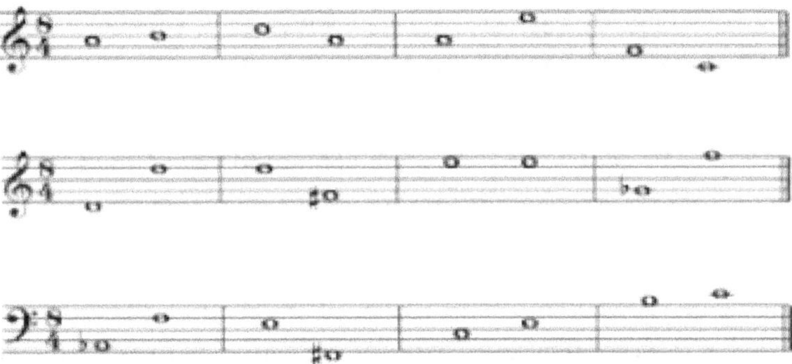

Chapter Summary

Here are the key points that you need to remember:

- Interval is the distance between two pitches.
- In order to name an interval, count the lines and spaces between the two notes. Don't forget to include the line or space the notes are standing on.
- The second phase of naming an interval must consider the half steps. The clef, key signature, and accidentals are important here.
- A simple interval is one octave or smaller, while a compound interval is greater than one octave.
- Intervals are considered perfect if their sound waves are closely related. Perfect intervals include primes, fourths, fifths, and octaves
- A perfect prime is also called unison.
- A minor interval is one half-step smaller than a major interval. These intervals include seconds, thirds, sixths, and sevenths.

In the next chapter, you will learn about key signatures and the circle of fifths.

Chapter Seven: Key Signatures

In this chapter, you will learn about how to use key signatures to make the performance of music much easier. You will also learn about the major and minor key signatures as well as how to read the circle of fifths.

Key signatures are a very important part of music. The key signature is what we use to know the pitches that a song will be performed. Every time that a piece of music is performed, it is played in a particular key or tonality. For example, if a song is to be played using the D key, then the entire song must be based around a D chord or a D note. Even the notes used will be from a D scale. The key signature represents all this information.

So how do we know the key that is being used?

If you look at the beginning of every line of written music, you will notice that there are sharps or flats (also known as accidentals) right after the clef symbol. These accidentals tell us the key to use. It is important to note that a key can either be a sharp or a flat, but it can never be both.

So, what is the significance of using keys? When you are writing a long piece of music in a single key, you will soon find it very tedious to keep repeating the accidentals all over the staff. Look at the image below to see what a simple melody in D major looks like if you don't use a key signature.

Figure 7.1

Now, this is just a short section of a piece of music. If you were writing a full song, the staff would get quite messy, not to mention the fact that you would get tired of writing all those sharps. So, to avoid this, music composers use key signatures only at the beginning of the staff to show the performers which pitches must have accidentals.

Below is the same simple melody in D major. But this time it has a key signature that indicates that the notes C and F should be sharpened.

Figure 7.2

The Circle of Fifths

This is a graphical way of arranging keys to show how closely related they are to each other. The circle of fifths has been part of music theory for centuries, and it provides a great method for summarizing the key signatures to be used for any key that has a maximum of seven sharps or flats.

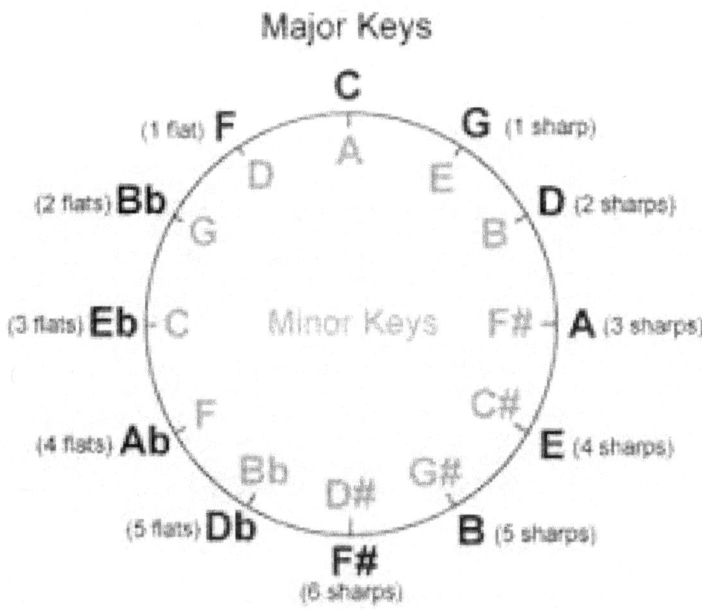

Figure 7.3

So how will you know which notes in the key are supposed to be sharpened or flattened? In order to use the circle of fifths to identify your key signature, you must use a mnemonic device to help you memorize the order of sharps and flats.

The first thing to do is memorize the order of notes on the following circle:

F C G D A E B

Most people use the mnemonic *Father Charles Goes Down And Ends Battle*

If you want to determine the sharp keys, you move clockwise around the circle of fifths. Then you read the mnemonic forward. For example, according to the circle of fifths, there are three sharps in the key A major. But which notes exactly are supposed to be sharp?

Moving clockwise along the circle and following the order of notes, you will identify the notes to be sharpened as F, C, and G.

If you want to determine the flat keys, you must move anticlockwise along the circle, and then read the mnemonic backward. For example, according to the circle of fifths, there are four flats in the key for A-flat major. But which notes should be flattened?

Moving anticlockwise along the circle and backward along the order of notes, you will see that B, E, A, and D are the notes that will have flats.

The reason why we call it a circle of fifths is because as you move from one section (or key) to the next, you are moving down or up by an interval of a perfect fifth. If you move clockwise by a perfect fifth, you will land on a key with one sharp more or one flat less than where you started. If you move anticlockwise a perfect fifth, you land on a key that has one flat more or one sharp less than where you started.

Minor Key Signatures

So far, we have been focusing more on the major keys. However, minor keys also have signatures. Every major key you see on the circle of fifths has a corresponding minor key with the exact same signature. Minor and major keys that have corresponding key signatures are referred to as ***relative keys***. For example, both F major and D minor have one flat. F major is regarded as the relative major of D minor while D minor is regarded as the relative minor of F major.

In other words, just because keys are next to each other on a keyboard (the chromatic scale) does not mean that they are closely related. The main factor that determines the relationship is having similar key signatures. The closer the keys are in the circle of fifths, the closer their relationship in terms of key signature.

This means that the next most closely related keys to F major and D minor are C major (or A minor), and B major (or G minor). Those keys that don't correspond at all with the key signature of F major are on the opposite side of the circle.

Exercise 6

1. Which keys in the circle of fifths are closely related to F sharp major and B flat major?

2. Name the major and minor keys for each key signature.

Chapter Summary

Here are the key points to remember:

- Key signatures tell us the pitches that a song will be performed in.
- To make writing music much easier, the key signature is placed at the beginning of the staff instead of between the notes in the staff.
- The accidentals indicate the key to be used in a piece of music.
- The circle of fifths is a graphical illustration of keys and indicates how closely related they are to each other.
- To determine the key being used, look at the number of sharps or flats in the key signature.
- To identify key signatures, use the mnemonic Father Charles Goes Down And Ends Battle (FCGDAEB).
- To identify the sharp keys, move clockwise around the circle and read the mnemonic forwards.
- To identify the flat keys, move anticlockwise and read the mnemonic backward.
- Major and minor keys that have corresponding key signatures are known as relative keys.

In the next chapter, you will learn about triads, chords, and chord progressions.

Chapter Eight: Building Chords

In this chapter, you will learn chords, which are the building blocks of the tone of a piece of music. Learning how to build chords can be a bit challenging for beginners, but the trick lies in taking it one step at a time. For that reason, we are going to focus on building triads, major chords, and minor chords.

Chords

A chord is simply a group of notes that are played together. Most of the sad songs you hear use what are known as minor chords. The upbeat songs tend to use suspended second chords or major seventh chords. Chords can either be used to make melodies or they can be arranged in specific sequences known as progressions to create a sense of direction and movement in music.

Triads

Chords are a set of three or more pitches that are played together. A chord that is made up of three notes that can be arranged as thirds is known as a ***triad***. The fastest way to know if a chord of three notes is a triad is to arrange the notes in a circle of thirds. If the pitch classes of the three notes sit next to each other, then they form a triad.

There are two ways of identifying a triad, i.e., according to its root and its quality. The ***root of chord,*** which is the note that gives the chord its name, is the lowest note. The second note in the triad is known as the ***third of chord***, while the last note in the triad is called the ***fifth of chord***. After you position the root of chord, you then place the third of chord a third higher than the root. The fifth of chord is then placed a fifth higher than the root, which coincides with a third higher than the third of chord. If you find this confusing, you may need to go to Chapter 6 (figure 6.3) where we learned about intervals.

In the figure below, the chord is written in the root position as a stack of third, which is the easiest way to write down a triad. Don't forget that in most cases, the root is the bottom note, unless you are dealing with an inversion.

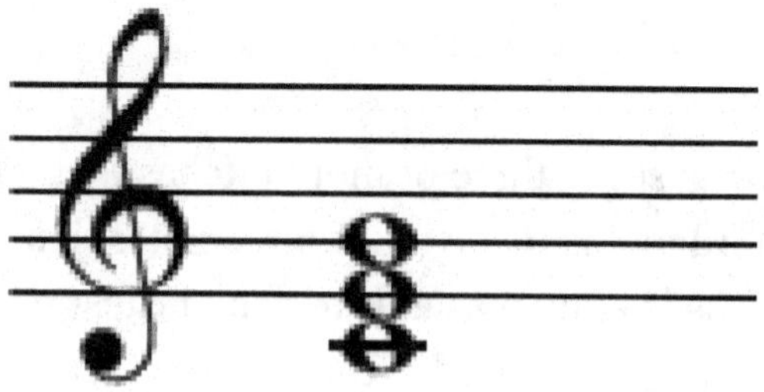

Figure 8.1

First and Second Inversions

First inversion occurs when the third of chord becomes the lowest note. In case the fifth of chord is placed at the bottom, then the chord is said to be in **second inversion**. The second inversion is also known as a **six-four chord** because the intervals are a sixth and a fourth.

The most important factor in a chord is not the distance between the top two notes from the lowest note. The number of notes also isn't an issue. The thing that matters the most is which note is at the bottom.

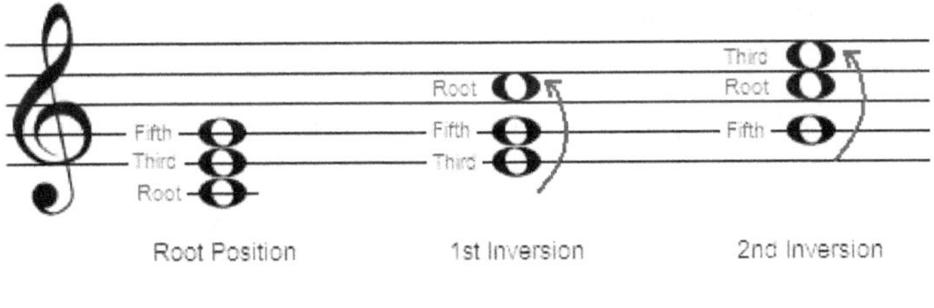

Figure 8.2

Triad Qualities

The first step in determining the quality of a triad is to identify the interval between the root and the other notes in the chord. The four qualities of triads that can be found in major and minor scales include:

- Major triad – M3 and P5 above root

- Minor triad – m3 and p5 above root

- Diminished triad – m3 and d5 above root

- Augmented triad – M3 and A5 above root

The two most common triads are the major and minor chords. In these two types of chords, the root of the chord and fifth of chord are at an interval of a perfect fifth, which are 7 half steps. This interval can be split into a major third, which is 4 half-steps, and a minor third, which forms 3 half-steps.

A ***major chord*** is formed when the major third falls between the root and the third of chord. A ***minor chord*** is formed when the minor third falls between the root and the third of chord.

On the other hand, diminished and augmented chords do not have a perfect fifth, which explains why they produce an anxious feeling in listeners. **Augmented chords** are formed when two major thirds are combined, thus creating an augmented fifth. **Diminished chords** are formed when two minor thirds are combined, thus creating a diminished fifth.

Figure 8.3

Seventh Chords

This is a chord that is formed when you take a triad and combine it with a note that is a seventh above the root. There are many different varieties of seventh chords, and we distinguish them according to the type of seventh and type of triad used. Here are some of the most common types of seventh chords:

- Dominant seventh chord – This is a combination of a major triad and a minor seventh

- Minor seventh chord – This is a combination of a minor triad and a minor seventh

- Major seventh chord – This is a combination of a major triad and a major seventh

- Diminished seventh chord – This is a combination of a diminished triad and a diminished seventh

- Half-diminished seventh chord – This is a combination of a diminished triad and a minor seventh

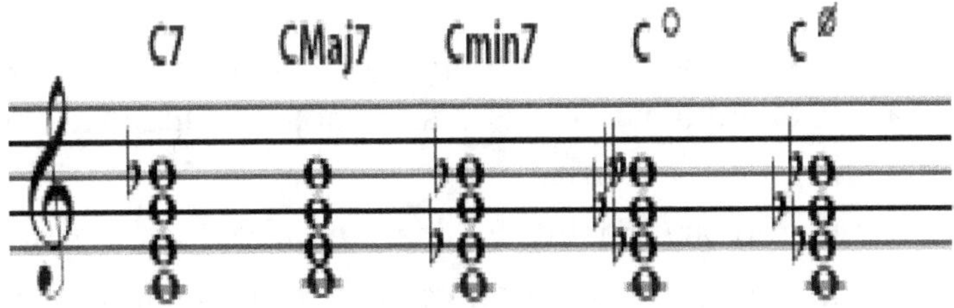

Figure 8.4

Exercise 7

1. Write these seventh chords – G minor seventh; B flat major seventh; F sharp minor seventh; and D diminished seventh.

Chapter Summary

Here are some of the key points that you need to remember:

- A chord is a group of notes that are played together.
- A chord that comprises three notes arranged as thirds is known as a triad.
- Its root and quality can identify a triad.
- In a triad, the lowest note is the root of chord; the second note is the third of chord, and the last note is the fifth of chord.
- First inversion occurs when the third of chord becomes the lowest note.
- Second inversion occurs when the fifth of chord becomes the lowest note.
- When the interval between the root and third of chord is the major third, a major chord is formed.
- When the interval between the root and third of chord is the minor third, a major chord is formed.
- When two major thirds are combined, an augmented chord is formed.

- When two minor thirds are combined, a diminished chord is formed.
- A seventh chord is formed when you add a triad and a note that is a seventh above the root.

Final Words

You have come to the end of the book. Though it was a long journey, I'm sure you now have a much better understanding of music theory than before. If you had never studied the subject previously, you should be ready to move on to the more complex theories of music. If you already had a background in music, then your knowledge of music theory will help you become an even better musician. For those who were seeking a refresher course in some of the elements you had forgotten, consider your mind refreshed.

Music theory is not really as hard as it looks or sounds. The bottom line is that you have to have a solid foundation that will always be there to guide you. The seven elements of music we have covered in this book are the keys to unlocking any musical composition. On top of that, there are seven good exercises in this book that will help you crystallize the knowledge you have gained in each chapter.

The questions provided in every exercise have covered the fundamentals that every music student and musician must know like the back of their hand. If you were keen when reading the book, I'm sure you had an easy time answering them. If you felt like you were struggling a little bit, then don't worry about it. Just go back to the chapter where you feel uncertain and reread it. Some of the concepts usually take time to sink in. Don't forget that the answers to every question are on the last page of the book.

Being able to read and write music is a very rewarding experience, and now you are ready to move onto the next phase of your musical journey. Yes, that was the easy part. Anybody can buy a book, read it, and toss it aside. All it will cost you is some time and money. However, you must now do the hard work necessary to integrate and incorporate this new knowledge into your music. This book has provided you with an opportunity to learn something that can help you going forward. Don't stop here. What is important is that you continue to practice and challenge yourself. Never stop learning and always make an effort to put into practice everything that you have learned in this book.

I am honoured that you took the time to read this book. It was a pleasure for me to walk with you through your musical journey. I hope you enjoyed reading and learning from this beginner's guide to music theory.

Thank you and good luck!

Solutions to Exercise Questions

Solutions to Exercise 1

1. Draw the staff on a piece of paper and practice writing the two clef symbols on the staff. Draw as many as you can until you learn it perfectly.

2. Draw the staff with a treble clef and name all the spaces on the staff.

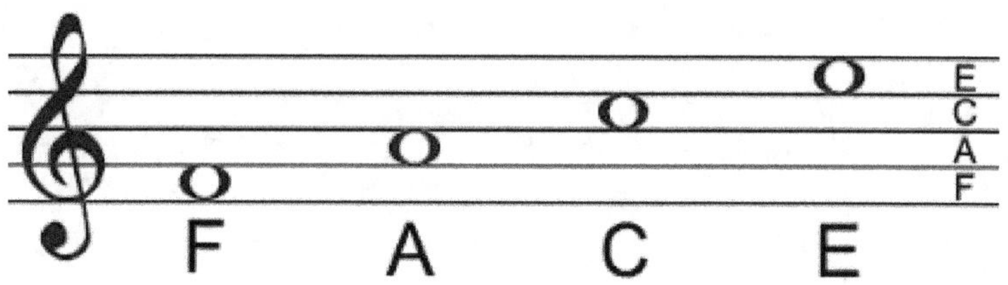

3. Draw the staff with a bass clef and name all the lines on it.

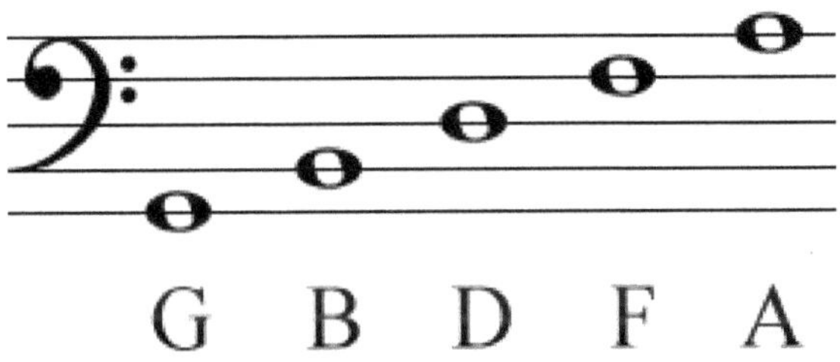

4. On a staff with a treble clef, name the ledger lines and spaces above the staff.

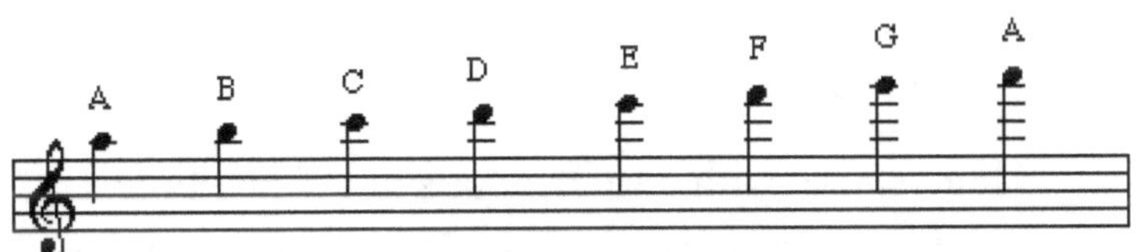

5. On a staff with a bass clef, name the ledger lines and spaces below the staff.

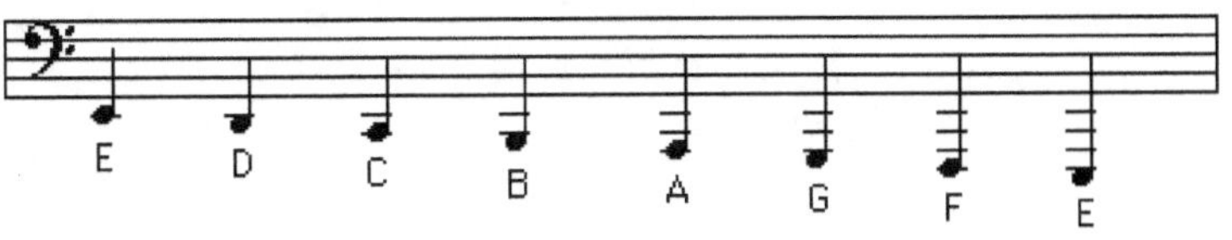

Solutions to Exercise 2

1. Complete the following series of natural notes: A B C D E F G A

2. Provide an alternative name for the following:

A♯ - B♭

D♭ - C♯

G♭ - F♯

E♭ - D♯

3. 1 semibreve = 8 quavers

4. 1 minim = 4 quarters

5. 1 minim = 1 quarter + 2 eighths

6. Three staves with a treble clef symbol and time signatures showing *two four time*, *three eight time,* and *six four time*. Fill in each measure with a different combination of note lengths. Use at least one dotted note per staff.

Solutions to Exercise 3

1. Italian tempo markings:

   - Poco piu mosso – a little more movement/motion

   - Piu vivo – more lively

   - Un poco allegro – a little fast

   - Molto adagio – very slow

2. In order from quietest to loudest: pp, mp, p, f, mf, ff

Solutions to Exercise 4

1. The staff with a treble clef and notes of the A major scale.

2. The staff with a bass clef and notes of the G flat major scale.

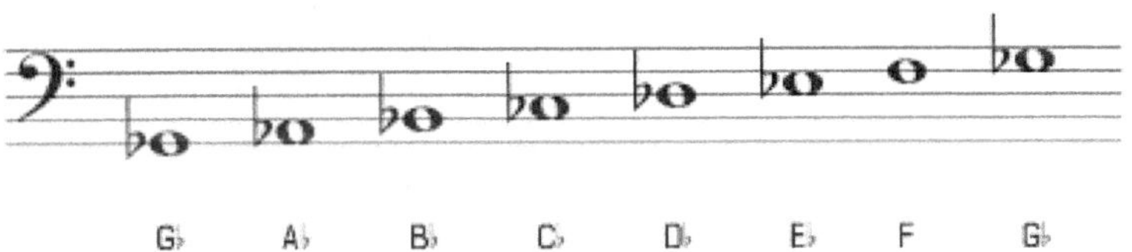

3. The staff with a treble clef and notes of the F minor scale.

F minor scale

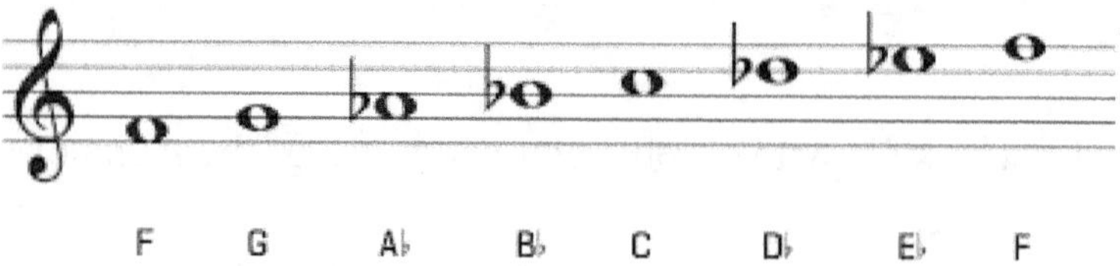

4. The staff with a treble clef and notes of the A flat minor scale.

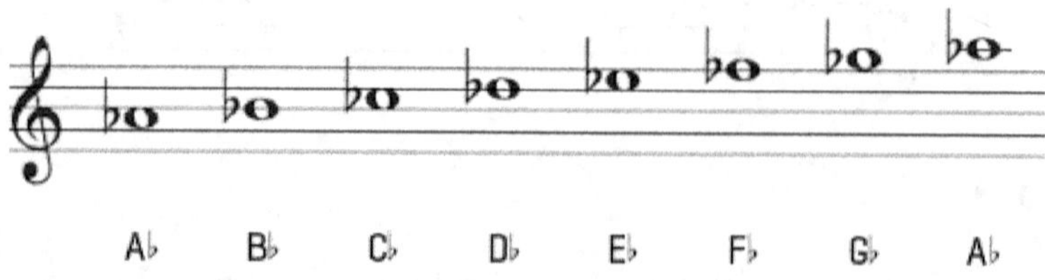

Solutions to Exercise 5

Names of intervals:

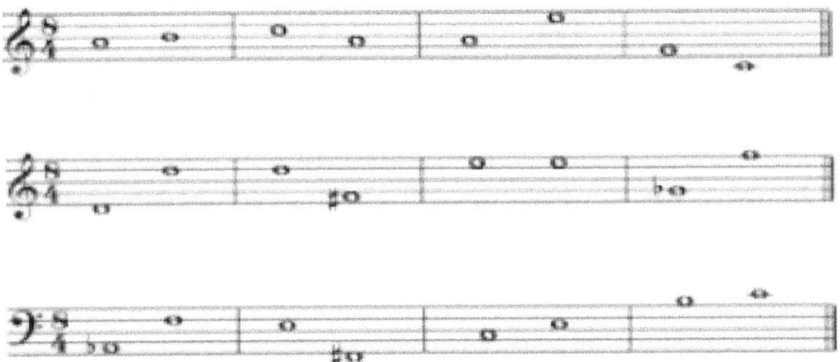

Top Staff:

Major Second - Minor Third - Perfect Fifth - Perfect Fourth

Centre Staff:

Perfect Octave – Minor Sixth – Perfect Prime (Unison) – Major Seventh

Bottom Staff:

Major Sixth – Minor Seventh – Major Third – Minor Second

Solution to Exercise 6

1. Relative keys to:

F sharp major – D sharp minor

B flat major – G minor

2. Major and minor keys for each key signature:

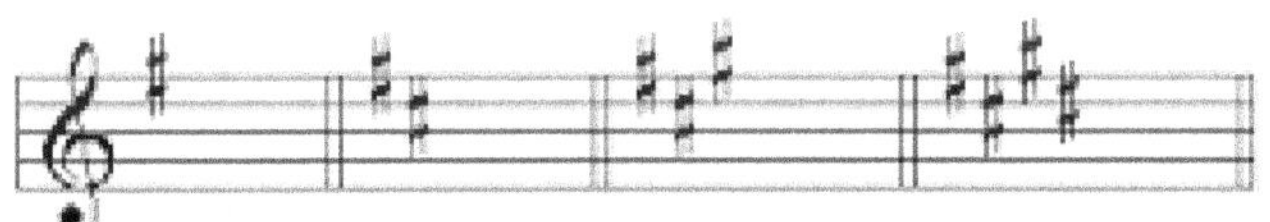

G Major – D Major – A Major – E Major

Solutions to Exercise 7

G minor 7th chord

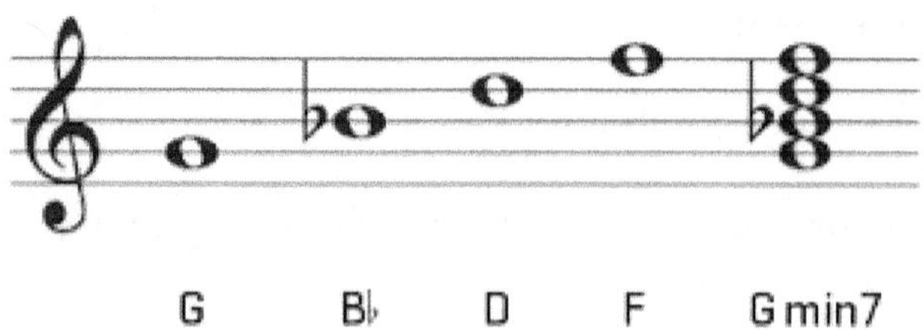

B-flat major 7th chord

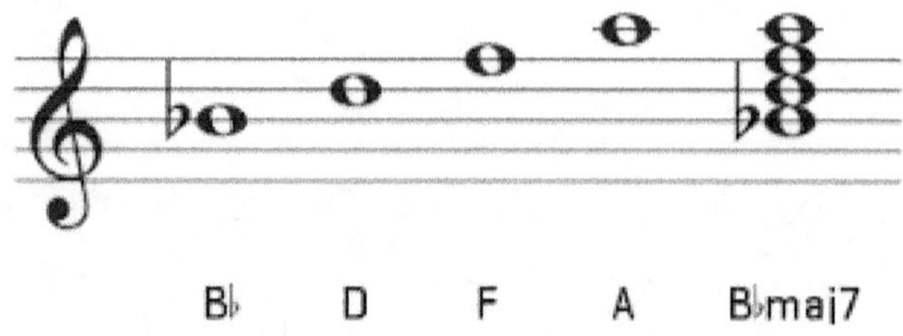

F-sharp minor 7th chord

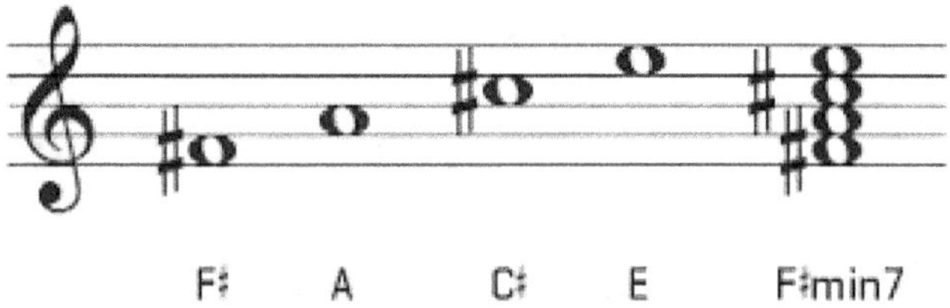

D diminished 7th chord

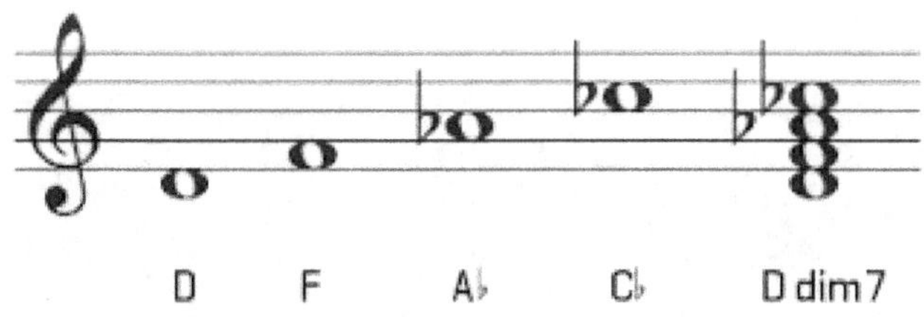

HOW TO READ
MUSIC
IN 1 DAY
The Only 7 Exercises You Need to Learn
Sheet Music Theory and Reading
Musical Notation Today
PRESTON HOFFMAN

BOOK 2

HOW TO READ MUSIC: IN 1 DAY

The Only 7 Exercises You Need to Learn Sheet Music Theory and Reading Musical Notation Today

Preston Hoffman

Table of Contents

Introduction

Music can be described as a chronological organization of sounds to create a beautiful form that is melodic, rhythmic and harmonious. Music has been a part of human culture long before recorded culture. It unifies the mind and soul and helps people express emotion. In the early days before the invention of audio recording and playback, people came up with a way of writing music as a way of communicating and preserving it. Written music is also referred to as sheet music. Written music language has been around for almost as long as the normal language we use to speak. It has undergone constant development through thousands of years. The written music language we use today has been around for over three decades.

Written music language is based on a system of notation that provides musicians with all the information they require to play a piece of music in the same way the composer intended it to be played. Music notation is a system that uses symbols to represent sounds and other aspects of music, such as timing, pitch, and duration. Music notation can also be used to represent more advanced aspects of music such as timbre, expression, and even special musical effects.

Learning how to read sheet music can be a bit of a challenging task, in particular for people who have not attended any prior music lessons. Like with learning most other skills, it is important to realize that there is no magic bullet for learning how to read music. However, with practice, anyone can learn how to read music, especially when it is broken down into small, simple steps.

This book will give you an introduction to the basics of reading music, give you a basic understanding of the fundamentals of music theory and notation and the elements of reading sheet music. It will also give you simple, step-by-step exercises that will help you learn how to read sheet music in one day.

Chapter One: Fundamentals of Music Theory

Before getting into sheet music and how it is written and read, it is important to have a very, very solid understanding of music theory. Music theory looks at various aural phenomena and how they are applied in music. It also considers the reasoning behind music – what makes music work as well as the rules followed by composers when creating music. Here are the basic aural phenomena that constitute the fundamentals of music.

Pitch

Pitch is a measure of how high or low a tone is. While pitch can be accurately measured, music theorists consider pitch to be subjective. This is because most natural sounds are comprised of a complex mix of several frequencies. In music, letter names are used to represent some specific frequencies. For instance, in most orchestras, the frequency of 440 HZ is referred to as the Concert A. However, this is not standard. There are no hard rules on how to assign letter names to different frequencies.

Most cultures allow pitch to vary in different pieces of music depending on mood, style, and genre. If you go back to France in the 1850's, the A represented 435 Hz. However, there is a specific convention that is followed. Pitches are assigned the first seven letters of the alphabet, from A all the way to G, with A representing the lowest pitch and G representing the highest pitch. Pitches higher than G start over again at A but with a higher octave. Pitches with the same name but different octaves are referred to as a pitch class. A frequency difference between two pitches is known as an interval.

Intervals

An interval refers to the distance between two pitches. Interval names consist of a number and a prefix. The number denotes the number of pitch names between the two pitches. For instance, there are two pitch names between the whole step F to G. These two pitch names are F and G. Since this interval has two pitches names, it is known as a second. However, the interval from F to A has three pitches; F, G and A. This interval is therefore known as a third. This goes on until we get to the pitch interval with eight pitch names. Intervals with eight pitch names (for instance, F to F or A to A) are known as octaves. Intervals between two notes of the exact same pitch are known as unisons.

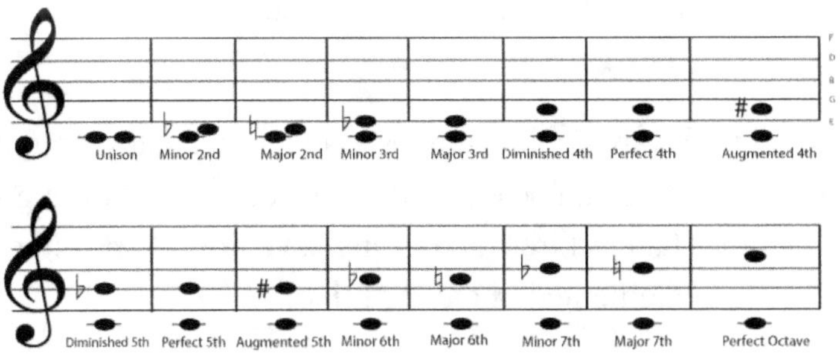

The different pitch intervals

The second part of an interval name is referred to as the prefix. The prefix is determined by the quality of the interval. There are five major prefixes that are used to describe intervals. A perfect interval is one that includes both an octave and a unison. Perfect intervals also have a fourth and a fifth. A perfect interval is labelled with the symbol 'P.' The next prefix is the major. This can only describe seconds, thirds, sixths and sevenths. A capital 'M' is used to label major intervals. Minor intervals are formed as a result of making a major interval smaller by half a step. This can be accomplished either by raising the bottom note by half a step or lowering the top note by half a step. A small 'm' is used to label a minor interval.

Another prefix that is commonly used to describe intervals is the augmented interval. This occurs when a major or perfect interval is made bigger by half a step without changing the interval number. Augmented intervals can be labeled using a capital 'A', the '+' symbol or the abbreviation 'Aug'. Finally, we have diminished intervals. These occur when a perfect or minor interval is made smaller by half a step, while maintaining its initial interval number. A small 'd', the abbreviations 'dim' or 'deg' or the symbol '°' can be used to denote a diminished interval.

From the above, it becomes evident that octaves, unisons, fourths and fifths can be either diminished, perfect or augmented. On the other hand, thirds, sixths and sevenths can be either diminished, augmented, major or minor.

Scales and Key Signatures

Musical notes are sometimes arranged in scales. A scale is a set of notes which are ordered per increasing or decreasing differences in pitch. The pitches in a scale span an octave. Scales that include both half and whole steps are known as diatonic scales. Each note within a diatonic scale has a specific name. The first and last notes in a diatonic scale are known as the tonic. Tonics are the easiest to find and the most stable. As a result, you will find that most diatonic melodies will often end with a diatonic note. The second note in the diatonic scale is known as the supertonic. The third note, which sits halfway between the tonic and the dominant is known as the mediant. After the mediant comes the subdominant, which is the fourth note in the diatonic scale. The fifth note is known as the dominant. Next to the dominant, we have the submediant. The seventh note is known as the subtonic. In the major, harmonic and melodic minor scales, if the seventh note is half a step lower than the tonic, it is referred to as the leading note.

The Major Scale

This is one of the most famous scales. This scale is made up of seven different pitches. The escalation of pitches on this scale is what is expressed by the familiar "Doh Re Mi Fa So La Ti Doh". The Major Scale has two half steps. One falls between the third and the fourth scale degrees while the other falls between the seventh and eighth scale degress. The other scale degrees are separated by whole steps. Below is an image of the C Major Scale.

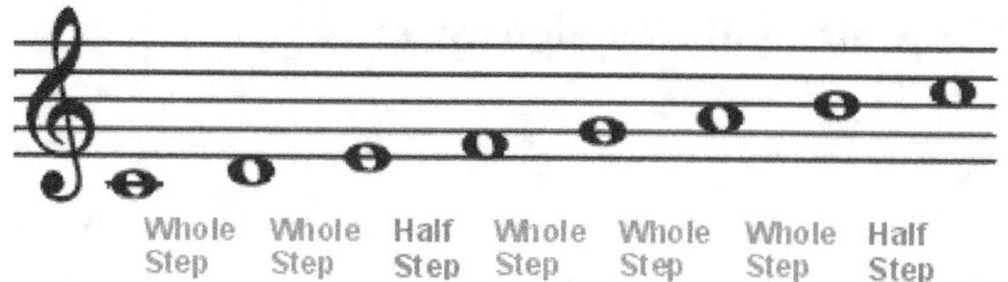

Whole and half steps in the C major scale

All major scales maintain the same pattern of whole and half steps. To construct another major scale, you only need to change the first note and then maintain the same sequence of whole and half steps.

The Natural Minor Scales

Natural minor scales consist of seven different scale degrees, with two half steps. The first half step falls between the second and third degree while the second falls between the fifth and sixth degree. The other scale degrees are separated by whole steps. Below is an image of the A minor scale. Just as with the major scales, you can construct other minor scales by changing the first note of the A minor scale and maintaining the same pattern.

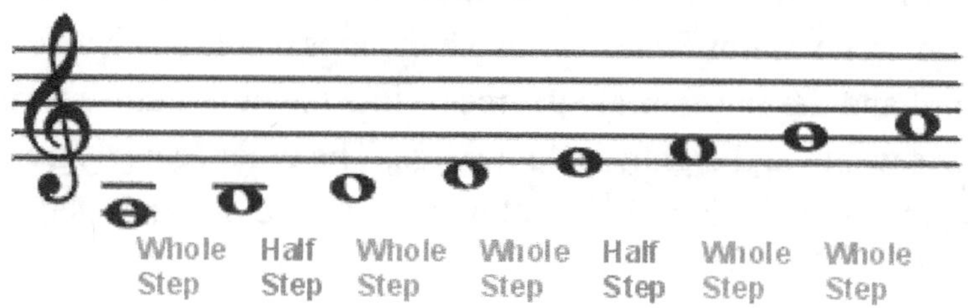

Whole and half steps in the A minor scale

The Harmonic Minor Scale

The Haromonic minor is similar to the natural minor scale. However, the seventh step of the harmonic minor scale is raised half a step. This means that the interval between the sixth and seventh notes becomes one and a half steps while the interval between the seventh and eighth notes becomes one half step. Below is an image of the harmonic A minor scale.

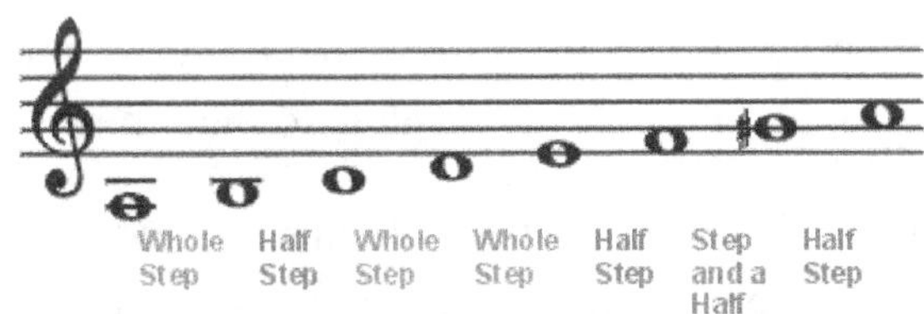

Whole, half and one and half steps in the harmonic minor scale

The Melodic Minor Scale

This is another scale that is the result of a slight variation of the natural minor scale. Here, the sixth and seventh notes are both raised by half a step. All the other notes maintain the same pattern as with the natural major scale. Below is an image of the melodic A minor scale.

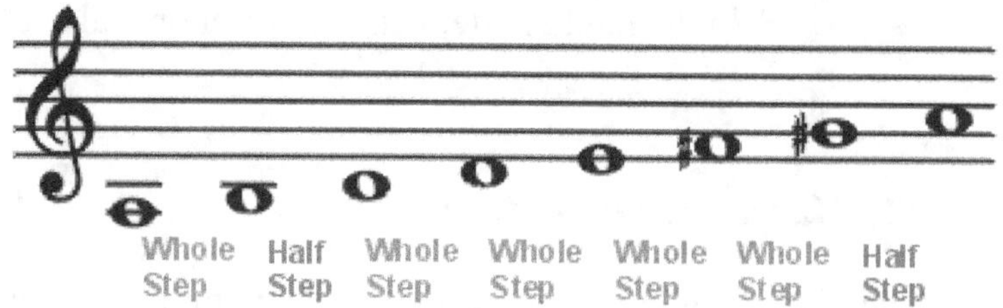

Whole and half steps on the melodic minor scale

Pentatonic Scales

As their name suggests, pentatonic scales consist of only five notes. Since they are a couple of notes less than the diatonic scales, pentatonic scales need intervals of more than half a step in order to get from one end of the scale to the other.

Some scales do not follow the interval sequences of either the diatonic or pentatonic scales. Such scales are known as nondiatonic scales. Most nondiatonic scales do not have an identifiable tonic.

An example of a well-known non-diatonic scale in Western music theory is the chromatic scale, which consists of an octave divided into twelve consecutive tones. This scale only consists of half steps. Since all the notes are equidistant, the chromatic scale does not have a tonic. Whole tone scales, on the other hand, are non-diatonic scales that are comprised of whole steps only. Whole tone scales also do not have tonics. The blues scale is another scale that is derived by adding a chromatic variation to the major scale. The blues scale has flat thirds and sevenths alternating with normal thirds and sevenths. The blues inflection occurs as a result of this alternation.

Transposition

It is possible to duplicate scale patterns at different pitches. This is known as transposition. For instance, if you write the major scale pattern but decide to start at the pitch G, the result becomes a transposition. However, you would still maintain the same pattern used by the major scale. It is possible to modify all the notes of a piece of music this way.

In some cases, however, some notes become sharp once they are transposed. In such instances, you might opt to place accidentals at the beginning of the piece. This modifies all the notes of a specific pitch. By placing the accidental at the beginning of the piece (instead of right beside the note), the accidental affects all the notes in the piece. For instance, placing a sharp at the beginning of line F makes all the Fs sharp. This designation of sharps and flats at the beginning of a piece is known as a key signature.

Key Signatures

In Western music theory, the pitches that make up a scale are designated by key signatures at the beginning of a composition. At times, the scale may shift as the music progresses. However, the interval relationships do not change even when the scale changes. To make key signatures easier to understand and remember, sometimes a chart known as the circle of fifths is used. On the outer side of this chart are the major key names. They are separated by fifths. On the inside of the chart are the minor key names. Between the two are staves showing the number and positions of the flats and sharps.

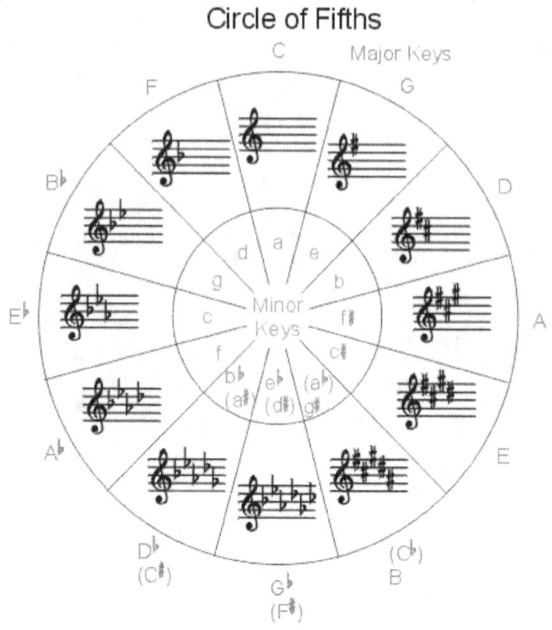

Modes

A mode refers to a type of scale that is coupled with specific melodic behaviors. Modes were developed in the middle ages as a way of organizing the melodic and harmonic parts of music. The usage of modes fell somewhat from the 17th to the 19th century. They were replaced by the major and minor scales. However, modes are still used in contemporary music. Unlike the tonic in a diatonic scale, the beginning tone of a mode is known as the final.

There are several modes. The most common is the Dorian mode, which resembles the natural minor scale with the sixth note raised. The half steps in the Dorian mode fall between the second and third and the sixth and seventh degrees. The Phrygian mode corresponds to the natural minor scale, with the second note lowered. The half steps fall between the first and second and fifth and sixth notes. The Lydian mode corresponds to the major scale, with a raised fourth note. The half steps fall between the fourth and fifth and seventh and eighth notes. The Mixolydian mode is similar to the major scale, with the seventh note lowered. The half steps fall between the third and fourth and sixth and seventh notes. The Aeolian mode is similar to the natural minor scale. Its half steps are placed between the second and third and fifth and sixth notes. The Ionian mode is similar to the major scale, with the half steps between the third and fourth and seventh and eighth notes. Finally, we have the Locrian mode, which corresponds to the natural minor, albeit with lowered second and fifth notes. The half steps on the Locrian mode fall between the first and second and fourth and fifth notes. However, Locrian modes are rarely used.

Just like scales, modes can begin on any tone, provided that the pattern of half and whole steps remains unchanged.

Identifying the identity of a transposed mode is easy since its final lies in the same position as the tonic of a major with a similar key signature.

Solfeggio

Solfeggio, sometimes referred to as solfege is a voice exercise which is used to teach pitch and sight singing. The solfeggio consists of syllables which are associated to specific notes in each scale. The syllable 'Do' corresponds to the first note or the tonic. The next syllable is 'Re', which corresponds to the supertonic. The mediant is represented by the syllable 'Mi'. The subdominant is represented by the syllable 'Fa'. The dominant is represented by the syllable 'Sol'. The next syllable is 'La', which represents the submediant. Finally, we have the syllable 'Ti', which corresponds to the leading tone.

Consonance and Dissonance

This refers to the categorization of sounds that are played simultaneously or successively. Consonant notes sound pleasant, sweet and stable when played together. Dissonant notes sound unpleasant or harsh. It is important to note that consonance and dissonance are subjective. What sounds good to one person may not sound pleasant to the other. These values may also be affected by context and other aspects such as tuning. However, there are common notes that are associated with consonance or dissonance.

Consonance and dissonance applies to both intervals and chords. The octave, the major and minor third, the perfect fourth and fifth and the major and minor sixth are simple intervals that are associated with consonance. They sound pleasing when played together.

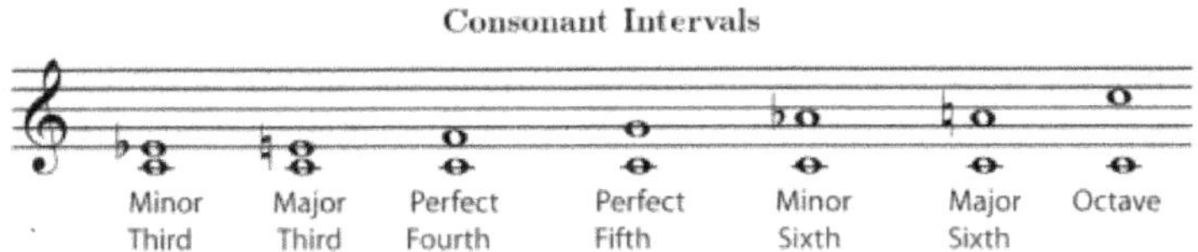

The major and minor second, the major and minor seventh and triton (the interval between the perfect fourth and fifth) are intervals associated with dissonance. They seem to clash when played together. When we hear dissonant chords, we expect them to move to a consonant chord. When a dissonance moves to a consonance, this is known as a resolution. A good pattern of dissonances and consonances is what makes music exciting.

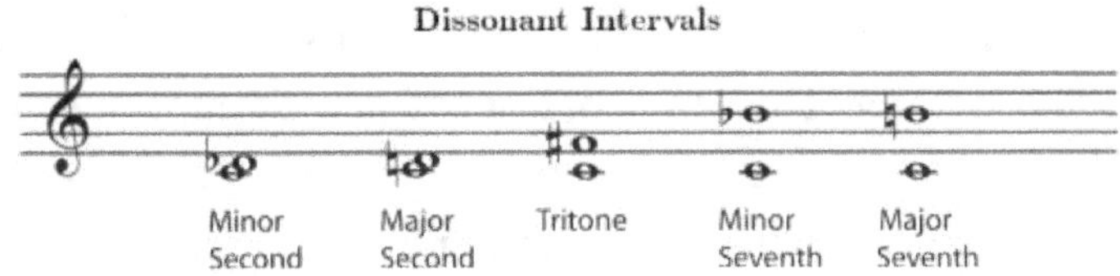

Rhythm

Rhythm in a piece of music refers to the sequential arrangement of sounds and silences as they progress through time. Rhythm can also be referred to as the basic pulse or pattern that is repeated through the progress of a piece of music. These pulses are referred to as beats. In a written piece of music, the beats are placed together in groupings known as measures or bars. In most pieces of music, the bars have an equal number of beats. The first beat in a bar usually sounds as the strongest. The bars in a piece of music set up the underlying rhythm of the music.

Melody

This is one of the foundational elements of music theory. A melody is a series of notes of a particular pitch and duration, stringed together to form a succession that typically escalates towards a crescendo of tension before resolving to a state of rest. However, a melody is more than a series of notes. A melody is the part of music that catches your ear. The basic elements that comprise a melody are the pitch, rhythm, duration and tempo of the string of notes.

There are some other important terms that are used to describe melody. The series of notes that make up a melody are known as the melodic line. Ornaments or embellishments refer to notes that the composer or performer adds to make a melody exciting and complex. They are not part of the main melodic line. They only serve to enhance the melody.

Melody affects how music sounds. A melody usually involves changes in pitch as it progresses to keep the music interesting. A melody that progresses on one pitch will quickly become boring. The rise and fall of the pitch of a melody written on the staff creates a line that rises and falls. This line is referred to as the shape or contour of the melodic line.

Melodic contour of a popular musical composition

Chord

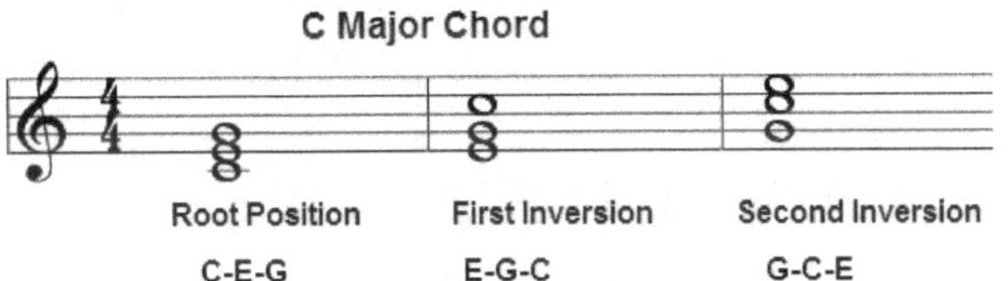

In music theory, a chord is a set of three or more harmonic notes that sound as if they are played simultaneously. They don't need to actually be played together. Chords and sequences of chords (ordered sequences of chords, also known as chord progressions) are common in most kinds of modern Western,

Oceanian and West African music. However, they are lacking in music from most other parts of the world.

The most common kind of chords are known as triads. Triads are made up of three distinct notes – the root note and two intervals of a third and fifth directly on top of the root note. More notes can be added to triads to form other kinds of chords like the extended chords, seventh cords or added tone chords. The most common chords include the minor and major triads and the augmented and diminished triads. The phrases minor, major, diminished and augmented are sometimes used to refer to the quality of the chord. The root note is usually used to classify chords. For instance, a major chord that is rooted on the note C is classified as chord C major.

Harmony

Harmony is another one of the key tenets of music theory. Harmony occurs in music when more than one pitches, tones, notes or chords are sounded at the same time. Harmony refers to how the tones and chords accompanying a melody interplay together to add meaning and depth to music. In music, harmony does have to actually sound "harmonious". The essence of harmony of the notes, pitches and chords sounding simultaneously. In some cases, harmony may actually be dissonant.

Harmonies in music come in different textures. When a melody is composed such that it strongly suggests a harmony that could go together with it – even without any other notes sounding simultaneously – is known as **implied harmony**. The easiest way of adding harmony to a melody is by playing it alongside **drones**. These are notes that do not change throughout the course of a musical piece. When different lines in a piece of music rise and fall together in accordance with the melody, this is known as **parallel harmony**. When a piece of music has one distinct melodic line while the rest of the notes are included simply to add harmony, this is known as **homophony**. When a piece of music has more than one independent and fairly equal melodic lines, this is known as **polyphony** or a **counterpoint**.

Timbre

Sometimes referred to as "color", this refers to the differences in musical sound resulting from the instrument used to play the sound. This is what enables us to distinguish between two different instruments. For instance, if a flute and recorder play the same note at the same pitch and volume, you can distinguish between the sounds from the two instruments. This difference between the two sounds is what is known as timbre.

The differences in timber between different instruments arises from the fact that each instrument produces sounds in a complex wave that has more than one frequency. As humans, we do not hear these different frequencies as separate notes. Instead, we hear them as a mixture of frequencies that form the color of the sound. In addition, the timbre of an instrument can be altered by employing different playing techniques.

Humans are capable of perceiving and appreciating very minute differences in the timbre of musical sounds. Not only can a person tell the difference between two instruments, they can also distinguish between two instruments of the same kind.

There are many different words used to describe various forms of timbre. Some of these words are interchangeable and have no specific definitions. Some of these include dull, clear, bright, rounded, harsh, mellow, warm, reedy, dark, shrill, piercing, brassy, strident, and so on.

Dynamics

In music, dynamics refers to how loud or quiet a performance is. While the volume of a musical performance can be accurately measured by audio engineers, dynamics are not given any absolute values in music notation. Instead, dynamics are considered as relative values. Since dynamics are a subjective value, the volume of a performance is determined by several factors aside from amplitude, including factors like timer and articulation.

In a written piece of music, dynamics are represented by symbols or abbreviations which show the volume at which different notes should be played. These symbols are derived from the Italian language and are used to indicate the different parts that require different volumes in the same way punctuation is used in a sentence.

Below are some of the symbols used to represent various levels intensity, together with their actual Italian and English meanings.

Abbreviation	Italian word	English meaning
ppp	Pianississamo	Very, very quiet
pp	Pianissimo	Very quiet
mp	Mezzopiano	Quite quiet
p	Piano	Quiet
f	Forte	Loud
mf	Mezzoforte	Quite loud
ff	Fortissimo	Very loud
fff	Fortississimo	Very, very loud
sf	Sforzando	Suddenly very loud
cres.	Cresendo	Getting louder
dim.	Diminuendo	Getting quieter

Articulation

In music, articulation refers to the performer's style and how it impacts the length or duration of a series of notes in relation to each other. Articulation is not quantified. Instead, it is only described, giving the performer room to interpret how to execute the articulation. Articulation marks are used to express articulations. These articulation marks establish a relationship between the notes in a piece of music and modify their execution.

Some common articulation marks used in music include the staccato, staccatissimo, marcato, legato, slur, detache, rinforzando and sforzando. There are symbols that are used above articulation marks to specify the type of articulation. For instance, a dot is used to indicate a staccato while a curved line connecting two or more notes indicates a slur.

Most types of articulations can be fitted into one of three general categories. Some articulations represent **dynamic change**. These show the need for a change in volume in relation to surrounding notes. The sforzando and marcato are examples of articulations that represent dynamic change. Articulations like the tenuto, staccato and staccatissimo represent **length change**. They are used to elongate or shorten notes. While every articulation changes a note in relation to the notes around it, some articulations affect a group of notes as a whole. These articulations represent **relationship change**. Examples of articulations that represent relationship change are the slur and detache.

Texture

The texture of a piece of music refers to how the composer combines the melody, rhythm and harmony to bring out the general quality of the piece. Put simply, texture describes how complex a musical composition is, or how different layers or elements are used in the piece to create a musical "tapestry." Texture is very often a relative term, though it can also be distinguished specifically depending on the number of elements in the compositions and how they relate to each other. Texture is affected by tempo, harmony and rhythm of a piece, the amount and richness of instruments used to play the piece as well as the timbre of these instruments.

The following terms are commonly used to describe texture:

Monophonic: This is a composition has a single melodic line. There's no harmony or counterpoint.

Biphonic: Biphonic music has two different melodies that play simultaneously.

Heterophonic: Consists of a single melody, with different variations of this melody being played or sung simultaneously.

Homophonic: Music that has a single melodic line with chords or accompaniment.

Polyphonic: This is a piece of music that has several harmonies and voices.

Form or Structure

Form refers to the overall plan or structure of a piece of music. In other words, form looks at the big picture in a piece of music. There is a great range of complexity in musical form. While most listeners will quickly understand the form of short, simple pieces of music, it can be difficult to understand the form of more complex or unfamiliar types of music. A person can still enjoy a piece of music without having to recognize its form. However, seeing the "big picture" makes the music even more enjoyable for the listener.

Musical form can be described by labelling it with letters or giving names to the very common forms. For instance, the first major section in the piece of music can be labelled A. If another section is exactly similar to the first section, it also gets labelled A. If it is quite similar but has some distinct differences, it could be labelled A' (A prime). Another distinct variation of A could be labelled A" (A double prime).

Expression

Musical expression refers to the art of expressing emotion through music and invoking emotions from the audience. Expression thus forms an emotional link between the performer and the audience. Musical expression explores how a performer brings a piece of music to life through the appropriate use of dynamics, articulation, phrasing, intensity, timbre, energy and excitement. The aim of musical expression is to elicit responses from the audience. Through a piece of music, the performer can calm or excite the audience and affect their physical and emotional responses in other ways.

Musical expression is not the result of a single element. Instead, it is the result of a combination of several musical elements used simultaneously. Musical expression also depends on the natural ability of the performer to express deep emotions and sentiment.

Notation

Musical notation refers to the symbolized or written representation of a piece of music. Music is represented in written form through the use of generally accepted graphic symbols as well as written instructions and their abbreviations. Different cultures and different ages use different systems of music notation. The Western notation in use today evolved during the middle ages. To this day, it is still undergoing various forms of experimentation and innovation. Sometimes, hand signs and spoken language can also be used to represent music. However, these are mostly used in teaching.

Western music notation uses symbols (notes) placed on a musical staff to graphically represent tones. There are different symbols for representing other musical elements like dynamics, articulations. Duration, keys, rests, accents, etc. The conductor usually uses verbal instructions to indicate aspects like technique and tempo.

Common Practice Part Writing

Common-practice part writing is a very crucial skill in music theory. While modern musical law does not incorporate practice-writing, knowing the rules on which practice writing is based can be very advantageous in analyzing and understanding music. Common practice has its foundations on the rules of counterpoint. This is a set of rules which were very popular in the 18th and 19th centuries. The aim of counterpoint was to come up with harmonies and progressions that people from that era found enjoyable and acceptable. Counterpoint was used by famous musicians like Beethoven, Brahms, Mozart, Handel and Bach. Music written in this style is often divided into two parts, each with four different species: 1st, 2nd, 3rd and 4th. Each of these parts defines a different way that the part interacts with different rhythms.

Common practice part writing is best represented in four-part writing, the most common of which is the chorale style which uses two voice parts per clef. The chorale style is based around bass, tenor, alto and soprano voices. The tenor and bass voices are written on the bass clef while the soprano and alto voices are written on the treble clef. The four different voices are then used together to come up with chordal progressions. There are several different rules which are used to define the movement of chordal progressions.

When writing a piece of music, the composer must concentrate on the spacing and range of each instrument or voice. It is very important for the composer not to stretch the range of an instrument higher or lower than it is usually used to. They must also be very careful of spacing, since wrong spacing can lead to voice crossing. This is where a voice or instrument goes higher or lower than the voice that is above or below it. Common-practice part writing strictly forbids voice crossing. For instance, the soprano voice is not supposed to go lower than the alto voice.

When part writing, it is important to use the Conjunct Melodic Motion, where the different parts generally move in stepwise motion. If you are using counterpoint, if a part jumps to a fourth or above, it should then progress in stepwise motion in the direction opposite the jump. The different voices are also required to progress together in contrary motion, which means that each voice goes in a different direction. This is preferable to having the voices move together in parallel motion, or having one voice move while the other doesn't, as in oblique motion.

In cases where the composer decides to use parallel motion, they must pay special attention to the intervals to ensure that they are in line with the counterpoint rules. Dissonant intervals should be avoided, whether they are melodic or harmonic. This includes seventh chords, tritons and diminished or augmented intervals. Using these intervals results in a jarring piece of music. The composer should also be aware of parallel intervals. These occur when two voices move the same distance, resulting in a similar interval twice in a row. However, this is not always a problem, unless the intervals are a perfect octave or perfect fifth, in which case the piece has a hollow or open sound which is a bit uncomfortable to the ear.

Chapter Two: Fundamentals of Music Notation

People invented language long before they learned how to write. Similarly, people started making music long before they came up with a system of writing down music. Before the advent of written music, people played music by the ear. To this day, some musicians still play music this way. However, written music has a number of advantages. It is much easier to study and share. Written music also makes it possible for bands and large groups of musicians to play long, complex pieces exactly as the composer intended. While there are many different types of music notation in existence, the most common and most popular is the use of the staff.

The Staff

The staff (plural staves) is the backbone of written music. It provides a backdrop on which musical symbols are placed. The staff is made up of five horizontal parallel lines and the four spaces between them. Below is an image of a simple unadorned staff.

Musical notations are placed on the staff, either on the lines or in the spaces between them. The notation of music on the staff is very logical. The higher a note is on the staff, the higher the pitch of the note. The lower the note on the staff, the lower the pitch. Sometimes, a note may have an extreme pitch that goes beyond the staff, either too high or too low. In this case, ledger lines are used to temporarily extend the staff vertically to accommodate these notes. You can think of a staff like the two dimensional mathematical plane, with the Y-axis representing pitch while the X-axis represents time.

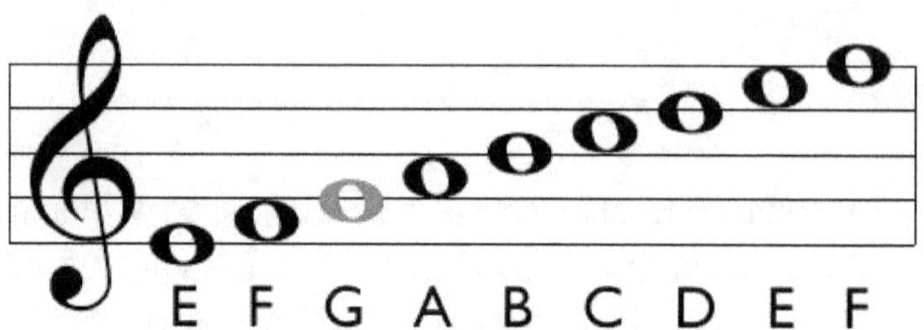

Staff adorned with notes

The notes and rests appearing on the staff are the actual written music. Notes represent sounds while rests represent silence. Vertical lines known as bar lines are used to divide the staff into short sections referred to as bars or measures, while double bar lines are used to signify the end of larger sections or even the end of a piece of music. Important symbols like clefs and time and key and time signatures are placed at the beginning of the staff. Other symbols are placed above the music to direct how other elements of the music should be executed.

Evolution of Staff Notation

The notation of musical notes and symbols on the modern staff evolved from the neumatic notations which was used between the 9th and 12th centuries for secular song and plainchant. Neumes were graphical symbols which were essentially used to indicate the rise and fall of the voice. Neumes themselves evolved from Greek and Roman symbols which were used to guide declamation. Different regions had different musical adaptations of these symbols. Unlike modern musical symbols, each neume consisted of two or more notes, with indications of their approximate relative pitches. The notes within a single syllable of text were represented using a single neume.

Unlike modern staff notation, neumes only acted as memory aids to singers who already knew a piece of music by heart. A singer who had no prior knowledge of the words and melody of a piece and music could not sing it by reading neumes. However, between the 10th and 12th centuries, there were significant developments towards a notation system that could allow people to sight-read music. 'Distematic' neumes, also known as 'heighted' neumes were used with varying spaces relative to each other, forming a continuous graph of pitch above the words of a piece of music.

Eventually, to make the pitch more precise, people started spacing the neumes on a horizontal grid of scratched lines. The degrees of a scale would then fall alternatively on a line or space in similar fashion to the modern staff. One line on the grid was colored red to represent the pitch F and another was colored yellow to represent pitch C. Eventually, the letters F or C started being used at the beginning of the appropriate lines to represent these pitches. By the 13th century, a four line staff was widely in use, with stylized forms of the letters F, C and G acting as clefs. By the 14th century, the five line staff had become the standard for polyphonic music.

In the 12th century, musicians in northern and north eastern France started adding more thickness to the thin, curved lines of neumes at specific points to define the separate notes within the neumes. This led to the rise of groupings of notes known as ligatures. Later, the ligatures were used to represent polyphonies which were without text. No longer tied to syllabic considerations, the ligatures attained rhythmic significance. However, the meaning of the ligatures still depending on context. In the 13th century, time values were codified for the ligatures, single notes and rests.

These new symbols with codified time values would form the basis for the mensural notation, which was popular between the 13th to 15th centuries. In the mensural notation system, the value of a note was determined relative to the value of its neighbors, based on several fundamental principles that were the basis of this system. This system would later evolve into the modern staff notation beginning in the 16th century. Longer note values became obsolete and shorter ones were introduced. The use of bar lines to measure meter, which had started in the late 15th century, became part of staff notation in the 17th century. Other aspects like regularly spaced barring and separate tempo indications become part of staff notation in the 18th and 19th centuries.

Groups of Staves

Just like normal text, music on the staff is read from left to right. Therefore, the notes to the left are played before those to the right. From the top of the page, each staff is read on its own, unless there is a group of connected staff. Connected staves should be played simultaneously. They are usually connected by a long vertical line on the left hand side. In other cases, bar lines may be used to connect staves. If a group of staves should be played by similar instruments or the same person, braces or brackets are used to group these staves together.

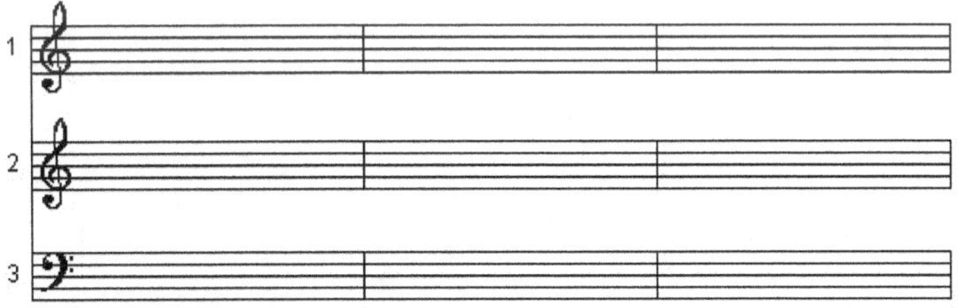

The Grand Staff

The grand staff is a combination of the bass and treble clef, connected together by a brace and line. This allows for notation of a wide range of pitches. The grand staff is commonly used in playing piano music, since it can accommodate the piano's wide range. It tells exactly which key should be played when.

Clefs

Clefs are the fancy symbols that appear at the beginning of each music staff. The clef symbol is used to associate the lines and spaces of the staff with particular pitches. There are many clefs in existence, many of which were used in the past. Today, only a couple of clefs are still used regularly. These are:

The Treble Clef

The treble clef, also known as the G-clef, is the most common clef in written music. It marks a treble sound. The treble clef, which is shaped like a stylized G, coils around the second the second lowermost line on the staff. It marks this line to be a G. From that, one can come up with the arrangement of the next letters on the staff. Each next letter is placed on a higher space or line. You should also note that the letter G is followed by an A. The lines on a treble staff in ascending order are E, G, B, D, F. You can use the following mnemonic to remember them: Every Good Boy Deserves Fudge. The spaces in ascending order are F, A, C, E, spelling the word FACE.

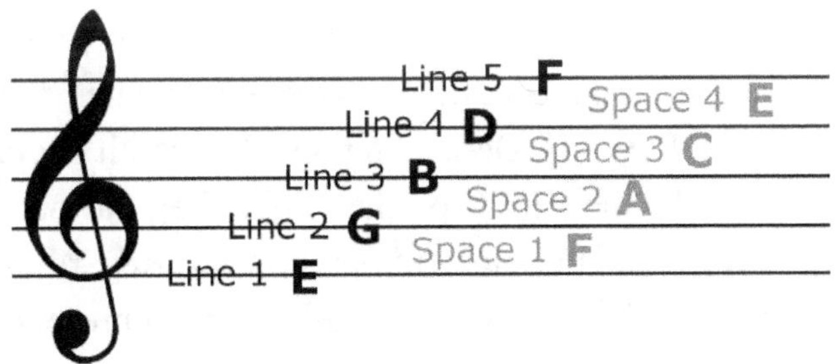

The Bass Clef

The bass clef is also known as the F clef. This clef designates the note F as the line bracketed by the two dots on the F-clef symbol. From there, one can identify the rest of the notes, which are still arranged in ascending order. This F-clef staff is usually used for low-pitched instruments. The lines on the bass staff, in ascending order are G, B, D, F, A. To remember the names of the lines on a bass staff, use the mnemonic "Good Boys Don't Fool Around". The spaces on this staff are A, C, E, and G. The spaces can be remembered using the following mnemonic: All Cows Eat Grass.

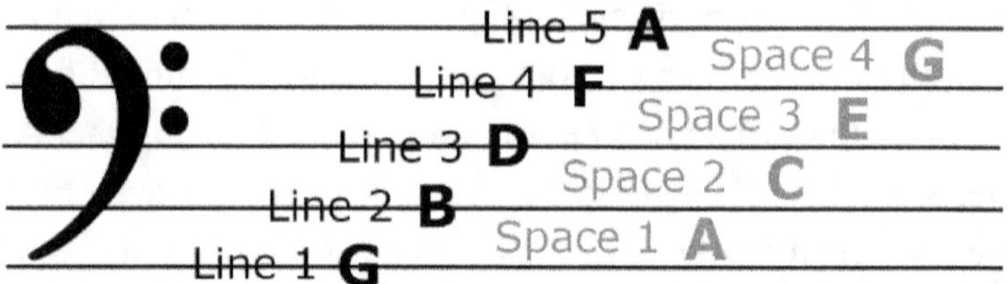

The C-Clef

Another clef that was popular is the C-clef, though its use is very infrequent nowadays. The C-clef is a movable clef. It can be placed anywhere on the staff. It has different names depending on its position on the staff. Depending on what line it is on, it is given names like the Alto Clef, the Tenor Clef, the Baritone Clef, the Soprano Clef or the Mezzo Soprano Clef. Regardless of its position, the line on which the C-Clef centers represents a middle C.

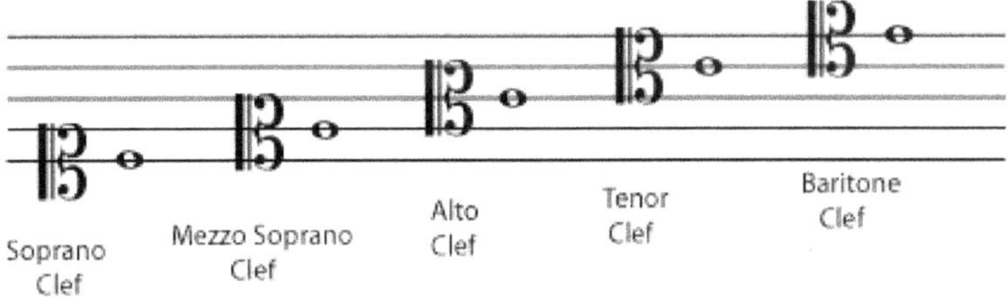

Measures

Measures, also known as bars, are marked by the vertical lines on the staff. They are used to organize music into sections. The number of beats in a measure is determined by the time signature. The beginning and end of a piece of music are marked using thick double bars. Sometimes, numbers are used to mark measures for easier navigation.

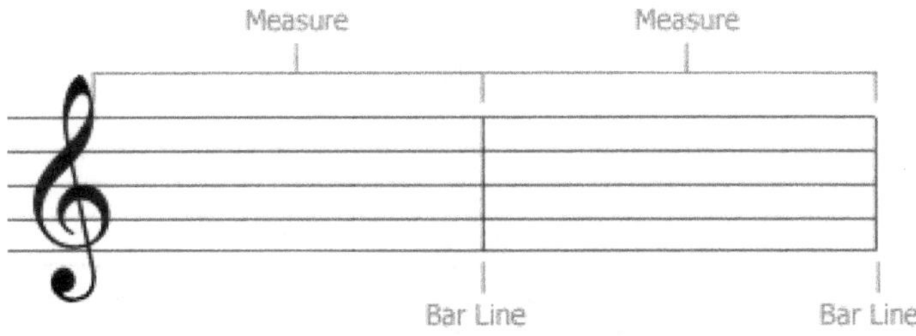

Notes

Notes are used to represent pitches on the staff, with letters being used to distinguish between the different pitches. The letters used to name pitches, in ascending order, are A, B, C, D, E, E, F and G. After G, the cycle starts again at A. The different lines of the staff represent different pitches, with lower lines representing low pitches and higher lines representing higher pitches. A note is represented on the staff using a small oval symbol.

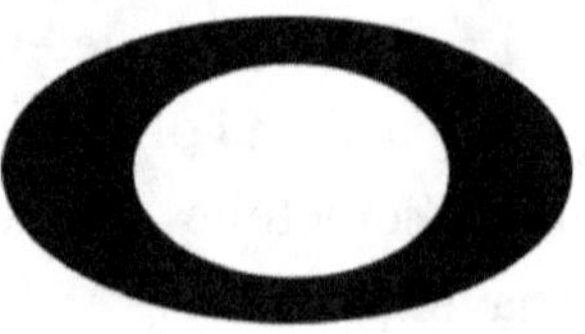

Notes on the Staff

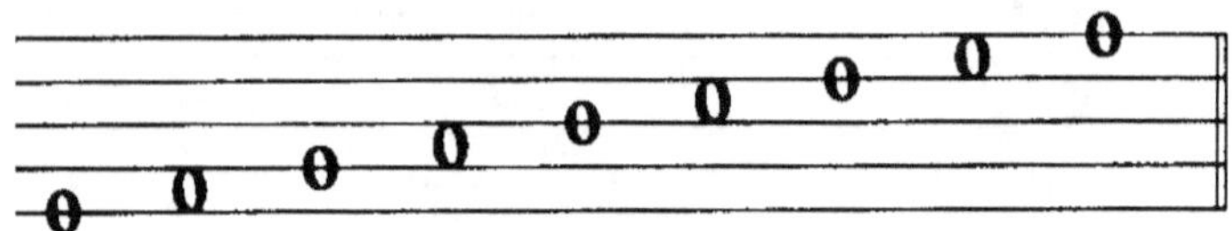

Notes are either placed on the lines or within the spaces on the staff. For notes with stems, the stems are placed on the left side of the note trailing down if the note is above the middle line. For those below the middle line, the stem rises upwards from the right side of the note. For notes on the middle line, the stem usually goes down, unless there are adjacent notes with flags that go up. The stems are usually one octave long (4 lines and 4 spaces). In case there are two melodies on the same staff, the stems for notes of one melody point up while those of the other melody point down.

Ledger Lines

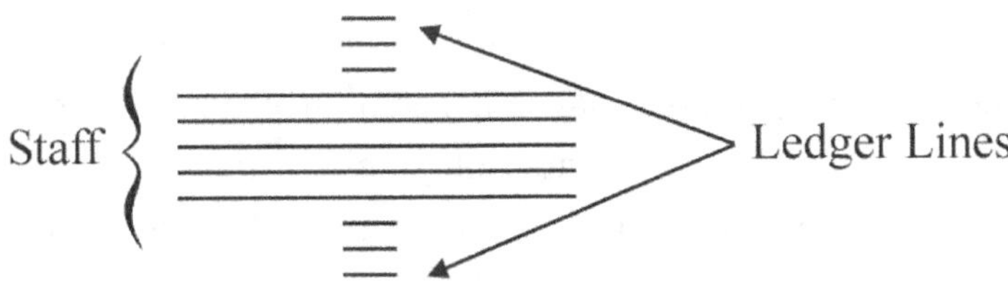

Ledger lines are lines that extend the vertical length of the staff, allowing for notes with higher or lower pitches than the staff to still be shown on the staff. The naming of ledger lines follows the same pattern used for the lines of the staff. The stems of notes placed on ledger lines point towards the center of the staff.

Note Durations

Each note has a specific duration.

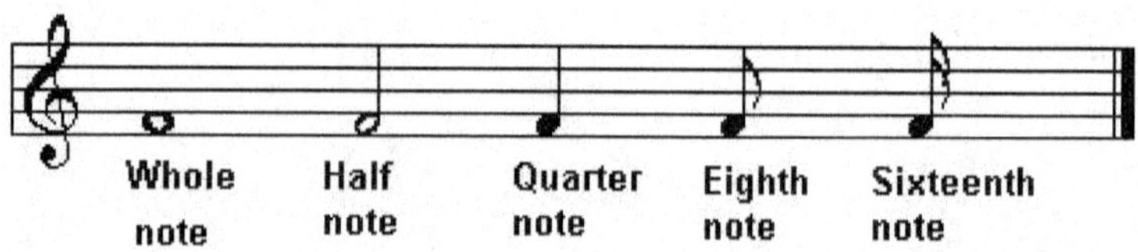

The largest note value is the whole note. A whole note has double the duration of a half note. Similarly, a half note has double the length of a quarter note, while a quarter note has double the length of an eighth note. An eighth note has double the length of a sixteenth note. This hierarchy can continue to infinity, with an addition of flags as the note is broken down into smaller units.

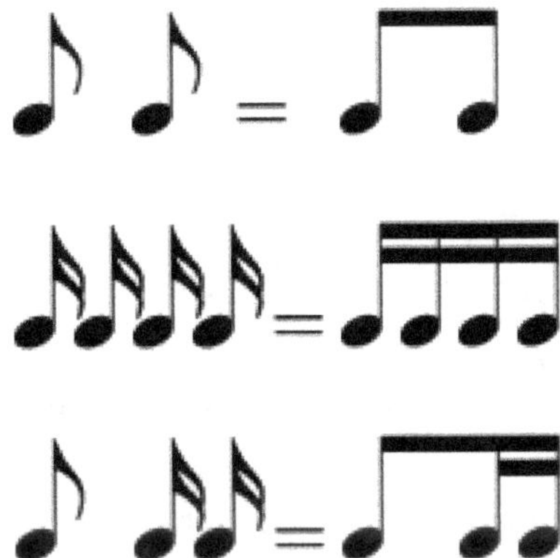

Two sixteenth or eighth notes can also be combined to look like the above image. Since eighth and sixteenth notes have flags, when they combine the flags are turned into connecting bars. An eighth and a sixteenth may also be combined.

Dotted Notes

Dots may be used besides notes. They increase the length of a note by half its original length. For instance, if a half note was worth 2 beats, placing a dot next to it makes it worth three beats.

Rests

Rests are periods of silence where the musician does not play any note. Rests are given values that correspond to those of notes. Therefore, just like notes, there are whole rests, half rests, quarter rests and so on. Unlike notes which change their vertical position depending on the pitch, rests always maintain the same vertical position.

Accidentals

Accidentals are used to modify the pitch of a note. They do this by either decreasing or increasing the pitch by half a step. Once an accidental appears on the staff, it affects all the notes of equivalent pitch for the remaining part of the measure. However, when they appear at the very beginning of a piece of music, accidentals are used to specify key signature.

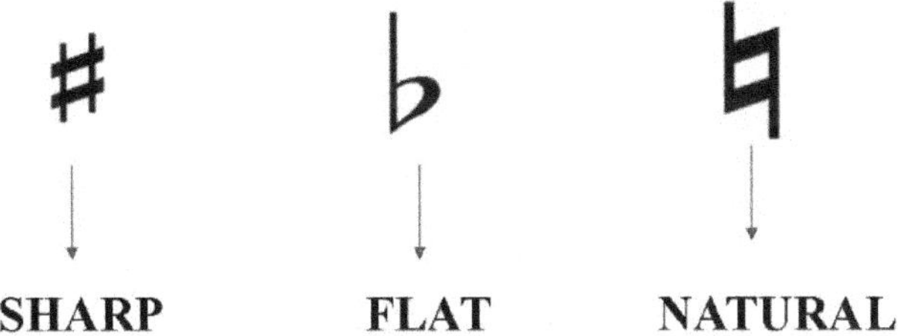

There are three types of accidental symbols. Flats are used to take the pitch of a note a half step lower. Sharps are used to raise the pitch of a note a half step higher, while naturals cancel out any previous accidentals. When a natural appears, the pitch goes back to normal.

Ties and Slurs

Ties and slurs are used to link together two or more notes. Ties link together notes of the same pitch to create a single but longer note. Slurs, on the other hand, link together notes of different pitches. In effect, this means that these notes should be played without any break between them.

Repeats

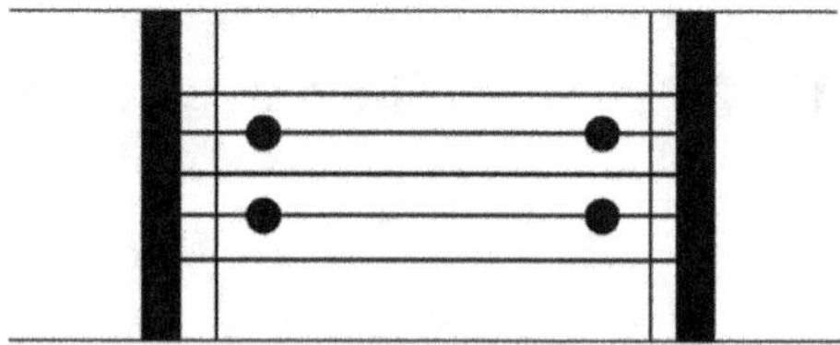

The above symbols are used to show the beginning and end
of a repeat. When you come across the second repeat sign, it
means that you should go back and repeat the music from the
point where the first repeat sign appeared. Repeat signs usually go
hand in hand with endings.

D.S.

This stands for 'Del Signo'. It is a directional marking.
When this appears in a piece of music, it directs the player to go
to the sign (Shown below). The Del Signo symbol usually goes
hand in hand with an 'al coda' or al fine'. When accompanied by
'al coda', it means that you should 'Go to the sign, from there go
to the coda'. If accompanied by an 'al fine', it means 'Go to the
sign, from there go to the end'.

This is the sign that was referred to above. From here, the music should be plated to the coda or wherever the Del Signo indicates.

The above sign represents the coda. It shows instances where the player is supposed to go to the special ending, also known as the coda.

Time Signatures

These are also known as meter signatures. They tell the player the number of beats in a measure and the notes that get the beat.

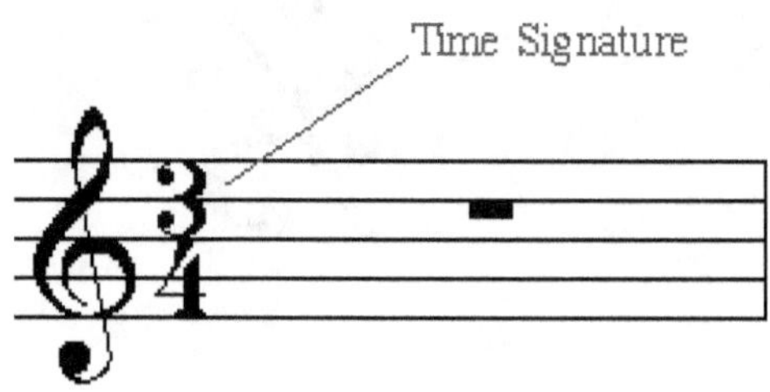

The top number in the time signature shows the number of beats in the measure. The bottom number, on the other hand, determines the note that gets the beat. For instance, when the time signature is 3/4, it means that each measure has 3 beats, while the beat goes to the fourth note.

Chapter Three: Elements of Reading Sheet Music

Sheet music refers to music where the different musical aspects of the composition – pitches, chords, rhythms, melodies, etc. – are represented in handwritten or printed form using modern musical symbols placed on a staff. Sheet music has different parts, comes in different types and is written for different purposes and uses.

Title And Credit

The first thing in a piece of music is the title of the song or composition. In most modern forms of sheet music, the title of the composition is indicated on the cover or title page. If there is no cover or title page, the title is indicated at the top of the first page. If the composition or song is taken from a bigger work such as a movie or opera, the title of the main work is also indicated. The name of the songwriter or composer is usually written along with the title of the composition. If the songwriter is unknown, this can be left out. If the lyrics of the song are written by a different person, the name of the lyric-writer may also be included. This is the same case for the name of the arranger. If the composition is an old folk music, a traditional hymn or spiritual or if it belongs to traditional genres such as blues, the name of the composer or songwriter is usually left out. This is because most of these songs

have no known authors. For such pieces, the word "Traditional"
is often used instead of the composer's name.

After the title and credit comes the actual written music, the
elements of which were discussed in detail in the previous
chapter.

Purpose and Use of Sheet Music

Sheet music is written for one of the following three
reasons:

- To act as a record of music
- To act as a guide to a piece of music
- To provide the means for performing a piece of music.

To understand sheet music, one needs to be able to read
music notation, which we discussed earlier. However, one does
not need to be able to read or write music in order to compose
music. Several famous songwriters and composers – the likes of
Paul McCartney, John Stanley and Lionel Bert – have produced
great music without being able to read music.

A popular skill when it comes to reading sheet music is
sight reading. This is the ability of a person to perform a piece of
music after viewing it for the first time, without prior practice.
Most professional musicians are expected to be well skilled in
sight reading. Some more experienced musicians can even hear
all the sounds in a piece of music in their head after looking at it
for the first time, without even having to hear the piece being
played.

Sheet music is very important when it comes to performing some forms of music, such as chamber music, orchestral works, singing choral works and sonatas. The musicians performing these kinds of music usually have the sheet music on a music stand in front of them. However, musicians performing solo pieces do not usually read from sheet music. Instead, they are expected to memorize the music. Jazz music also uses an improvised form of sheet music known as a lead sheet to give indications of the different elements of the music.

Traditional forms of music rarely depend on sheet music. Instead, traditional musicians usually learn how to play music by the ear, or by being taught by another person. While sheet music often serves as a platform for new music and helps in the composition of new music, it can also act as a visual record of existing music.

Types of Sheet Music

Written music comes in different types. If a composition is meant to be played using only one instrument or voice, it is usually written as a single piece of sheet music. In other cases, a piece may be intended to be performed by different persons. In this case, each performer will have a different piece of the sheet music, which is known as a part.

Sometimes, separate vocal and instrumental parts of a piece of music may be written together, resulting in what is known as a score. There are various formats of musical scores:

Full score: This refers to a large book that shows the parts of the instruments and voices in a piece of music. Full scores are mainly used by conductors to lead an ensemble. They may also be used as a basis for studying a given work of music.

Miniature score: This is a smaller version of a full score. For this reason, it cannot be used by a conductor. However, it is still a handy tool for those looking to study a piece of music.

Study score: Study scores are sometimes similar in size and can be difficult to distinguish from miniature scores. However, study scores may include comments about the music for study purposes.

Piano score: This is a piece of sheet music that has been simplified or compressed such that it can fit on the grand staff and is therefore playable by piano. Reducing a score into a piano score takes considerable skill, since the score needs to be detailed enough to present all the elements of the composition while still remaining playable on the piano.

Vocal score: This is a full score that has been reduced to only show the vocal parts on their staves. Vocal scores make it easy and convenient for vocal performers to learn and rehearse music separately.

While these are the main types of scores, there are other minor types of scores, such as:

Short scores: These refer to scores that take a piece of music meant for many instruments and compress it to just a few staves. Short scores are typically used when composing music, then get expanded later to complete the orchestration.

Open score: This is a piece that places each voice on its own staff.

Chapter Four: Seven Step-by-Step Exercises to Help You Learn How to Read Sheet Music

Having learnt the basics of music theory, the fundamentals of music notation and the elements of sheet music, now is the time to put your knowledge into practice. Like with learning any other language, learning how to read sheet music needs lots of practice. Below is a list of step by step exercises that will speed up your learning process

Step One: Practice Full Concentration

While this may seem very obvious, it has a huge impact on your success in reading sheet music. However, without full concentration, you will easily miss notes, fly over accidentals, mess up rhythms and make a ton of other mistakes. If you are a beginner, this can be very frustrating and may even cause you to give up. Often, while trying to read a piece of music, you may find yourself reading with only half your concentration. The worst part is you might not even realize it. It's important that when you start practicing, you should clear your mind of any other distractions and focus wholly on the task at hand. The key to maintaining total concentration is to challenge yourself to complete reading an entire piece of sheet music perfectly. Try and avoid making mistakes as much as you can. If you find your mind wandering, refocus and start all over again.

Step Two: Start with Elementary Material

When starting to learn how to read sheet music, some students are often too ambitious and choose to start by reading complex musical pieces. This is not a very good approach. When learning a new language, a student starts by reading short material with simple phrases they can understand easily. As their expertise in the language grow, they graduate to reading more complex literature in the language. Similarly, you cannot learn by reading complex pieces of music. Starting with short, simple compositions allows you to acquire habits of fluency. As you get better, gradually step up the difficulty and complexity of you read. The best way to do this is to consult a qualified music teacher who can continually assess your level of knowledge and recommend suitable material.

Step Three: Divide the Music Into Chunks

During their first attempts at reading sheet music, many students try to read the music singularly. They count every single beat and take note of every single rhythm. Doing this can be very exhausting and is outright impossible. Your brain is hardwired to divide things into groups for easier comprehension. For instance, as you read this book, you are not focusing on every single letter.

Instead, your brain groups letters into words and reads them as a whole. You should do the same when it comes to reading sheet music.

A good way of practicing how to read music in chunks is to divide each bar into two parts and take note of where the downbeats fall. This allows you to interpret music in a more relaxed manner and free up your mind to focus on other aspects of the piece you are reading. This also allows you to learn how to "hear" a melody by just looking at it.

Step Four: Look for Familiar Rhythms and Patterns

Each piece of music is unique different from another. However, there are certain repeated patterns that are common in many pieces of music. Some common scale fragments are found in many musical scores. These are a great start for learning how to recognize patterns in larger music sections. Try and identify different melodic lines in the music that contain ascending or descending scale fragments. Just like children have to read multiple books to get improve their word reading skills, you should also read multiple pieces of music and strive to identify the common patterns in each. You can find practice pieces online or ask a music teacher to provide you with some.

Step Five: Practice Looking Ahead

One of the main reasons that students make mistakes when reading sheet music is the simple fact that they are not ready for the upcoming notes and are hence caught off guard. A student encounters a measure that they are supposed to play immediately and they are unable to process all this information quickly. This causes them to falter as they have to think of what is required of them at that point. Such a pause ruins the flow of the whole piece of music. To avoid being caught off guard, students should get into the practice of continuously scanning ahead to be aware of the notes and rhythms coming up. Always scan a beat or two ahead of whatever you are currently playing. This skill requires you to use a combination of all the other skills mentioned above. You have to focus fully on reading the music, divide the music into chunks and look for familiar patterns. All these allow you to be aware of whatever is coming up ahead.

Step Six: Learn to Continue Through Mistakes

As you learn how to read sheet music, it is inevitable that you are going to make some mistakes here and there. While you should aim for perfection, you should accept that you are going to make some mistakes. However, you should not let mistakes deter you. The most important thing is to always keep the tempo of the piece in mind, since this is what holds the whole music together. You might miss a note or an accidental, but just keep going and get the flow of the whole piece. Once you are done, restart the whole piece and try to eliminate the mistakes this time round.

Step Seven: Keep a Practice Journal

Like I noted earlier, the secret to becoming good at reading sheet music is practice. You should practice as many times as you can. This helps you to increase your skills and helps you build confidence in your skills. Ideally, you should practice reading sheet music at least 20 – 30 minutes each day. Each day, note down how long you spent practicing and what you practiced. Apart from practicing on your own, try to get together will friends or colleagues and practice together. This will help you improve your skills and increase your motivation.

Conclusion

149

The ability to read sheet music is a great skill to have. While learning how to read sheet music is a somewhat challenging task, it is something that one can teach themselves. All it requires is concentration, attention to details and lots of practice. I can't emphasize this enough. Practice is what will make you a skilled sheet music reader. As you get better, you will adopt to your own ways of reading music. This book has provided you with the fundamentals of music theory and music notation. It has also given you a basic introduction to sheet music and seven step by step exercises you can use to improve your sheet reading skills.

HOW TO PLAY
GUITAR
IN 1 DAY
The Only 7 Exercises You Need to
Learn Guitar Chords, Guitar Scales
and Guitar Tabs Today
PRESTON HOFFMAN

BOOK 3

HOW TO PLAY GUITAR: IN 1 DAY

The Only 7 Exercises You Need to Learn Guitar Chords, Guitar Scales and Guitar Tabs Today

Preston Hoffman

Table of Contents

Introduction

Thank you for purchasing this book. You are now already on your way to becoming a guitarist.

The guitar is one of the most versatile instruments that there is and one of the most straightforward to play. Becoming a player opens you to a world of fun, relaxation and satisfaction.

For some, it might lead to a bit of extra income, if you join a band. Making music is a wonderful thing; making it in the company of others is even better.

By buying this book, you have made the first move to acquiring lifelong skills, which will provide much laughter, much joy and immense satisfaction.

We suggest that you work through this book a chapter at a time, spending long enough in each lesson to have secured the skills before moving on to the next chapter. It may seem hard at the outset, but it will quickly become easier.

This is a very practical book. You will be playing straight away. There are two useful chapters at the end, which offer more detail on questions that might arise, and a glossary of terms. There are also some songs to get you playing.

Mostly, this book will introduce you to playing the guitar. Give yourself a day, and you will be well on your way.

Chapter One: Getting Started – Lesson One - The Parts of the Guitar, and How to Hold It

The saying goes that there is no time like the present, so if your aim is to learn to play the guitar quickly, let us get straight into it.

Essential Information

A few notes, though, before we start. There is a glossary at the back of this book. Any term followed by an asterisk (*) will be defined in the alphabetical glossary at the end.

Secondly, a very useful tip is to get your head around each chapter before moving on to the next. The better understanding you have of each section, the more rapid your progress will be.

In addition, the learning will stick, and you will not have to constantly look back to re-learn the skills that this book will help you to acquire.

Next, don't worry if you get sore fingers on your left (fret*) hand, especially if you are playing a steel string guitar. The skin on the end of your fingers will quickly harden and the soreness will disappear.

OK, let's get on with it. For the purposes of the rest of the chapter, the assumption is made that you already have your guitar, and that it is stringed and tuned*. If not, there are sections on choosing your guitar, stringing it and tuning the instrument later in the book.

The Parts of the Guitar

The guitar is formed from a few basic parts, each of which has their individual role. It doesn't really matter which kind of guitar you own, because the make-up is the same. If you have an electric guitar, there will be extra knobs and levers, but we will look at these later.

Guitar Head and Tuning Pegs

The head has two primary purposes. It is there to help sustain, or lengthen, the sound of the strings.

If you put your hand on the head, and play the open* strings with the other hand, you will sense the vibrations of the notes continuing to make a sound.

The second role of the head is hold the tuning pegs. These are the pegs connected to the rollers around which the strings are held tight. Turning these pegs changes the note. See the section on 'tuning' for more details.

Heads look different on the various types of guitar; do not worry about this, as they all perform the same task.

Guitar Neck and Nut

The picture above shows the nut. This is the part of the that holds the strings in place.

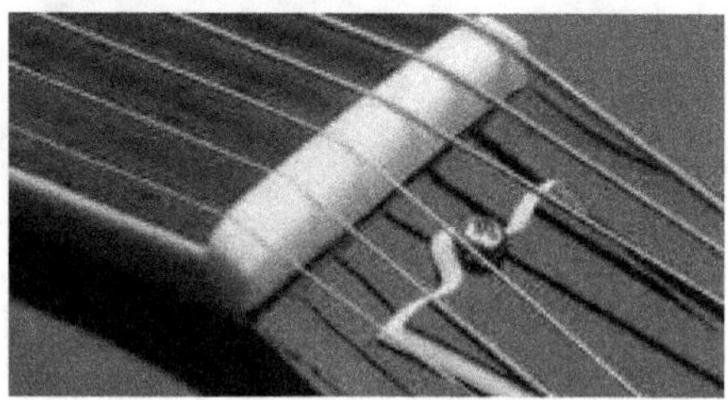

The nut has six little slots into which a string fits. It ensures that a full sound is heard by keeping the string away from the neck and frets.

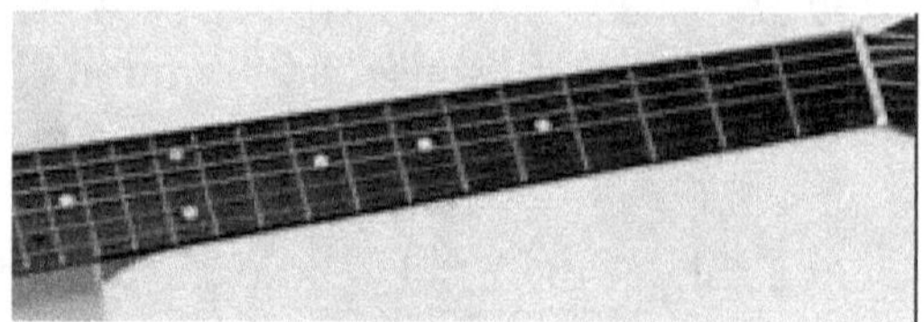

The picture above shows the neck of a guitar. This is the long section on which the frets are located. The example above has fret markers – the little dots that help the player to locate the appropriate fret when playing down the neck, which is more difficult than playing up at the head end. Not all guitars have these markers.

Here we can see the body of the guitar. The hole in the middle is called the sound hole, which is there to amplify the sound of the guitar. Electric guitars do not have these, as they have pick-ups (raised metal bars) to send the vibrations electronically to the amplifier.

Note that the body shape of a guitar can take many forms, especially with electric guitars. The final part of the guitar to identify is the bridge, into which the ends of the strings are fitted.

Holding the Guitar

As a beginner, it is best to start with a sitting position. As players become more experienced, then it is possible to play standing up, but the extra support offered when sitting helps the new player.

The position above is the classical stance when playing the Spanish* guitar. Note that the left foot is raised. A footrest can be purchased to facilitate this, but a pile of books or a block of wood works just as well. The guitar sits on the left leg, with the right just offering support. Both hands then fit into the natural position.

For larger guitars, such as acoustics*, then the picture below offers a more usual position. Here, the guitar is on the right leg, with the two legs close together. Of the two, the better one for the beginner is the Spanish guitar position. However, comfort is the most important thing of all.

Chapter Summary

So now we have the basics.

- You know the names of the parts of the guitar
- You know how to hold the instrument

In the next chapter you will begin to learn how to play.

Chapter Two: Lesson Two - Chords

In this chapter we will learn about the basic chords* which will allow you to begin to play songs almost immediately.

For a right-handed person, or somebody who plays right handed (most people do…) chords are formed with the left hand. Many songs can be played with just a collection of three or four chords, and in this chapter, we will look at the main ones.

There are seven notes in music, and chords are named after these. Chords are MAJOR* chords unless otherwise stated. Major chords make a kind of complete sound, whereas the other main form, MINOR* chords, make a sort of questioning, unfinished sound. Once you play one of each, the difference will be clear.

There are numerous varieties after that, but for this book, as it is for beginners, we will stick to just one alternative, a 7th chord*. This is a chord with an extra note (a seventh above the base note, for those interested).

The chords below are the ones that appear most commonly. Some, such as for example, the B Major chord (B) will appear in later chapters because they require a barre to play.

A Chords

Here, the lowest E string is not strummed*, the other five strings are. Use your first finger to cover the four strings on the second fret, then press the bottom string with your little finger

A

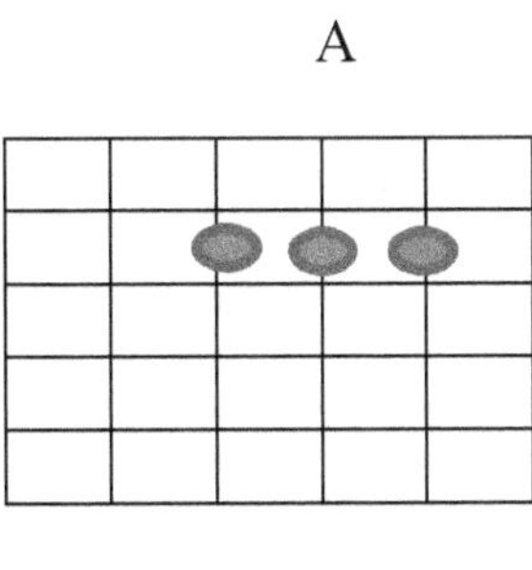

Am (A minor)

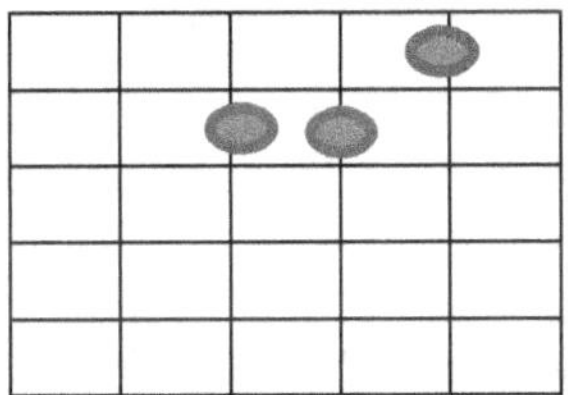

A7

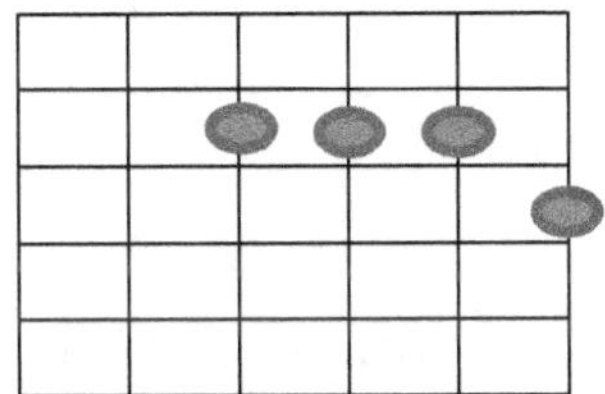

Use your first finger to cover the four strings on the second fret, then press the bottom string with your little finger

Am7

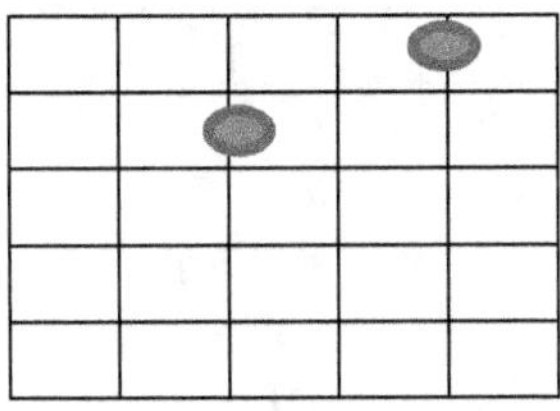

C Chords

As with A chords, the lowest E string is not strummed.

C

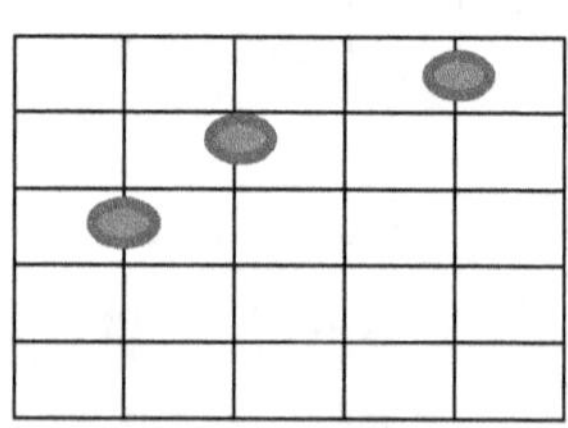

C7

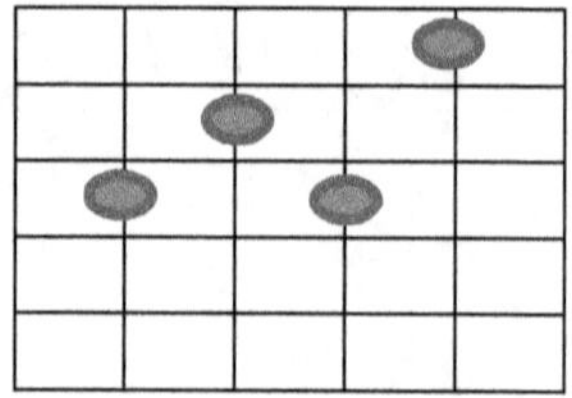

D Chords

Here, the lowest two strings, E and A, are not strummed.

D

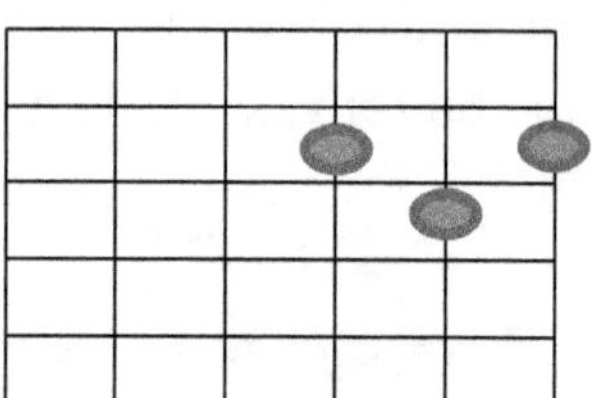

Dm

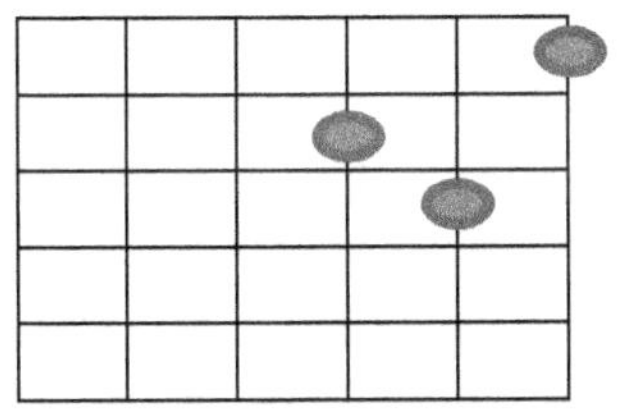

D7

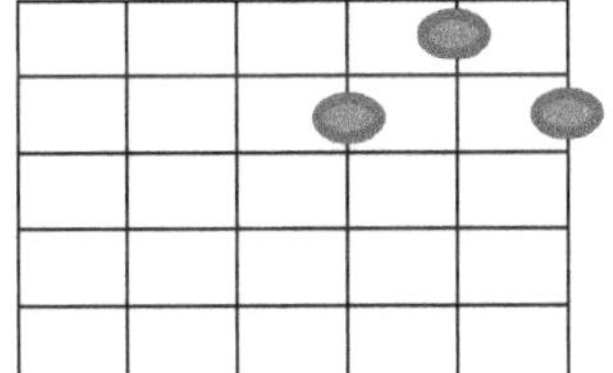

Dm7

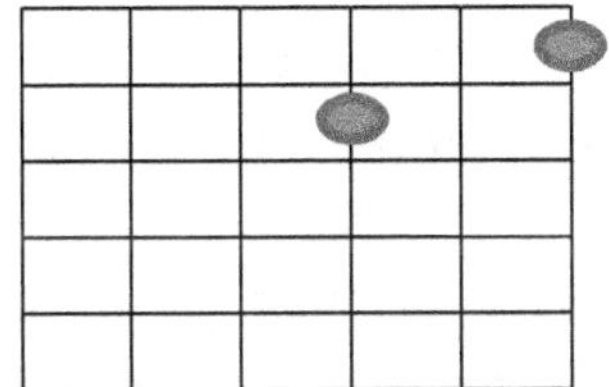

E Chords

Here, all strings are strummed.

E

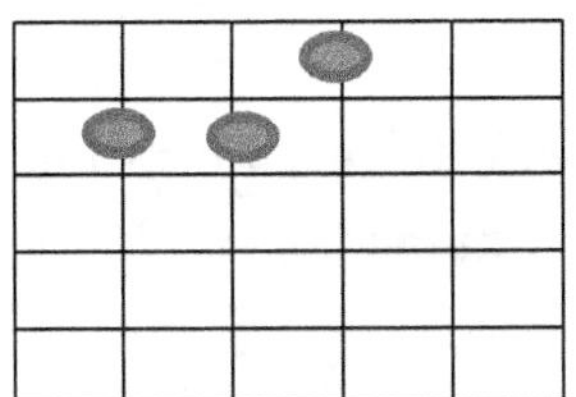

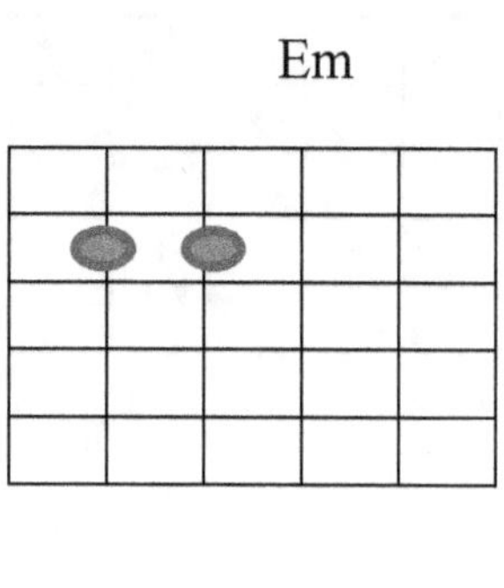

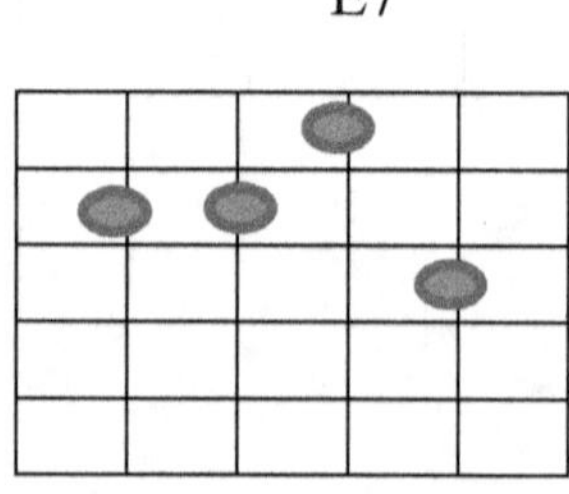

Use your first finger to cover the four strings on the second fret, then press the bottom string with your little finger

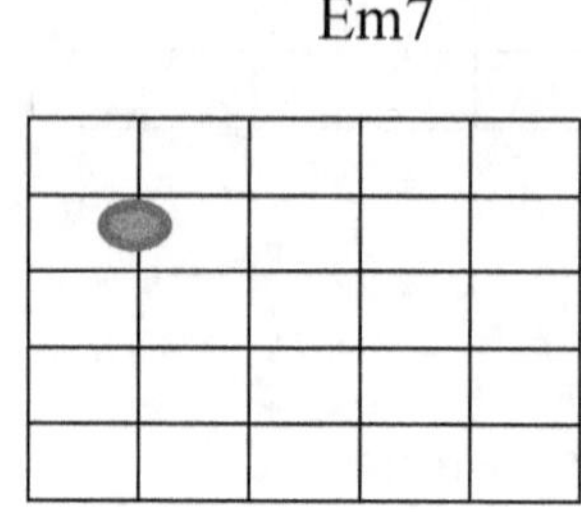

F Chords

If a barre is used, all strings are strummed, if not then the E and A strings are not strummed.

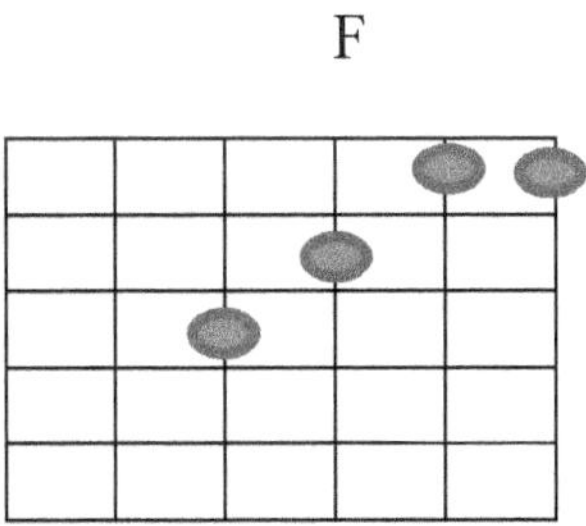

Use your first finger to hold down the first two strings. If you can, the first finger can create a bar by stretching over all six strings. It takes a bit of strength, but that soon develops.

G Chords

All strings are strummed.

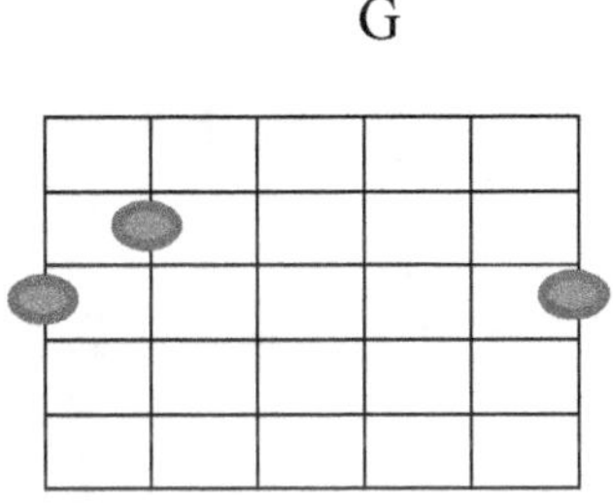

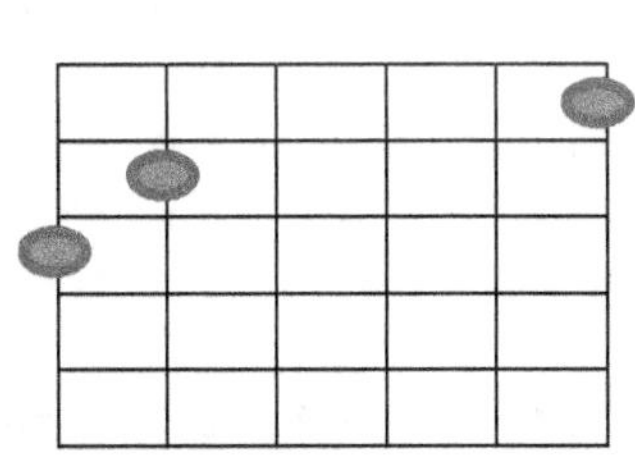

The key with these chords is to practice them. Get them so that you can form each chord and play them so that there is no buzzing of the strings, or 'flat' sounds of a string not being pushed down firmly enough.

Progressions

Songs are often built around chord progressions. These are chords that simply go together well. Practice these and you will be able to use them in a wide range of songs.

The Most Common Progression

This works in any key, but for our purposes we will practice C, F and G

C C C C F F F F G G G G C C C C

Songs such as John Lennon's Imagine follow this progression.

Pop Progressions

These chord combinations work in popular songs such as Someone Like You by Adele. The chords are C, G, Am and F.

C C C C G G G G Am Am Am Am F F F F C C C C etc

Jazz Progressions

Everything from Boyfriend, the Justin Bieber, ummm, song and some of Queen's Bohemian Rhapsody follow this progression, which features the chords Dm, G and C.

Dm Dm Dm Dm G G G G C C C C Dm Dm Dm Dm etc

The Progression from the Fifties

Common in fact from the 1940s to the 1960s for both ballads and more upbeat songs, there are two progressions here. Firstly, is C Am Dm and G and songs such as the Beatles' The Fool on the Hill used this.

C C C C Am Am Am Am Dm Dm Dm Dm G G G G C C C
C

Similar to this is the second progression which was used by the late great Leonard Cohen in the much-recorded Hallelujah. Here, the chords of C Am F and G are used.

C C C C Am Am Am Am F F F F G G G G

Chapter Summary

In this Chapter, we have presented all the most common chords that do not require a barre.

- These chords come in the major form, which is usually known just by its letter, that is, C is the same as C major
- They come in a seventh form
- The can also come in a minor form as well as a minor seventh version

- Chords are often put together in what are called progressions, and which form the basis of many songs.

In the next chapter you will learn a little bit about strumming.

Chapter Three: Lesson Three - Strumming

Before reading any further, give yourself a bit of a treat. Put your favourite CD, record, iPod song or whatever on to play. Listen carefully to the rhythm and count the beats of the drum. Sometimes, you can hear this on the guitars as well, but the drum is usually clearest.

What you are listening to is the beat of the song, sometimes called the time signature. In other words, the number of beats in a bar of music. If you learn to read music, this will be very important to help you play, but for the moment, just understanding about different rhythms in the simplest form is all that is needed.

Tap along to the beat, get that rhythm in your bones. What you will notice is that most, but not all, songs are written in 4/4 timing, that means that there are four beats in the bar. They might be played as eight quick beats, or two heavy and two light ones, or just 1,2,3,4; by counting or tapping your foot along you will see that the song is divided into blocks of four.

There are other rhythms, 3/4 is the beat of the waltz – **dum**, dee, dee, **dum**, dee, dee, **dum**, dee, dee, **dum**, dee, dee, etc. But we will start with four beats to the bar.

One tool here that can be very useful is a metronome, which is a device which ticks a steady rhythm out. You can buy a modern digital one from about $16, or a traditional one with a lever for about $100, which also makes a great ornament.

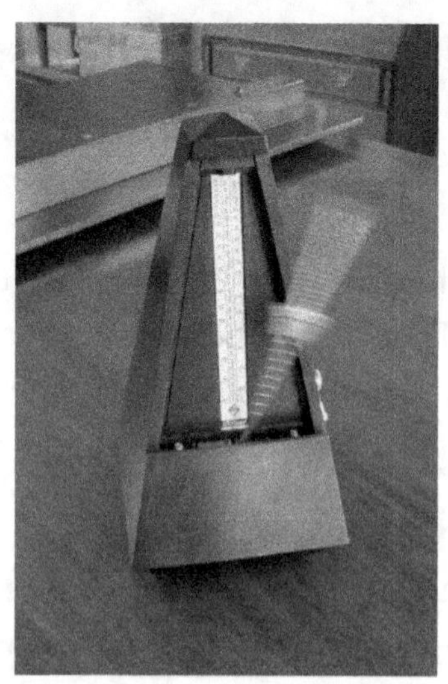

Or, there are apps available for your phone and free online versions. What the metronome will do, as it clicks away at the speed you set, is to help you keep a constant beat. This is really important as the guitar frequently supplies the rhythm for a song.

Basic Four-Four Rhythms

For each of the following, start by using you thumb, then add in a forefinger if it feels comfortable, finally, try it with a plectrum*.

Hold a chord that you feel comfortable making, and when you get the feel change the chord after ever bar, or four beats.

Set the metronome to sixty beats per minute, then when you get the hang of the rhythm, increase it to eighty beats per minute.

Example One

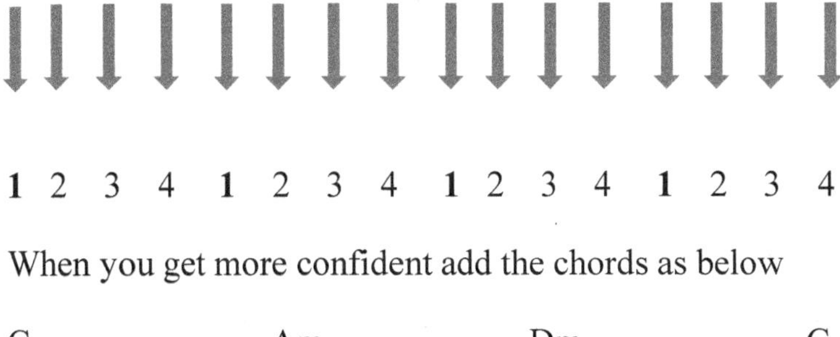

1 2 3 4   1 2 3 4   1 2 3 4   1 2 3 4

When you get more confident add the chords as below

C   Am   Dm   G

Example Two

This time you will strum twice as quickly, getting eight strokes in each four beats. Start with a down beat / strum and follow it with an upbeat. Once again, add the different chords when you have the hang of it. Don't forget to use your metronome to make sure you maintain a rhythm and keep time.

Example Three

Once you have these basics, then we can go for something very complicated. After you have mastered this and the chords we have shown you, you really will be able to call yourself a guitar player. Perhaps not yet an Eric Clapton, Jimi Hendrix or Paul Simon, but definitely someone who can bash out a beat, play the chords and make it sound good.

As before, start with the single chord and the slow speed, then build things up. Note the direction of the strokes.

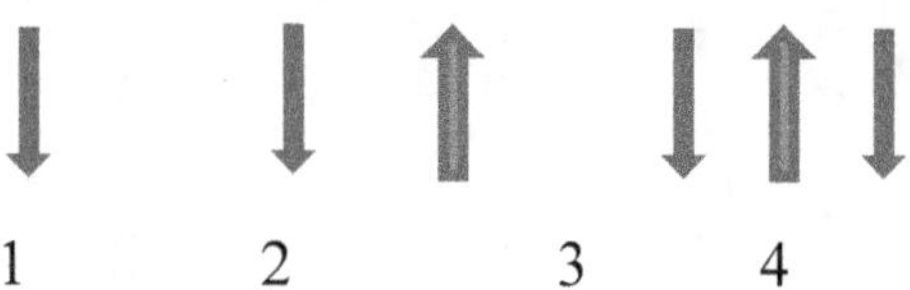

1   2   3   4

Note that here the first 'stroke' of the third beat does not happen. The effect you are looking to achieve is **DUM   DEE DEE pause DEE DEE DEE DUM   DEE DEE pause DEE DEE DEE** etc.

A Tip for the Plectrum

It is best to start with a medium weight plectrum, as they are easiest to manipulate. Heavy ones can get caught on the strings, and lightweight ones can be harder to control. Hold the plectrum between your thumb and first finger, and curl the other fingers up into a loose fist. Hold the plectrum towards the top, so just over half is exposed to strike the strings. You do not want the strings to catch on your fingers.

Finally, remember when strumming that the movement comes from the wrist, not the whole arm. The great arm flashing helicopter rotors of Pete Townshend and other performers are for show, not effect. Just a small rotation of the wrist leads to controlled, pure strumming with a great sound.

Chapter Summary

In this chapter we have learned a little about strumming, the technique and some rhythms that can be played.

In the next chapter we will learn something a little more technical: reading tabs.

Chapter Four: Lesson Four - Reading Tabs

There are four basic ways to play the notes and chords, found in a piece of music, on the guitar. These are:

- Reading the Music
- Playing by Ear
- Reading Chord Names
- Playing by Tab

Reading Music

The guitar is unusual when it comes to instruments. First, compared to most, it is relatively easy to learn. There is none of the complex finger movements of the piano, breathing challenges of wind and brass instruments or judgement of tone and pitch associated with the likes of the violin and cello.

That means that players are often self-taught, from books such as this, or have picked it up from friends. Learning to read music is a very useful skill indeed, but it is time consuming and needs a lot of practice. It tends to be an element left out when learning the guitar without the benefit of formal tutorage.

However, there is a use in knowing where the various notes are located on the guitar. These are presented in the table below. Along the top are the fret positions, down the side are the strings to which the fret position is related and finally in the middle is the note played. The logical pattern will quickly become apparent. Remember that the following pairs of notes are the same:

A# and Bb, C# and Db, D# and Eb, F# and Gb, G# and Ab

Open	First	Second	Third	Fourth	Fifth	Sixth	Seventh	Eighth
E (first)	F	F#	G	G#	A	Bb	B	C
B (second)	C	C#	D	Eb	E	F	F#	G
G (third)	G#	A	Bb	B	C	C#	D	Eb
D (fourth)	Eb	E	F	F#	G	G#	A	Bb
A (fifth)	Bb	B	C	C#	D	Eb	E	F
E (sixth)	F	F#	G	G#	A	Bb	B	C

Playing by Ear

There are some natural musicians who can just hear a piece, and know how to play it and which chords or notes to use. Sadly, not many of us fit into that category.

Playing by Chords

This is the easiest way of playing. Here, the chords to play are written above the lyrics of the song. The only problem is that if you do not know the song, it can be very hard to play. Getting the placement of the actual chord changes is also very difficult. Simply placing the fingers in the exact place is a challenge. There are some songs using this method later in the book, to get players started.

Playing by Tab

This might seem complicated at first, but with a bit of time, can be a very helpful way of overcoming the difficulties listed above.

The tab is a horizontal box with six lines, each one equating to one of the guitar's strings. The lowest represents the low E string, next is the A string, the D string, G string, then one from the top is the B string, with the top line equating to the higher pitched E string.

Numbers printed on the strings relate to the fret that the string should be played on. A '0' means that the string should be played open.

Chords are a little more complicated, but still quick to learn. Here, numbers appear on all the strings.

Can you work out which chord the following tablature represents?

It is, of course, E major. Strings 1 (E), 2 (B) and 6 (E) are open, then the G string is played on the first fret, and strings 4 and 5, (D and A) are played on the second fret.

To help even more, tablature, or tabs, will usually feature the chord's name as well.

A little later we will learn a bit about finger picking. This is when the notes of the chord are played individually by the fingers of, for right handed players, the right hand. The proper name for this is an arpeggiated chord*.

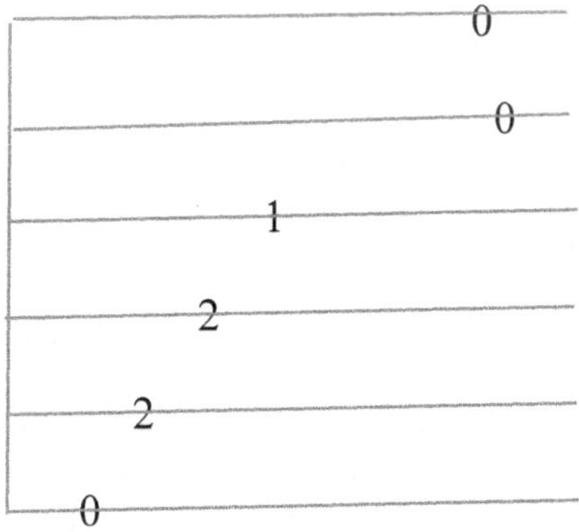

The arpeggiated E major chord will look like the diagram above.

Where a string should not be played, it is indicated by an X. There are numerous other signs in tablature, which can be investigated when a player is more competent with their instrument, but this is enough information for the first stages of playing, especially as this book aims to get players up and running, at the most basic level, within a day.

Chapter Summary

In this chapter we have learned four ways of playing the guitar. By chord, by ear, by music and by tab.

- Playing by chord is the most straightforward, but is a rough science.
- Tab and music are accurate, but trickier (especially by music).
- Playing by ear is an aptitude all musicians would like, but few possess.

In the next chapter we talk about barre chords, the method by which any chord can be played.

Chapter Five: Lesson Five - Barre Chords

In this chapter you will learn about how the barre can turn the basic chord shapes into any chord.

Creating the barre can be tiring at first, and strength needs to build up in the hand. It is easiest on an electric guitar, where the neck is slim and the strings are usually lightweight. The Spanish guitar is hardest because of the width of the neck and the bulkiness of the strings.

Below we can see how the basic E chord fingering turns into the chord of F when it is shifted down a fret, and the index finger makes a barre behind it.

F

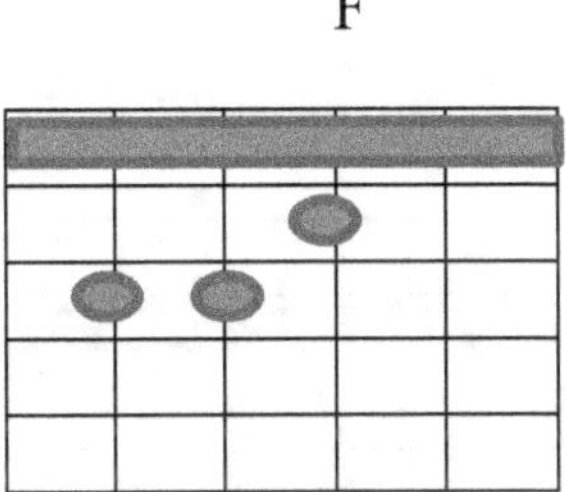

Here are some of the chords that we did not show earlier, with their barre in place

B Chords

B

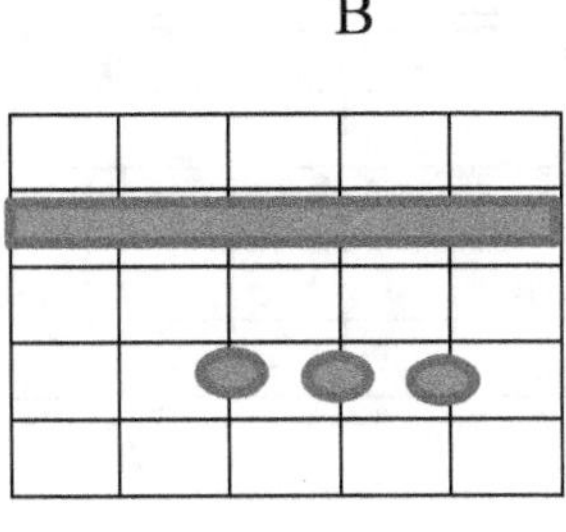

Bm

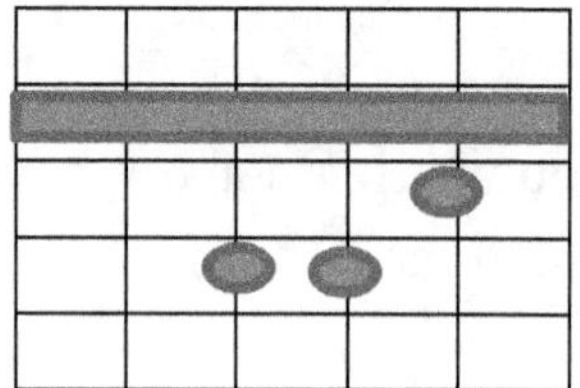

B7 (no low E strummed)

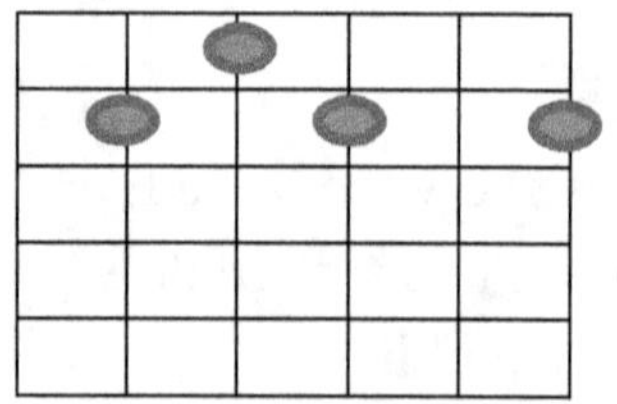

Bm7

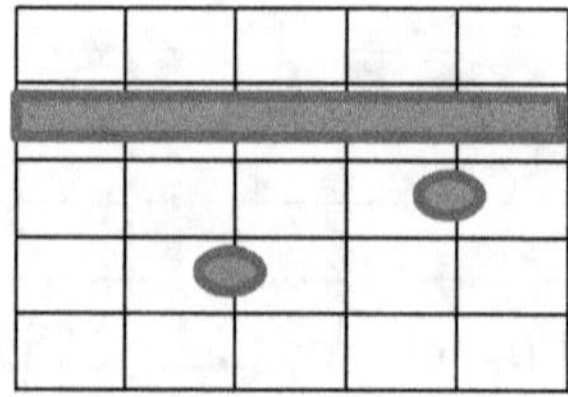

F Chords

Fm

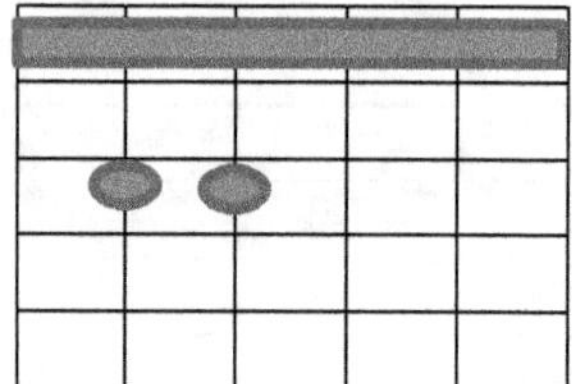

F7

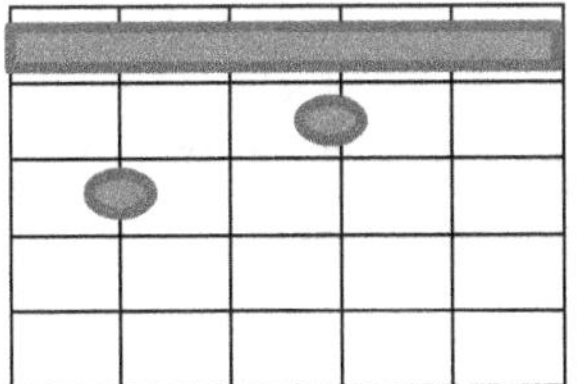

Fm7

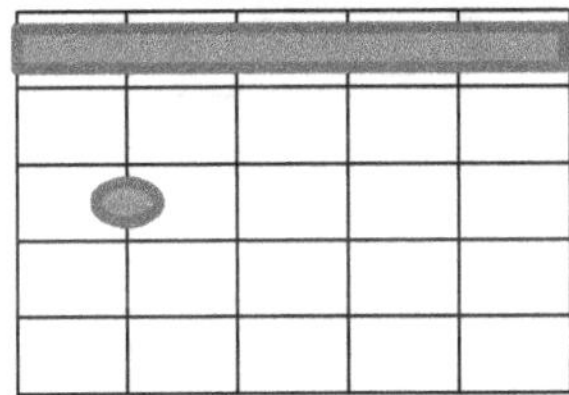

G Chords

Gm

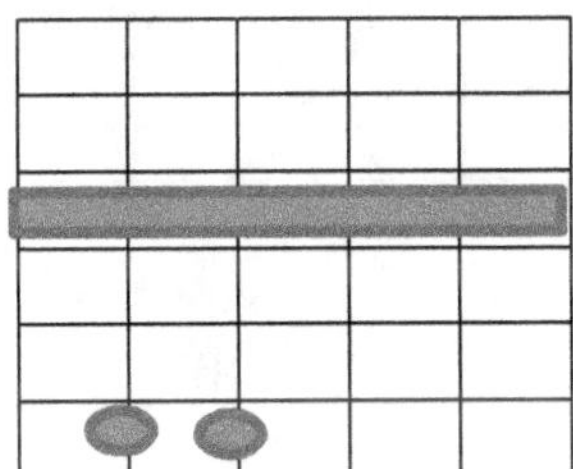

Gm7

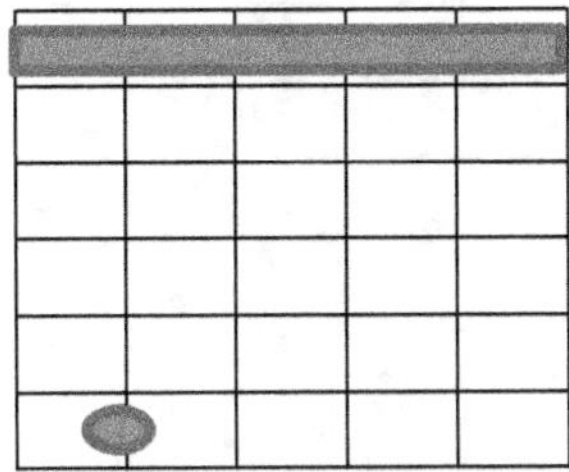

Sharps and Flats

Sharp and flat chords tend to be made using a barre. The most common chords here are F sharp (F#), C#, B flat (Bb) and Eb, although there are several more.

F#

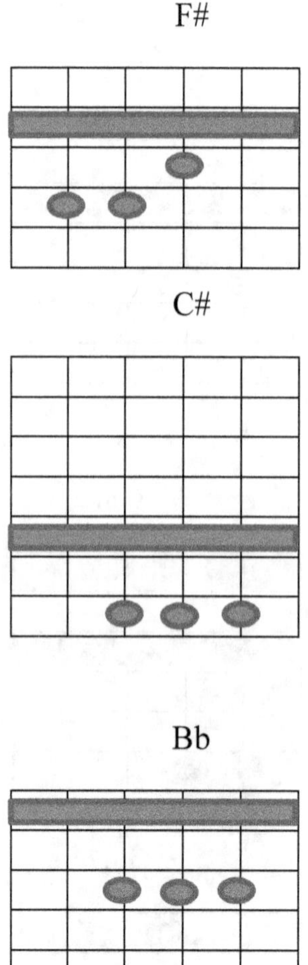

C#

Bb

Eb

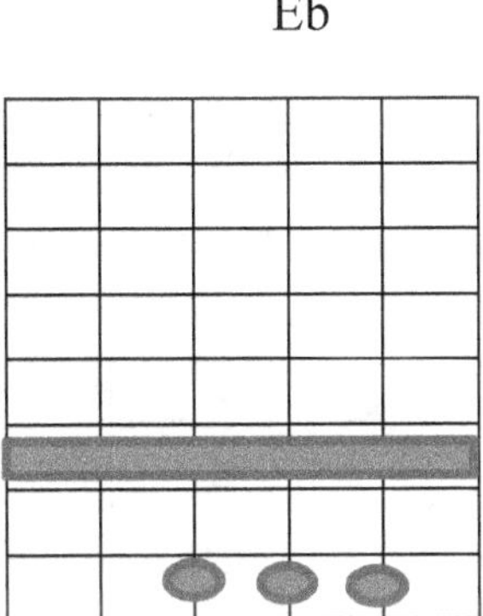

As many of you will have spotted, it is possible to play the same chord in many ways using a barre. This can make chord changes easier as players become more experienced. Although the chord is the same, the pitch and quality of sound will vary depending on where on the fretboard* the chord is played.

Chord Table

The table below shows how various chords are formed depending on where they are played on the fretboard. Chord shapes are listed across the top, and the fret on which the barre is held down the side.

In the middle is the chord that is formed. The pattern can be repeated for any cord shape, although these are the shapes that are usually to be found used with a barre.

	E	Em	Em7	A	Am	Am7
	E	Em	Em7	A	Am	Am7
1st	F	Fm	Fm7	Bb	Bbm	Bbm7
2nd	F#	F#m	F#m7	B	Bm	Bm7
3rd	G	Gm	Gm7	C	Cm	Cm7
4th	Ab	G#m	G#m7	C#	C#m	C#m7
5th	A	Am	Am7	D	Dm	Dm7
6th	Bb	Bbm	Bbm7	Eb	Ebm	Ebm7
7th	B	Bm	Bm7	E	Em	Em7
8th	C	Cm	Cm7	F	Fm	Fm7

Chapter Summary

In this chapter we have looked at the barre.

- We have seen that the barre accompanied by the shapes of other chords can create new chords.

- Practising with a barre makes chord changes easier.

In the next chapter you will learn more about those essentials of instrument playing, scales.

Chapter Six: Lesson Six - Guitar Scales

Quite a short chapter this one, but a very important one. Scales are the notes that are contained within a particular key in music. Songs are written in keys, and by knowing the notes that are involved in that key, it is possible to play accompaniments and lead guitar to go with it.

A great way to warm up is to run through a couple of scales, it gets the fingers of both hands working, and over time the notes will become engrained in your head. You will then know, even if you are just reading the chords involved in a piece, the key in which it is based.

The tables below show the notes involved in all the major and minor keys. The numbers on the left indicate the place of that note in the scale, while the keys are across the top.

Major Keys

	A	Bb	B	C	Db	D	Eb	E	F	F#	G	Ab
1	A	Bb	B	C	Db	D	Eb	E	F	F#	G	Ab
2	B	C	Db	D	Eb	E	F	F#	G	G#	A	Bb
3	C#	D	Eb	E	F	F#	G	G#	A	Bb	B	C
4	D	Eb	E	F	F#	G	Ab	A	Bb	B	C	Db
5	E	F	F#	G	Ab	A	Bb	B	C	C#	D	Eb
6	F#	G	Ab	A	Bb	B	C	C#	D	D#	E	F
7	Ab	A	Bb	B	C	C#	D	D#	E	F	F#	G
8	A	Bb	B	C	Db	D	Eb	E	F	F#	G	Ab

Minor Keys (Harmonic Minors)

	A m	Bb m	B m	C m	C# m	D m	Eb m	E m	F m	F# m	G m	G# m
1	A	Bb	B	C	C#	D	Eb	E	F	F#	G	G#
2	B	C	C	D	D#	E	F	F#	G	G#	A	A
3	C	Db	D	Eb	E	F	Gb	G	Ab	A	Bb	B
4	D	Eb	E	f	F#	G	Ab	A	Bb	B	C	C#
5	E	F	F#	G	G#	A	Bb	B	C	C#	D	D#
6	F	Gb	G	Ab	A	Bb	C	C	Db	D	E	E
7	G#	A	Bb	B	C	C#	D	D#	E	F	F#	G
8	A	Bb	B	C	C#	D	Eb	E	F	F#	G	G#

There are many different types of minor scales, such as harmonic (which is printed), melodic and natural scales. However, the harmonic is fine for using at the level we are currently at.

One of the most common and popular scales for the guitar is the blues scale.

The blues scale in C includes the following notes:

C	Eb	F	Gb	G	Bb	C

In the key of D, it looks like this:

D	F	G	Ab	A	C	D

Finally, we will learn the classic series of notes that, once mastered, lead to the classic 12 bar blues themes that underpin so many songs.

In tab form, it looks like this:

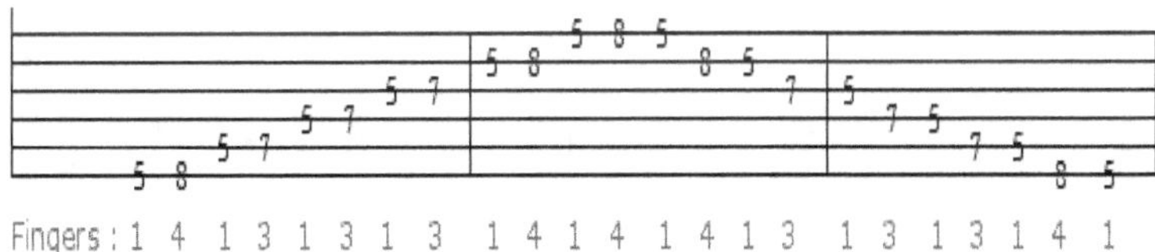

In notes, it is played as follows:

⬆	A	C	D	E	G	A	C	D	E	G	A	C	⬇
A	G	E	D	C	A	G	E	D	C	A			

Chapter Summary

Chapter six has introduced you to the concept of the musical scale. You have been given the notes involved in the different key signatures in which music is written.

In the next chapter you will learn more about plectrums or picks, and a little about finger picking.

Chapter Seven: Lesson Seven - Using a Plectrum and Finger Picking

As we saw earlier, there are many different weights of plectrum. It is best to start strumming with a middle weight one, and over time players will find the weight that suits them best, and which works for the kind of music they are playing. Heavy plectrums tend to be easier for picking notes if, for example, a combination of picking and strumming is required. Lightweight plectrums are handy for faster, smoother strumming. They are handy for electric guitars, where the sound is created electronically.

There are also thumb and finger picks which can be worn when picking notes. They can be tricky to use, catching on the strings, and a light action is needed. As a beginner, it is probably best to start picking using the fingers, rather than the picks shown below, but it is a matter of choice. A sharper sound is created with the picks.

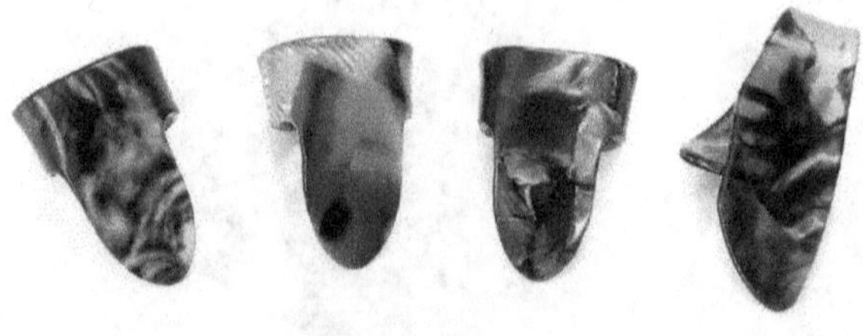

Whether picking or strumming, a different tone is created depending on where the action takes place. Playing over the sound hole (or pick up, with an electric guitar) creates the fullest, and loudest sound.

Move towards the bridge, and a harsher tone is produced. Unsurprisingly, playing closer to the neck makes for a softer, more mellifluous sound.

Finger Picking

Sometimes called finger style*, or plucking*, this is the method by which individual notes of a chord are played one after the other, often quite quickly. It is a style often associated with folk style music, and ballads.

Listen to Paul Simon playing the opening to the Simon and Garfunkel hit, The Boxer, to hear finger picking at its best.

Picking usually works as follows. The thumb plays any notes on the low E, A and D strings, while the first, second and third fingers pick notes from the G, B and E strings. Normally, the index finger will pluck the lowest string being played, usually the G string, with the middle finger next, usually the B string and the third finger used for the top E string. The little finger is not used, and many players place it under the sound hole on the body of the guitar to provide support and help the other fingers to remain in the correct place. The only time it would come into play is if there is a need to pluck five strings simultaneously.

Picking can be used with arpeggiated chords, and for playing pairs of notes together

An advantage of finger picking is that it turns the guitar into more than a percussive rhythm keeper. It allows for melodies to be interspersed with chords, and for the playing of harmonies (notes combined to produce a pleasing effect). Hammers* and pull offs* can also be incorporated into playing, as the guitarist becomes more competent. Tapping the body of the guitar to create a percussion effect is also easier than when working with a plectrum.

It is still possible to strum, using the thumb or first finger, but the sound created has a different quality to that created with a pick, and therefore it is not suitable for more upbeat rockier numbers.

Finger pickers need to keep their hands in good condition. The right hand always needs short finger nails for pressing the strings, and the same is true for the finger picker, unless they choose to use artificial picks. A nail too long will catch on the string, spoiling the effect being sought.

Another advantage with finger picking is that a greater variety of sound can be created. Generally, the volume will be lower, but varying the position of where the strings are plucked, and the force with which this happens, can alter the timbre*, to create mood and atmosphere in a song.

More flexibility is offered when playing, flamenco style strumming, plucking of multiple strings, arpeggios and such like all are easier to play with fingerpicking. However, the strings used should be nylon or light gauge steel, unless an artificial pick is attached to the fingers, to prevent nail and finger damage.

All the above makes it clear that finger picking lends itself to classical, solo guitar playing or playing as an accompaniment to voice or just perhaps one or two other instruments.

When finger picking is notarised in a piece of music, it will usually adopt the following notations:

Thumb = B

Index = I

Middle = M

Ring = A

Little = C or X or E

What's Next

As with everything else when learning the guitar, practice is all.

There are two simple finger picking exercises that can be practised to get the player into the swing.

For each, use the thumb for the E, A and D strings, the index finger for the G string, middle finger for the B string and third finger for the top E.

Use the chord progressions from earlier to practice. Set the metronome for 60 – it can get faster as you progress.

The first pattern is for 3/4 timing, the second for 4/4.

We will use the Dm, C, G, Dm progression in the example below. We will be playing two strings for each beat of the bar.

It goes something like this:

3/4 Example

The top row represents the chord, the second the finger playing and the third is the beat.

Dm						C						G						Dm					
T	I	M	A	M	I	T	I	M	A	M	I	T	I	M	A	M	I	T	I	M	A	M	I
1		2		3		1		2		3		1		2		3		1		2		3	

And so on…

4/4 Example

Dm								C								G							
T	I	M	A	M	I	T	I	T	I	M	A	M	I	T	I	T	I	M	A	M	I	T	I
1		2		3		4		1		2		3		4		1		2		3		4	

Chapter Summary

In this chapter we have learned a bit about finger picking, its uses and tools that can help.

- We know about how the notation is present
- We have undertaken some practice
- We know the kind of music with which it works best.

In the next chapter we will present some songs for you to play.

Chapter Eight: Some Songs to Play

Below are some songs along with their chords. They are well known, and if one is unfamiliar, they can be found easily on the internet. For legal reasons, we can only print songs that are out of copywrite, but there are hundreds of examples of popular music on the internet, plus countless books available from your local music stores.

Sing along with the songs, it will help you to 'feel' where the changes take place and keep you in time.

Happy Birthday

```
    A       E
Happy Birthday to you
    D      A
Happy Birthday to you
    A7         D
Happy Birthday dear Billy (please feel free to substitute a
name!)
    A   E   A
Happy Birthday to you.
```

Morning Has Broken

          C Dm G   F   C
Morning has broken, like the first morning
(C)   Em Am D7   D   G
Blackbird has spoken, like the first bird
C   F   C   Am D
Praise for the singing, praise for the morning
G   C F G7   C   F
Praise for the springing fresh from the world
[Interlude]
G E Am G C G7
          C Dm   G   F C
Sweet the rain's new fall, sunlit from heaven
(C)   Em Am D7   D   G
Like the first dewfall, on the first grass
C   F   C   Am D
Praise for the sweetness of the wet garden
G   C F G7   C   F
Sprung in completeness where his feet pass
[Interlude]
G E Am F# Bm G D A7/D D
        D Em A   G   D
Mine is the sunlight, mine is the morning
      F#m Bm   E7   A
Born of the one light, Eden saw play
D   G   D   Bm E
Praise with elation, praise every morning
A   D G A7   D
God's recreation of the new day

G A F# Bm G7 C F C

       C Dm G   F C
Morning has broken, like the first morning
(C)   Em Am D7   D G
Blackbird has spoken, like the first bird
C   F   C   Am D
Praise for the singing, praise for the morning
G   C F G7   C   F
Praise for the springing fresh from the world
[Outro]
G E Am F# Bm G D A7/D D

She'll Be Coming Round the Mountain

G
She'll be coming 'round the mountain
    G
When she comes.
     G
She'll be coming 'round the mountain
    D7
When she comes.
     G
She'll be coming 'round the mountain,
     C
She'll be coming 'round the mountain,
    G   D7
She'll be coming 'round the mountain,
     G
When she comes.

[Verse 2]
     G
She'll be driving six white horses
     G
When she comes
     G
She'll be driving six white horses
    D7
When she comes
      G
She'll be driving six white horses
       C

She'll be driving six white horses
          G   D7
She'll be driving six white horses
       G
When she comes

[Verse 3]
        G
Oh, we'll all come out to meet her
        G
When she comes
        G
Oh, we'll all come out to meet her
       D7
When she comes
        G
Oh, we'll all come out to meet her
       C
Oh, we'll all come out to meet her
       G   D7
Oh, we'll all come out to meet her
        G
When she comes

[Verse 4]
       G
We will kill the old red rooster
        G
When she comes
        G
We will kill the old red rooster
       D7

When she comes
    G
We will kill the old red rooster
    C
We will kill the old red rooster
    G   D7
We will kill the old red rooster
    G
When she comes

[Verse 5]
    G
We'll all have chicken n' dumplin's
    G
When she comes
    G
We'll all have chicken n' dumplin's
    D7
When she comes
    G
We'll all have chicken n' dumplin's
    C
We'll all have chicken n' dumplin's
    G   D7
We'll all have chicken n' dumplin's
    G
When she comes

Swing Low, Sweet Chariot

```
C
I looked over Jordan,
  F        C
And what did I see,
                G7
Comin' for to carry me home,
 C          F         C
A band of angels comin' after me,
        G7      C
Comin' for to carry me home.


       C        F  C
Swing Low, sweet chariot,
               G7
Comin' for to carry me home;
       C        F  C
Swing low, sweet chariot,
C          G7       C
Comin' for to carry me home.
```

The Drunken Sailor

Em
What shall we do with the drunken sailor?
D
What shall we do with the drunken sailor?
Em
What shall we do with the drunken sailor?

[Chorus]

Em D   Em
Ear-ly in the morning
Em
Hooray, and up she rises
D
Hooray, and up she rises
Em
Hooray, and up she rises
Em D   Em
Ear-ly in the morning

[Verse]

Em
Put him in the long boat 'til he's sober
D
Put him in the long boat 'til he's sober
Em
Put him in the long boat 'til he's sober

[Chorus]

Em D   Em
Ear-ly in the morning
Em
Hooray, and up she rises
D
Hooray, and up she rises
Em
Hooray, and up she rises
Em D   Em
Ear-ly in the morning

[Verse]

Em
Pull out the plug and wet him all over
D
Pull out the plug and wet him all over
Em
Pull out the plug and wet him all over

[Chorus]

Em D   Em
Ear-ly in the morning
Em
Hooray, and up she rises
D
Hooray, and up she rises

Em
Hooray, and up she rises
Em D   Em
Ear-ly in the morning

[Verse]

Em
Put him in the bilge and make him drink it
D
Put him in the bilge and make him drink it
Em
Put him in the bilge and make him drink it

[Chorus]

Em D   Em
Ear-ly in the morning
Em
Hooray, and up she rises
D
Hooray, and up she rises
Em
Hooray, and up she rises
Em D   Em
Ear-ly in the morning

[Verse]

Em
Put him in a leaky boat and make him bale her
D
Put him in a leaky boat and make him bale her
Em
Put him in a leaky boat and make him bale her

[Chorus]

Em D   Em
Ear-ly in the morning
Em
Hooray, and up she rises
D
Hooray, and up she rises
Em
Hooray, and up she rises
Em D   Em
Ear-ly in the morning

[Verse]

Em
Tie him to the scuppers with the hose pipe on him
D
Tie him to the scuppers with the hose pipe on him
Em
Tie him to the scuppers with the hose pipe on him

[Chorus]

Em D   Em
Ear-ly in the morning
Em
Hooray, and up she rises
D
Hooray, and up she rises
Em
Hooray, and up she rises
Em D   Em
Ear-ly in the morning

[Verse]

Em
Shave his belly with a rusty razor
D
Shave his belly with a rusty razor
Em
Shave his belly with a rusty razor

[Chorus]

Em D   Em
Ear-ly in the morning
Em
Hooray, and up she rises
D
Hooray, and up she rises

Em
Hooray, and up she rises
Em D   Em
Ear-ly in the morning

[Verse]

Em
Tie him to the topmast while she's yardarm under
D
Tie him to the topmast while she's yardarm under
Em
Tie him to the topmast while she's yardarm under

[Chorus]

Em D   Em
Ear-ly in the morning
Em
Hooray, and up she rises
D
Hooray, and up she rises
Em
Hooray, and up she rises
Em D   Em
Ear-ly in the morning

[Verse]

Em
Heave him by the leg in a runnin' bowline
D
Heave him by the leg in a runnin' bowline
Em
Heave him by the leg in a runnin' bowline

[Chorus]

Em D   Em
Ear-ly in the morning
Em
Hooray, and up she rises
D
Hooray, and up she rises
Em
Hooray, and up she rises
Em D   Em
Ear-ly in the morning

[Verse]

Em
Keel haul him 'til he's sober
D
Keel haul him 'til he's sober
Em
Keel haul him 'til he's sober

[Chorus]

Em D   Em
Ear-ly in the morning
Em
Hooray, and up she rises
D
Hooray, and up she rises
Em
Hooray, and up she rises
Em D   Em
Ear-ly in the morning

Greensleeves

Am   C
Alas my love,
  G   Em
you do me wrong,
  Am   E
to cast me off so discourteously,
  Am   C   G   Em
for I have loved you so long,
  Am   E7   Am
delighting in your company.

[Chorus]

C   G   Em
greensleeves was all my joy,
Am   E
greensleeves was my delight,
C   G   Em
greensleeves was my heart of gold,
  Am   E7   Am
and who but my lady greensleeves.

[Verse 2]

  Am   C   G   Em
Thy gown was of the grassy green,
    Am   E
Thy sleeves of satin hanging by,

     Am   C   G   Em
Which made thee be our harvest queen,
  Am   E7   Am
And yet thou wouldst not love me.

[Chorus]

C   G   Em
greensleeves was all my joy,
Am   E
greensleeves was my delight,
C   G   Em
greensleeves was my heart of gold,
    Am   E7 Am
and who but my lady greensleeves.

[Verse 3]

   Am   C   G   Em
Well, I will pray to God on high,
     Am   E
That thou constancy mayst see,
   Am   C   G   Em
And that yet once before I die,
Am   E7   Am
Thou will vouchsafe to love me.

Jingle Bells

```
C
Dashing through the snow
                F
In a one horse open sleigh
            G
O'er the fields we go
            C
Laughing all the way
C
Bells on bob tails ring
              F
Making spirits bright
F           G
What fun it is to laugh and sing
G           C
A sleighing song tonight

C
Oh, jingle bells, jingle bells
C
Jingle all the way
F           C
Oh, what fun it is to ride
G
In a one horse open sleigh
C
Jingle bells, jingle bells
C
Jingle all the way
F           C
```

Oh, what fun it is to ride
G   (F)   C
In a one horse open sleigh

Chapter Nine: Stringing and Tuning Your Guitar

Playing the guitar when it has new strings is always a treat. The beautiful sounds of the strings and the quality of the notes make it seem as though you are playing a new instrument. However, fitting the little blighters is not such fun.

Remember, classical or Spanish guitars have nylon or gut strings, other varieties take steel strings. Put steel strings on a Spanish guitar and the stresses will be too much, resulting in damage to the body and neck.

If you are not going to be playing the guitar for a while, loosen the tension on the strings, it helps to take the pressure off the guitar's frame.

Restringing a Guitar

Little intricacies around the bridge can vary from guitar to guitar, but the basics are below.

Step One

Turn the tuning peg, loosening each of the existing strings, until all are quiet slack.

Step Two

Starting with the Low E string, keep loosening until the string can be pushed through its hole. Then, pull it out from the bridge. This may involve untying a knot, pulling by the little nut on the end of the string, or removing a string holder from the bridge by pulling, it will depend on your guitar.

Step Three

Repeat step two with all the other strings, starting with the A string, then through D, G, B and finishing with E.

Step Four

Take the bottom E string, the lowest note (it will be the thickest string, in its own little pack). Push the end through the hole in the bridge, and pull tight. Secure the string with whatever means the old string was secured by. Slide the string through the hole in its tuning peg, making sure that you have it in the correct peg. This first string will go through the first hole in the head at the top of the guitar.

Step Five

Pull the string tight, then feedback about 4-6 cm to create some slack.

Step Six

At the head end, angle the string slightly upwards and turn the tuning peg to tighten it. When the string is taught enough, position it in its slot in the nut of the guitar. That is the small, slotted strip where the neck meets the head. Tighten further until the string is sufficiently tense to remain in place in the nut. Don't worry about tuning yet.

Step Seven

Repeat steps four, five and six with the other strings, starting with the A string, then the D, G, B and finally the top E.

Step Eight

If you have excessive amounts of string hanging loose at the neck end, get some cutters and trim the strings. Leave about 3-4 cm showing.

You now have a restringed guitar…one that is very out of tune.

Tuning the Guitar

Unless you have purchased expensive, pre-stressed strings, then your guitar will go out of tune very quickly. You will need to retune regularly for a week or so. You will find that the guitar stays in tune for longer and longer periods.

First Tune

Unless you are blessed with perfect pitch, you will need something to tune the guitar to. A piano, tuning fork or measuring device attached to the head will do help you with this. Just as easy is to go online and search for a free guitar tuner. These work perfectly well.

Tuning the Guitar to itself

Once the instrument has settled after its re-stringing. It is much quicker to tune it to itself. This can be done in two ways.

Note Method

The fifth fret on the string is the same note as the open string on the next. So, pressing and playing the fifth fret on the A string, gives the note D, which is the same as the open D string.

The only exception is from the G string to the B string. Here, the fourth fret needs to be played to get the same note, B, as the open string after it.

Tune the string while holding down the note and letting both it and the open note ring on. Although requiring a bit of contortion, this allows you to hear the notes blend together.

Harmonic* Method

Harmonics are played by placing the finger of the left hand lightly on the string directly over a fret marker. The string is plucked and the finger lifted simultaneously. A bell like ringing sound is created.

Listening to the harmonics is a great way to tune, as rather than judging pitch, you will hear the vibrations of the harmonics. They will synch together when the notes are the same.

You will need to play harmonics on the fifth fret of the lower string, and seventh fret of the higher string to get the effect required. Unfortunately, this method does not work with the G to B strings, although it does with all other combinations.

Hearing Method

If you play a chord slowly, or two notes an octave* apart (use the table of notes in the earlier chapter to find where the same notes can be found) those with a good ear can hear whether their guitar is in tune or not. This gets easier with experience.

Tuning a Twelve String Guitar

If re-stringing a normal guitar is tricky, that is nothing to a 12 string. Tuning, too, is a little different.

For normal pitch, the main six strings are tuned as normal, but between each of the low E, A, D and G a string is fitted and pitched to an octave above the main note. The top two strings, B and top E, have their partners as identical pitch to themselves.

So, starting from the lowest string, the tuning is:

E (as per normal guitar)

E (up an octave)

A

A (up an octave)

D

D (up an octave)

G

G (up an octave)

B

B (same note, NOT up an octave)

E

E (same note, NOT up an octave)

Hard work, but a great sound.

Types of Guitars

The main types are:

- *Spanish guitar*, usually the smallest kind, with nylon or gut strings, and a soft but precise sound. Usually finger picked, but can be strummed, usually with the thumb or fingers.
- *Acoustic Guitar*, steel stringed and usually finger picked or strummed with a plectrum.
- *Electric Acoustic*, as above with the addition of an electronic pick up to allow it to be played through an amplifier.
- *Electric Guitar*, often with one or two pick-ups, usually strummed or played as lead guitar – see below.
- *Bass Guitar*, four stringed electric with different tuning. Notes are usually plucked.
- *Combo*, a guitar with two necks allowing bass and normal guitar to be played.
- *Hollow Bodies Guitars* – these are electric guitars where the sound is enhanced with a hollow body. See below for an example.

- *Twelve String,* a steel strung acoustic usually strummed.
- *Hawaiian,* a guitar really in name only, although the steel tube with which the notes are formed can be bought for other guitar types.
- *Four and A Half String,* yes, really! Some of the earliest instruments were four stringed, with an extra, open string attached from the bridge to half way along the neck.

Looking After Your Guitar

You can get a decent, second hand model for $10, or you can pay thousands. Whichever, a guitar is a precision instrument and deserves to be treated as such. It is worth investing in a case to protect from everyday life. A soft one is fine if the guitar is to be kept at home, a hard one if it is going to be moved around, or the toddler can get access to it.

A soft, lint free duster can give the guitar a once over after it is played, removing finger marks, and specialist cleaners can be used to make it sparkle.

When the guitar is not in use, store it in a dry room, out of direct sunlight, away from a radiator and in a moderate temperature. Properly looked after, a guitar will last for life. In fact, for generations.

Buying a Guitar

Some things better with age. Cheese, fine red wine, Jane Fonda…many musical instruments also fit into this category. The guitar is no different. As the wood matures and settles, so the sound improves in quality. Therefore, there is no real need to buy new when $50 at a second hand will get a decent and very usable model. Double that for a new one.

But whether buying new or second hand, try out the instrument. Check that its weight is comfortable, and it is the right size. Elvis Presley played on a ¾ size instrument through the early part of his career, but he was a little special. Basically, make sure the guitar feels right when you hold it.

Check for cracks anywhere – if you find one walk away; a guitar is an instrument designed to take the stresses of tight strings, if there is a fault, it won't last for long. Check that there is no bowing on the back, and that the neck is straight.

Surface damage such as light scratches won't matter if they have not damaged the wood but if there are buzzes when played and the cause is not obvious (such as too much overhanging string at the head) then look elsewhere.

Make sure that the bridge is secure and the tuning parts are all in good condition.

Playing Lead

The lead guitarist is the quarter back, the centre forward, the Ferrari, the Tom Cruise of the guitar world. In other words, the glamour player. Listen to Pink Floyd or Dire Straits or Eric Clapton and hear the astonishing lead guitar melodies and riffs that take the music to that ultimate destination. Of course, just as Mr Cruise needs his support players and the quarterback (his team mates), so the lead is nothing without his rhythm back up.

But if lead is what you want, then a number of skills need to be developed. Some musical knowledge is needed, as lead improvisations come from an understanding of the constituent parts of the chord structure and key signatures being played.

Competency with both hands is needed. The left often picks notes at the end of the neck close to the body, where the frets are narrower, and more precision is needed. At the same time, picking notes with a plectrum is harder than doing it with the fingers.

But, as always, practice makes perfect and that starring role comes to those who want it and work for it.

If it is for you, start by grasping the first position. This is where notes are played using the first four frets, with the index finger on string one, and so forth ending with the little finger on fret four. Once tunes, melodies, harmonies and riffs* can be picked from here, then you can move on to working further down the fret board.

Accessories

Here is a list of some helpful accessories. Not all of these are required, so we have listed a usefulness factor after each. 1/5 means you may not need this item whereas 5/5 means you should have that item for playing regularly.

- *Stand* - frame for holding the guitar when it is not being used. It will add protection to the guitar and help preserve its life.   4/5
- *Footstool* – a handy device for serious Spanish guitar players and beginners as they get the guitar position right. To be honest, though, a pile of books works as well.   1/5

- *Plectrums and Picks* – essentials, especially plectrums, for the acoustic and electric guitar player. 5/5 (plectrums) 2/5 (finger picks)
- *Tuning Paraphernalia* – necessary in the old days, when a tuning fork was the only way to get into tune if there was no piano in the house. Nowadays it is all available online. 3/5 (because an portable tuner is always handy)
- *Metronome* – a handy tool for the beginner. A good, old fashioned metronome does the job and looks great, but as with tuning equipment, a metronome can be found for free through an app or online. 3/5 (but only for its decorative qualities)
- *Guitar Cover* – it will prolong the life of your instrument. 5/5
- *Strap* – depends on the type of guitar. Classical or Spanish guitars rarely come with strap holders as they are meant to be played sitting down. But if you have an electric, then you look a bit silly playing while sitting, at least if there is an audience. 3/5
- *Amplifier* – in the old days, your amp could double as a nuclear fallout shelter, so big and sturdy was the speaker. Now, for $50, a tiny amp capable of filling a large hall with sound is readily available. Pay more, and all kinds of effects will come as well. 5/5 for electric guitars.
- *Effects Pedals* – as spectacular as it looks, stamping on pedals while sweat pours of your face staining the silver lycra and making the Bowie Make Up run, these are a bit, well, seventies. Just get a decent amp. 0/5

- *Music Stand* – from the mad to the sensible. A music stand will hold your music at the right level whether you stand or sit. Admittedly, a table also works, as does a chair and, if your eyesight is good enough, the floor. But, a music stands makes you look professional 2/5

Chapter Ten: Glossary – In Very Simplified Terms

Acoustic Guitar – Steel stringed and slightly larger than a classical guitar. Associated with folk music, some pop music. Ideal for strumming or picking.

Arpeggiated Chord – a chord where the individual notes are picked out one at a time.

Barre – Using the first finger to cover all six strings. This has the effect of allowing the basic chord shape to be played anywhere on the guitar neck. So, for example, the E shape creates the chord E when there is no barre. With a first fret barre, and the same shape after it, the chord moves up from an E to an F, one more and it becomes F#, next G, G#. A, A# (usually called Bb of B flat), C, C#, D, Eb (the same as D#) and then back to E.

Bass Guitar – Not covered in this book, but a four-stringed variety, with each string of a lower pitch than in the six-string variety, usually electric.

Chord – a combination of notes played together.

Classical Guitar – sometimes called Spanish Guitar, these are slightly smaller than other types usually. They are nylon stringed and can be used for classical music, finger picking and, sometimes, strumming.

Clef – the symbol in music which gives an indication of pitch. The guitar uses the treble clef, but never the bass clef. The clef appears at the beginning of a sheet of music.

Electric Guitar – Played through an amp. The easy action of electric guitars makes them comfortable to play. Ideal for lead or rhythm work. Less good for finger picking.

Finger Picking – playing notes individually, occasionally in pairs, with the thumb and fingers of the right (for right handed guitarists) hand.

Finger Style – see Finger Picking

Fret – The zones marked on the neck of the guitar. Each fret is marked by a narrow strip which runs perpendicular to and below the strings.

Fretboard – the frets on the neck of the guitar.

Hammer – playing a note by banging the left hand onto the string at the correct fret for the note.

Harmonics – bell like sounds played by placing the finger of the left hand lightly on the string directly above the fret marker. As the string is plucked, the finger lifts. A good place to practice is on the 12th fret for each string, where harmonics are easy to play.

Hawaiian Guitar – often played flat, they are tuned by using a hollow tube, which creates a unique, smooth and tropical sound. It is possible to buy the tubes and use them on other kinds of guitars.

Jamming, or Jam Session – informal playing with others.

Key – music is written in a 'key' – it tells you the combination of 'rules' that make the piece sound 'right'. The guitar is tuned to the key of E minor 7 with a suspension. There, that makes a lot of sense. It is possible to tune a guitar to a different key, but there are risks; the strings have a limit to which they can be stretched, and will snap if over tightened. Equally, if too slack, they will 'buzz' when played. It is best to stick in the natural key, which is changed through utilizing the frets and different chord placements.

Major Chords – those that sound full and complete.

Minor Chords – those chords that have a kind of questioning quality to them.

Notes – a note is the individual note that is made by playing a string. The notes change when the finger pushes down a string in a fret.

Octave – the group of eight notes between the same notes at different pitches. So, from C to C is an octave where D, E, F, G, A and B all fit between the two C notes.

Open String – this is the string when played with no notes pressed down on the frets. Starting from the string at the TOP of the guitar, the thickest string (which, confusingly, is the lowest note) they are E A D G B E.

Pick – sometimes called a plectrum, this is a triangular piece of thin plastic that comes in different widths – thin or light, medium and thick or heavy. It is used to strike the strings in an upwards or downward motion when strumming.

Plectrum – sometimes called a pick, this is a triangular piece of thin plastic that comes in different widths – thin or light, medium and thick or heavy. It is used to strike the strings in an upwards or downward motion when strumming.

Plucking – the action by which a note or notes are played by the right hand pulling the strings with a plucking action.

Pull off – a note played by the finger of the left hand pulling away from the string with a sharp, plucking action.

Riff – a repeated pattern of notes or chords.

Seventh Chords – a chord with an extra note.

Spanish Guitar - sometimes called Classical Guitar, these are slightly smaller than other types usually. They are nylon stringed and can be used for classical music, finger picking and, sometimes, strumming.

Strumming – the action of striking down the strings either with the thumb or plectrum (occasionally the first finger) when playing a chord.

Timbre – the musical quality of the sound created, often connected to mood and atmosphere.

Tuning or Tuned - these are the individual notes of the open strings. When played open (see above) they produce the following notes (see above). Starting from the string at the TOP of the guitar, the thickest string (which, confusingly, is the lowest note) they are E A D G B E.

Twelve String Guitars – as it suggests, twelve strings with clever tuning, creates a very full sound when strummed. Often used for country or folk type music.

Final Words

You have now reached the end of this introduction to the guitar. You could well be an expert player, about to organize your first gig in front of 1000 people at the local concert hall.

Much more likely is that practice, practice and more practice is what is needed next.

But competence will come quickly, given a bit of time. Twenty minutes a day will help you see rapid improvements in your playing and the acquisition of more and more skills.

Guitar playing is common, so it is easy to find advice from friends or the world wide web when you hit a problem. And that is a part of the joy of playing a guitar, or indeed any musical instrument.

You become a part of a community; a non-competitive, supportive and interesting one. There is enormous pleasure in playing your guitar by yourself, but even more by joining with others in a band, or just a friendly jam session* can be a lot of fun.

Make that your next step and now you are on the road to becoming a musician!

HOW TO PLAY
PIANO
IN 1 DAY
The Only 7 Exercises You Need to
Learn Piano Theory, Piano Technique
and Piano Sheet Music Today
PRESTON HOFFMAN

BOOK 4

HOW TO PLAY PIANO: IN 1 DAY

The Only 7 Exercises You Need to Learn Piano Theory, Piano Technique and Piano Sheet Music Today

Preston Hoffman

Table of Contents

Introduction

Have you always wanted to learn to play the piano? Have you been hesitant about doing so because of the thought of having to spend endless hours practicing? Maybe you took some lessons but gave up because it was too hard.

What if there was a much easier way? What if I were to tell you that you could learn all the basics in seven simple lessons and that you could learn to play a proper tune in less than a day?

Does that sound a little too good to be true? Here are a couple more facts for you – playing the piano is not that complicated. It's just that the way that we are traditionally taught to play is a lot more complicated than it needs to be. Normally, you have to start by learning one note at a time, and have to learn all the theory before you get to actually start practicing what you have learned.

There is a lot of work to do before you even get close to seeing real results and that can be very disheartening.

What we do in this book is to break it down for you into simple but essential steps. You will learn the basics of music theory quickly and easily and will be able to play your first tune within hours. This will give you the motivation to carry on and keep practicing.

Will this book turn you into a maestro? No, but then it is not designed to do that. It will, however, get you started and teach you the foundations that you can build on.

You'll get to show your friends and family just how smart you are by being able to play your favorite songs – and save yourself a bundle in sheet music too.

If you are looking for an excellent introduction to playing the piano, this is the book for you. If you decide to carry on learning from there, this gives you a solid base to do that as well.

Chapter One: The Keyboard and Keys

In this chapter, you will learn about all the keys on the keyboard. This is the first step in our seven-point plan to teach you how to play the piano.

Your piano keyboard will look like this:

Looking down at the keyboard for the first time can be a bit intimidating. The keyboard is made up of a set of 52 white long keys, and a set of 36 shorter, more raised black keys. You should have 88 keys in total. (Some older pianos have smaller keyboards.)

Have a look at the diagram below – it is a smaller section of the keyboard, and contains all the basic information that you need to know. Once you get to know this information, you can basically apply it to the rest of the keyboard.

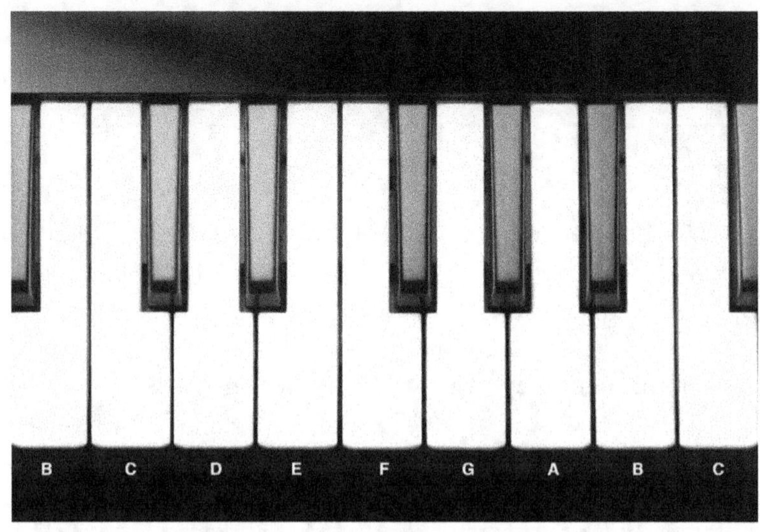

The White Keys

The white keys, as shown above, each play a particular note in music. These are named for the first seven letters of the alphabet – A through to G. There are a lot more keys than there are notes, so the letters are repeated over and over again. So, starting at the very left edge of the keyboard, you start with the letter A. The repetition makes it a lot easier – there are the same seven notes over and over again.

The next key represents the "B" chord, and so on, until you get to the key after the "G" chord. Then the keys start at "A" again. Each set represents one octave.

So, do you have to sit down and count each key from the start to determine which letter it represents? Fortunately, there is an easier way, and that is part of the reason that we have the black keys.

The black keys are divided into groupings of twos (twins) – marked in green on the diagram above or threes (triplets) – marked in red on the diagram above. The "C" note is always to the left of a set of twins. The "F" note is always to the left of a set of the triplets. To remember this more easily, you can think of the "C" as having two points to it and the "F" as having three points to it. From there, it is easy enough to fill in the remaining letters.

Whereabouts the keys are positioned on the board indicates how high or low the note is. The lowest notes are on the left, and you move up the scales as you move over to the right.

Quick Exercise: Play each key now and see how different they all sound. Find each of the "C" keys on the keyboard. Follow with all of the "D" keys and so on. Then play the following notes on any set of the keys:

B, D, B, E, D, B.

Do you recognize the tune at all? Does it remind you of when you were a kid? It should – it's the start of "It's Raining, It's Pouring." Well done, you have just played a tune without a single music sheet in sight. Didn't I tell you that this was going to be easy?

Play it again in a different octave so that you can hear how it sounds higher or lower. Repeat on all the different octaves to note the differences in sound.

The Black Keys

The black keys are different musical notes to the white keys. Play them, and you will notice a distinct difference. The names of these keys are also the same letters of the alphabet and take on the names of the white keys nearest them. The distinction is that keys to the left of the white key are known as flats and to the right of the white key are known as sharps. So, you have "B Sharp" or "B Flat," for example.

An easy way to remember this is to think about how your cutlery is laid out on the table. Your knife is sharp and always laid out to the right of your plate. That makes it easy to remember that right is sharp.

Now, because the black keys have a white key on either side of them, they can be called sharps or flats interchangeably. If you look to the right of a white "B" key on your keyboard, the black key is "C Sharp." But it is also left of the white "D" key and so is "D Flat." Don't overthink it too much – it is not all that important right now, and we go into it in more detail in Chapter 6 anyway.

What is more important is to learn your way around the keyboard – think more in terms of the letter, rather than it being a sharp or flat.

Quick Exercise: Now you know how to find your "C" and "F" notes and, because of this, how to find the others as well. Play each "C" note on the black and white keys and listen to how each sounds. Do the same for all the other keys as well.

Now try something a little more complicated. Position your thumb over any white key and your forefinger over the corresponding black key. Play each in quick succession. Then try playing them together. Experiment a little until you find the tones that match one another more closely.

Intervals

These are the distance between the different notes. A semitone, or half-step, will always separate the black key from the white key next to is. Where the white keys are not broken by black keys, like between "B" and "C" or "E" and "F", the difference in the note is a semitone.

A full tone is the space between two white keys that have a black key in between them, like "C" and "D".

Chapter Summary

- Your keyboard is made up of 52 white keys and 36 black keys. (Some older keyboards have fewer keys.)
- Each key represents a particular musical note.
- There are seven musical notes that we use in music – these are named A through to G.
- The black keys are grouped in twins or triplets to help you locate the different notes more easily.
- The white key to the left of a twin is always "C." The white key to the left of a triplet is always an "F."

- To remember the difference, remember that "C" has two points to it and "F" has three to it.
- The black keys take their names from the white keys closest to them.
- The black key to the right of a white key is called sharp. The one to the left of a white key is called flat.
- An easy way to remember this is that knives are sharp and are always put to the right of your plate when the table is laid.
- Intervals refer to the difference in sound between the white and black keys.

In the next chapter, you will learn about the pedals on your piano and how to use them.

Chapter Two: The Pedals

In this chapter, you will learn how and when to use the pedals on your piano. This is the second step in our seven-point plan in helping you learn to play the piano.

The pedals on the piano are not just there for decoration. You use the pedals for sounds that are not possible using just your hands. Most standard pianos will have two such foot pedals – the Una Corda on the left and the Sustain on the right. Some pianos have three pedals. The extra pedal in the middle is called the Sostenuto, but it is seldom used.

The Una Corda Pedal (The Soft Pedal)

Use your left foot to play this pedal. It helps to soften notes, so could be used when you are first starting to build up to a crescendo. It will not work on very loud notes, so the range is limited somewhat.

The Sustain Pedal

You will use your right foot with this pedal. It elongates your note's sound and causes it to resonate after you have lifted your fingers from the key. The resonance will be held until you take your foot off the pedal. This is usually used to bridge harmonies. With this pedal, as long as you are pressing the pedal, all the notes you play will be sustained.

The Sostenuto

As mentioned before, this is not something that you will use very often. You would normally use your right foot to play it, and it is similar to the Sustain Pedal in that it sustains the notes played. The difference between this pedal and the previous one is that the Sostenuto pedal only sustains the notes that you were playing when you pressed the pedals. Any notes played after that will play as normal.

Using the Pedals

When you start playing, get into position and position the balls of your feet above the pedals. Your heels should still touch the ground; this will help you maintain a good posture and also allow you to keep a light touch when it comes to depressing the pedals.

What you need to keep in mind is that this is not a stomping contest. You need to practice lifting your foot off the pedals gently. If you take your foot off too quickly, it can create a noisy bang; It can take a little practice to get used to using the pedals smoothly. Just think of it like parking your car – you don't smash the accelerator to the ground when parking, you ease into the parking slowly.

If the music calls for the use of the pedal, you will see the word "Ped" marked where you need to apply the pedal. Alternatively, the composition may call for the use of it all the way through the piece. You can release the pedal when you see an asterisk on the sheet. This will look like:

Quick exercise: Try using the pedals in conjunction with the lines of "It's Raining it's Pouring" that you learned in the previous chapter. Mix it up a little, play the same tune using the Una Corda pedal from time to time and then listen to how it sounds when you use the Sustain pedal instead. If you do have a Sostenuto panel, play around with that one as well.

Chapter Summary

- Most pianos have two pedals – the Una Corda pedal and the Sustain pedal.
- Some pianos have a third pedal – the Sostenuto pedal.

- The Una Corda pedal is always on the left; the Sustain pedal is always on the right. If the Sostenuto pedal is there, it will be in the middle.
- You will not use the Sostenuto pedal very often.
- The Una Corda pedal helps to soften notes.
- The Sustain pedal keeps the notes going for as long as you have the pedal down. It will do this for all notes played, while the pedal is down.
- The Sostenuto pedal isolates the note that was played when the pedal was first pressed and sustains only that particular note. The rest are played as normal.

In the next chapter, you will learn how to read some basic sheet music for yourself.

Chapter Three: Reading Sheet Music

251

In this chapter, you will learn what many of those dots and lines mean when it comes to sheet music. This is the third quick step in the program.

You need to know something about reading music in order to progress. Think of sheet music like a script for a movie, except that it is written using musical symbols rather than words. The composer could, technically, write out the words but it would make playing the music much slower and difficult because you would have to read each word.

Symbols are a lot easier to read, once you understand what they mean. The composer tells you which notes you should play, when to pause, how long to pause for, and even the pace at which you should play.

A sheet of music will look something like this:

Everything You Need to Know About a Piano Score

If you look at the score above, you will see a lot of dots, dashes, and other symbols. It looks a little confusing, but it's not so bad if you take it a note at a time. Each of the notes tells you which key you need to play and how long you need to play it for.

To keep the notes in some semblance of order, they are written on a five-line stave.

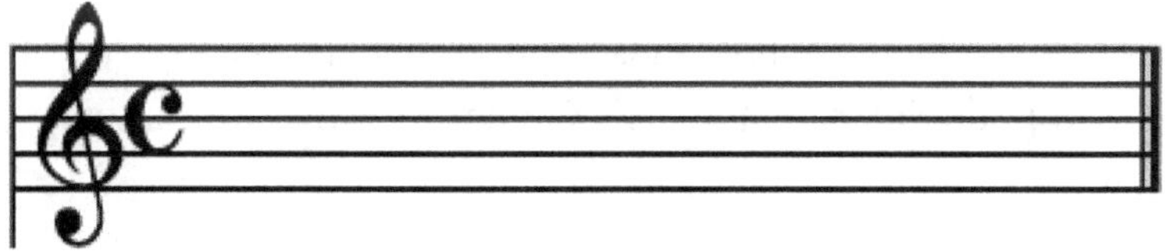

Starting with the Stave

The notes can be placed on the lines, or in the spaces between lines. Each line or space represents a specific note. The notes are divided up into equal sections called measured. These are separated from one another by bar lines – vertical lines at the end of that particular measure. The stave will normally start with some type of clef (The stylized "G" in the illustration above), and this may be followed by a sharp or a flat (The "C" in the illustration above.)

In addition, the markings above the stave will usually tell you what speed to play at. The markings underneath the stave will tell you what volume that section is to be played at.

You will see that there are usually two staves joined together with brackets, with different symbols at the top and bottom. This is known as a grand stave. It is denoted like this because you need to play both staves together – one set being the notes to play with your right hand, the other the notes to play with your left hand.

Don't worry about this too much at this stage – the main tune is usually shown in the stave for the right hand, so you don't need to pay attention to both now. In fact, as you will see later, you don't even have to have these two to play a tune so if you find it confusing, don't stress about it. We have a way around that.

The Basic Symbols to Learn

The Treble Clef

This is the stylized G that we were talking about in the previous section. There are a number of different ways that this is written. The treble clef shown below will denote which keys you need to play with your left hand. X

The treble clef looks like:

The Base Clef

This shows the part of the music to be played with your left hand. (To start out with, we are not going to worry too much about the left-hand section.) The base clef looks like:

The Key Signature

This is another thing that might appear at the start of the music. It shows which of the notes need to be played as flats and which need to be played as sharps.

This is what this will look like on your sheet music:

$$\sharp \quad \flat$$
or

The Time Signature

This can be any two numbers. The numbers tell you how many beats there are in each measure. (We go over this in more detail in Chapter Seven.) This will look like:

$$\frac{2}{2}$$

Tempo Marking

This is a way of showing you what tempo the piece should be played at. The notation below shows the number of crotchet beats to play in a minute. Alternatively, they could write out what speed the piece is to be played at. This will often be in Italian like "Presto". (We go over each of these in more detail in Chapter 7).

This will look like:

Dynamics

This lets you know what volume you need to play at. The "P" in the above diagram means Piano, or quiet. The "F" in the above means Forte or loudly. If the symbol has an "M" after it, it means moderate volume. (We are not really going to worry too much about that in these lessons though.) These symbols look like:

$$\boldsymbol{p}$$
$$\boldsymbol{f}$$

The Notes

These relate to the actual notes that you are playing so let's go into them in a little more detail. A note is generally made up of a head (the dot) and a stem, the vertical line that is either above or below the dot. Your notes will look something like:

Whole Notes

This is a whole note and will be one of the only ones that doesn't have a vertical line. This is meant to last four beats.

Half Notes

These are half notes or minimums and are played for two beats. You can tell that they are half notes because the dot is not filled in.

Quarter Notes

These are quarter notes – you will normally play four of these in one measure. (More about that in Chapter Seven).

Quavers and Semi-Quavers

These are eighth notes or quavers and sixteen notes or semiquavers.

Where the Notes Are Displayed

There are two shortcuts that you can use to remember which line or space each note is displayed in. Remember how we said that some of the notes are displayed on the lines, and some are displayed in the spaces in between them, this is how you remember what notes go where.

For The Lines

Remember the mnemonic device, Every Good Boy Deserves Fruit. In this case, the "E" note is recorded on the top line, the "G" note on the next line down, the "B" note on the middle line, the "D" note on the next line down and the "F" note on the final line.

For The Spaces

Remember the word FACE to keep this one straight but this time start from the space at the bottom and work your way up. So, the "F" note is in the final space of the stave, the "A" note is in the next space up, the "C" note is in the space second from the top, and the "E" note is in the space right at the top of the stave. In this case, the "F" note is an octave lower than in the previous example.

A Quick Shortcut

I am now going to teach you a shortcut to playing popular music. This only works with music that has words to it, but it is a great shortcut and is more than enough if you just want to be able to play some tunes for the family.

The sheet music example we displayed previously was made up of grand staves. When you have lyrics as well, these are displayed in the vocal line. This is a stave that is directly above the grand staves and is a much more simplified version of the notes. It will usually have a treble stave at the very front.

If you want to start playing music quickly and easily, concentrate on the vocal line only. This allows you to play at the pace that suits you and is a lot easier than having to read the more complex staves beneath it.

The additional advantage of doing this is that you can buy music sheets that only have the vocal line on them. If your main aim is to be able to play a few tunes, this can save you a lot of money and space because the grand staves are not usually included in these copies.

Quick Exercise: Go to http://www.music-for-music-teachers.com/silent-night-sheet-music.html, and you can download the sheet music for "Silent Night" for free, in a simple format. It's a fairly simple composition and one that you probably already know the melody for. See how well you can follow along on your piano.

Chapter Summary

- You need to know what the different symbols on sheet music are in order to be able to interpret it.

- Sheet music is set out in a five-line stave. You can see which note to play based on where it is placed in the stave and also the symbol used.
- Things like the general tempo of the piece will be listed at the beginning of the stave.
- Notations above and below the stave can show the speed at which a piece is to be played and what volume to play it at.
- A stave will usually consist of at least two separate sections, one for the notes to be played with the left hand and one for the notes to be played with the right hand. These two staves should be played at the same time and so are bracketed together to form a grand stave. (We are not going to do that right now, though.)
- The symbol for the note will tell you what note to play and how long to play it for.
- Each note is displayed on a different line, or space, in the stave.
- An easy way to remember which note goes on which line is to remember "Every Boy Deserves Good Fruit." This is read from the top line to the bottom one.
- An easy way to remember which note goes into what space, is to remember the word "FACE." In this case, the spaces are read from the bottom up. The notes used in this case are an octave lower than in the previous instance.
- To make things a lot easier for yourself, you can read the music from the vocal line. This is a much more simplified stave meant to be read by singers so

it does not have all the symbols a grand stave would have and does not have them separated into notes to be played by the left hand and notes to be played by the right hand.

In the next chapter, you will learn about more about practicing scales and why it is not a boring time waster.

Chapter Four: Practising Scales

In this chapter, you will learn about scales and why you should look forward to practicing them. This is your fourth lesson – you are almost there now.

Now that you understand about which keys are which, know when to use the pedals and know something about reading sheet music, we are ready to move on to playing scales. This is the fourth step in our program.

How did you do with playing "Silent Night?" It should have been relatively simple for you – you might have made a mistake or two here or there, but, overall, you should have been able to follow it. See how easy it is to start playing real music? And you can play popular songs like that without ever having to worry about learning scales.

However, there is a good reason that one of the first things you normally learn to play on a piano are scales. Now, admittedly, this can seem a little boring, but it is good practice. Scales are a great way for you to build up a working knowledge of the melodies in a song and to also give your fingers more practice. So, while you can play without practicing scales, if you really want to start getting better, you will have to spend some time on this.

The most important thing about scales is that you should repeat them over and over again. Think of it like a putting green in golf – you are there to practice your swing, not to actually play a game. The more you practice, however, the better your swing gets and the better you are able to play when you actually head out to the course. The same applies for practicing scales on your piano.

What is a Scale?

It is a series of notes that follow on from one another in a particular order. The most commonly encountered scales are major scales and minor scales. They both have the following commonalities:

- They are both eight notes in length.
- The topmost note and the bottommost note are only an octave apart.
- Each note is done in order from lowest to highest or highest to lowest. You do not mix up the order of the notes at all.
- Scales are made up of a combination of half- or whole steps.

If you understand how the scales work, you are able to build any type of scale you want, just by adding in the right sequence of steps. Scales form the basis for creating chords and allowing you to learn to improvise. You will need to know these if you want to start composing your own music.

The scales that you choose to practice will be dependent on what musical style you are most interested in. It is, however, a good idea to start by learning the major scales and then move on to practicing the minor scales.

Major Scales

The pattern here will be a tone, a tone, a semitone, a tone, atone, a tone, and a semitone. It is pretty easy to work out, as long as you start on the right note. All major scales will be based on the same principle.

You can, for example, play an "C" scale in major. You can start on "C" and then move up through the other notes, using only the white keys. The "C" major scale is one of the easiest to start with because you only need to concentrate on the white keys.

Major scales are generally thought to be livelier in nature.

Minor Scales

Once you are more comfortable with major scales, you can try your hand at minor scales. The minor scales are available in three separate versions – the harmonic or the natural or the melodic scales. What this means is that every minor scale has three separate formats to learn.

The Natural Minor Scales

This is the key minor scale to practice. The difference between it and your major scale is that you start with the A note and then finish off again with the A note.

The Harmonic Minor Scales

This also follows a set pattern, but it is slightly different. It is a tone, a semitone, a tone, a tone, a semitone, a tone + a half and a semitone. This pattern is often described as a bit eerie in nature and will lend something of a haunting quality to your work.

The Melodic Minor Scales

This is more complex because you will use the pattern, a tone, a tone, a semitone, atone, a tone, a semitone and then a tone when working your way up the scales. When working your way back, it changes to a tone, a tone, a semitone, a tone, a tone, a semitone, and finishes on tone.

What makes this scale useful, is that it teaches you to be more flexible when it comes to your other scales. When practicing your minor scales, it is best to start with the A minor scales because these are easiest.

Quick Exercise: Practice this now - find the Middle C and practice working your way through all seven notes. You would start by using your thumb and the rest of the fingers on your right hand and then bring in your left hand for the final two keys. Practice this working your way up the scales, and then down them again.

When you have mastered that, you can move on to practicing more scales. You can try starting with a different note, always remembering to move up either half a step or a whole step. Here is an illustration of the different C Scales that you can use to get you started with your practicing.

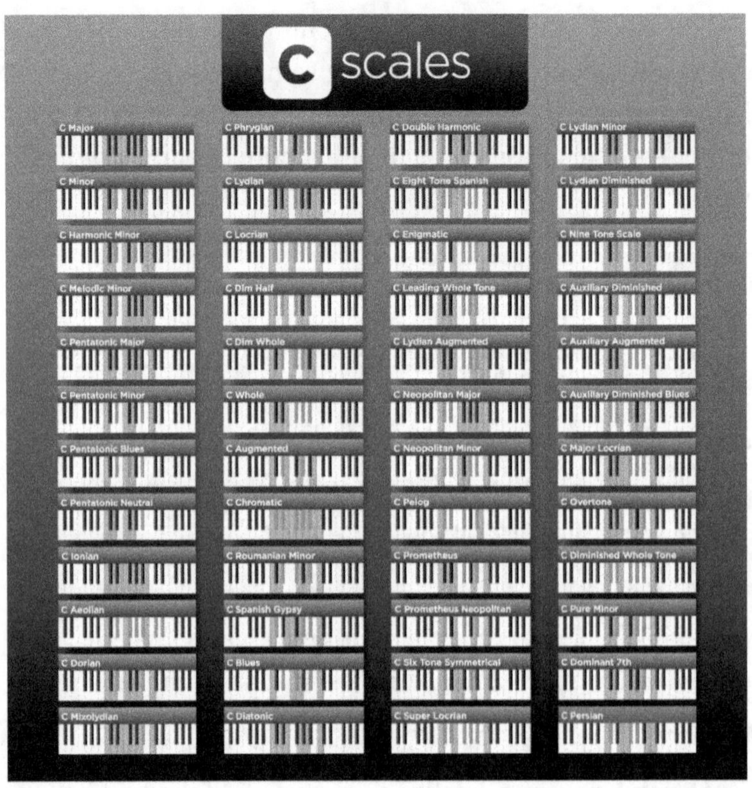

Most of the C scales shown above can be accomplished using your right hand only. It is also important to practice scales using your left hand, so don't just focus on one type. Try to practice at least three different scales a day for at least ten minutes overall in order to get better at them.

Chapter Summary

- Scales are seen by a lot of people as boring, but they are essential exercises when it comes to getting to know the keys.
- They can also be used as warmups or to help build up the strength in your finger.
- The key to getting scales right is to know your intervals really well. Every successive key is either a half- or whole step up or down from the previous one.
- There are minor scales and major scales, each with their own unique pattern.
- There are three varieties of minor scales – the natural, harmonic and melodic.

In the next chapter, you will learn about using chords to make the melodies sound richer.

Chapter Five: Adding in Chords

In this chapter, you will learn about adding in chords. This is the fifth step in the program.

Chords are important in creating harmonies. You will distinguish them on your music sheet because they will have three or four notes stacked on top of one another.

What is a Chord?

A chord is made up of at least three tones, played simultaneously, where the intervals are based on a set formula. So, slamming your fingers down on four or five random keys may be fun, but is not a chord.

Three-Note Chords

These are the simplest ones to work with and are also known as triads. You will normally play these by using your pinky, thumb, and forefinger. Chords begin very simply. Like melodies, chords are based on scales.

Chords are essentially based on scales, the difference being that with scales, each note is played in succession. With chords, all of the notes are played together.

The root note is the note that you start with. The chord will be named for this note. If you are using a basic triad, you will have your root note and two other notes, notes that are at a third interval from the first note and at the fifth interval from the first note.

You can add to the chord by moving up a step or a half-step, or by adding extra notes in. To make things easier for you, though, I have included a list of all the basic chords at the end of this chapter.

Major Chords

These are the ones that you will use most often and are the easiest to play. A lot of the songs that you play, including Silent Night, consist of major chords. Major chords are based on your major scales. The first example in the illustration below is an example of a major chord.

Most of the time, composers will omit writing "Major" when using a chord. They simply use the symbol for chord above the staff of it to show which chord it is. If you see the symbol for a chord, and nothing naming it, you can assume that it is a major chord.

Other Chords You May Encounter

You are mostly going to be dealing with major or minor chords, but that does not mean that these are all that there is.

Other chords are formed by adding extra notes to your standard major or minor chord.

Augmented Chords And Diminished Chords

The only real difference in a major or minor chord is the third interval. The fifth interval, however, is always the same and it is here that you can play around to create a new chord altogether.

Augmented chords consist of the root note, your major third interval, and an augmented fifth interval. With augmented chords, you raise the final note by another half-step and always work with a major chord to start with. Here are examples of augmented chords.

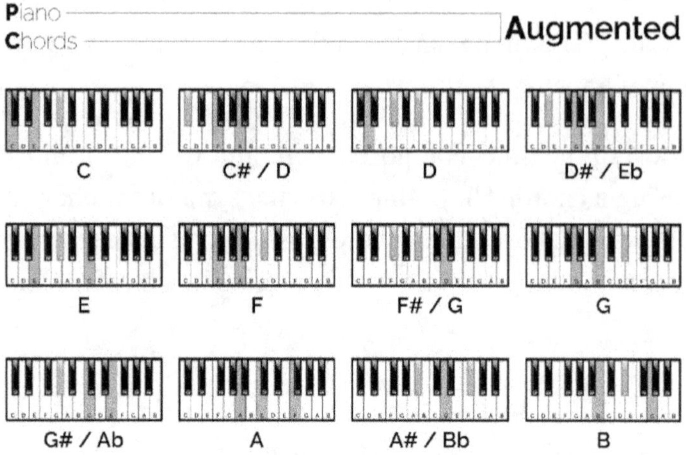

Diminished chords consist of the root note, your minor third interval, and your diminished fifth interval. In this case, you lower the final note by half a step and always work with a minor chord to start with. You would normally see them with "Dim" in the name.

Here are some examples of diminished chords:

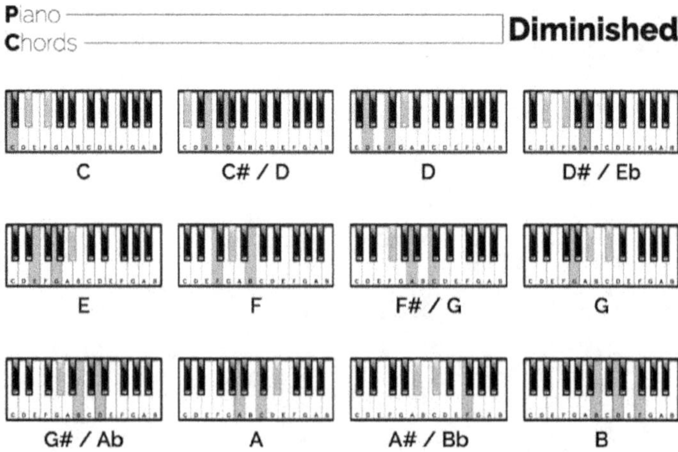

Suspended Chords

This is considered a three-note chord, but it is not really a triad. In this case, one of the notes is left hanging, meaning that you need to wait for the next one. There are two options when it comes to suspended chords – The second and fourth suspended chords. They will have "Sus" in the name.

A suspended two chord is made up of the root note, the major second interval, and the fifth interval. A suspended four chord is made up of the root note, the fourth interval, and the fifth interval.

Generally speaking, a suspended chord will usually be followed by another note, but they can also be used on their own.

Here are examples of suspended chords:

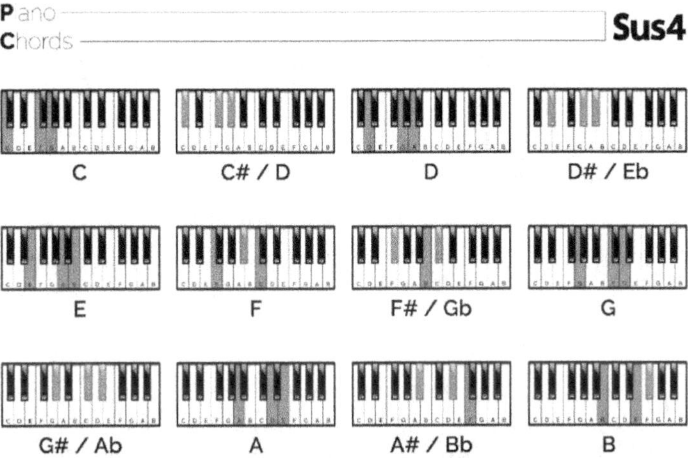

Adding a Seventh Interval

A triad is a basic kind of chord. In order to make it more interesting, you can add other notes at the end in the form of a seventh interval. It is usually used in a composition to help create suspense and will usually be followed by a major chord or minor chord. On its own, it is not likely to sound great, but when added to a triad, it improves the sound.

You can choose to add any of the chords we have discussed here to create this seventh interval.

The Chord Symbols

Chord symbols let you know the type of chord and what the root note of the chord is. These will start with the letter of the root note. (Keep in mind that with a major chord, this will be all there is.)

With other chords, you will have either a letter in the name, such as "M" to indicate a minor chord and/ or a letter like "7" to indicate the seventh chord. So, if, for example, you see the name Dm6, you know you have that you are playing the D minor chord with a sixth interval.

The chord is played along with the note that is shown underneath it. You will hold this chord until you see a new chord symbol or change of cord marked in the music.

Chord Inversions

It's not the most interesting exercise to play the same chords over and over again. You really don't need to do this at all. It doesn't matter what you do with the basic chords; they will always sound exactly the same.

That is where chord inversions come into play. They allow you to change up the sound of a chord. So instead of playing the root chord, and following it with the third chord and fifth chord, as usual, you could change things up by starting with the final chord and ending on the root chord. So now what you are doing is to play the root chord an octave higher than the standard chords.

Inversions can also help you to transition from one chord to the next. Let's say you are playing a C major chord, followed by an A minor chord. This would mean playing the C chord and then moving your hand over to play the next set of keys – it would be somewhat clumsy.

If you use an inversion, though, your hand will end up in the correct position as you end off the C chord, allowing you to play with a lot less effort.

Using Chord Progressions

Chord progression means moving through a range of chords in the same key signature. Imagine how boring it would be if you played the same chord throughout the entire piece. You can use chord progressions to liven things up a bit or to move from one signature to the next.

Arpeggios

You don't always have to play the notes that make up your chord at the same time. You can also rather play them one after another in sequence. Arpeggios help to keep the piece moving. You would, for example, instead of playing a typical C major chord, play each note, starting with the "C," individually. You would then play the "C" in the next octave before reversing the order of play and going back down to the first "C" you played.

This would just be one possible version so try changing it up a bit. This is also possible using minor chords – you just would not need to descend at the end of the structure again.

A Round-Up of Different Chords That You Might Come Across

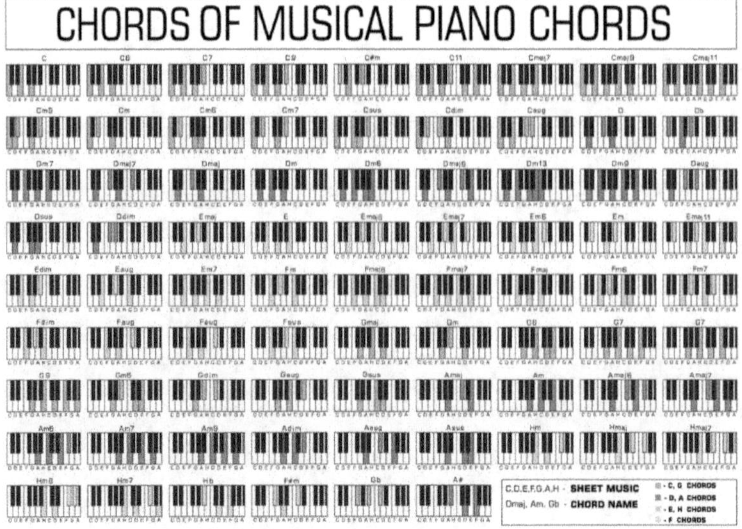

Chapter Summary

- Chords are notes that are played together to create a more harmonious composition.
- On the music sheet, a chord is denoted if there are three notes stacked together.

278

- Chords are at least three notes long and are calculated according to set formulae rather than just being chosen at random.
- A chord is usually based on the scales that you use.
- There are many different kinds of chords.
- Augmented chords are created from major scales and have the last note going up by half a step.
- Diminished chords are created from minor scales and have the last note dropping by half a step. They will have "Dim" in their name.
- Suspended chords leave you hanging and need to be finished off with another note. They will have "Sus" in their name.
- You can add another interval in order to make the chord more interesting.
- Major chords are named after their root note. So, a C major cord is simply named "C."
- You can invert cords to make them more interesting and to make the play smoother. This means starting with your top note and carrying on into the next octave with your root note.
- Chord progressions can make the piece more interesting and can help bridge one signature line with another.
- Arpeggios are another way to change things up – you play exactly the same notes, except this time you change things up by playing the notes in sequence rather than together.

In the next chapter, you will learn more about sharps and flats.

Chapter Six: Sharps and Flats

In this chapter, you will learn how to start incorporating the black keys and how to recognize when to do so. This is your sixth lesson.

The symbols that we deal with in this chapter are also known as accidentals. These "accidentals" tell you when to use the black keys, or how to modify your note's pitch.

As mentioned previously, the black keys are called sharps or flats, and named for the white keys directly next to them. Let's do a quick recap. If the black key is to the right of the white key, it will be that key's sharp. If it is to the left of that key, it will be that key's flat.

Here's a diagram of how this would look on your actual keyboard:

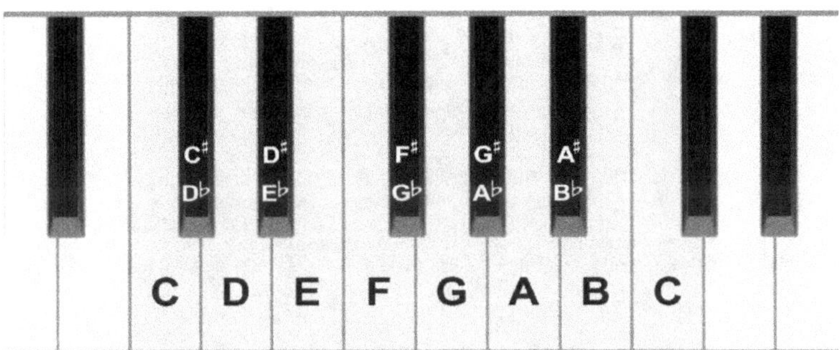

On the sheet music, you will see the symbol for the sharp or the flat directly before the note, next to the head of the note that it applies to.

Sharps

Sharps raise the pitch by a half-step or semitone. The symbol for a sharp is:

♯

Flats

Flats lower the pitch by a half-step or semitone. The symbol for a flat is:

♭

The Natural Key

This tells you that it is time to stop using the black keys. It will precede the natural note and tell you that you should play all the remaining notes in that series as natural notes. The symbol for the natural key is:

♮

The Key Signature

You will also see these notes directly after the clef or base staves and before any time signature. This is what is referred to as the key signature, and it lets you know what key to use for the tune, and how many sharps and flats there are in the piece. You will need to look this over before starting.

Once you have been practicing your scales, this gets a whole lot simpler to do. All of the keys except for A minor and C major have both flats and sharps.

Chapter Summary

- Accidentals are used to change the pitch of notes – they change the pitch by a half-tone or semitone.
- The three accidentals are Flat, Sharp and Natural.
- To get the flat and sharp notes, you have to use the black keys on the keyboard.
- The flat takes its name from the white key to its left and reduces the pitch.
- The sharp takes its name from the black key to its right and increases the pitch.
- So, every black key is both a sharp and a flat.
- The natural symbol tells you to revert to stop using the black keys.

In the next chapter, you will learn why timing is so important and how you can get this critical aspect right.

Chapter Seven: It's All About the Timing

In this chapter, you will learn the final and possibly most important element in this book – how to get the timing right. This is the final step in our program.

There is more to music than getting the notes and chords right. (Sure, that is obviously a big piece of the puzzle, but you also need to be able to get the timing and beat right.) In fact, you might be able to slip an incorrect chord or note past your audience without them noticing, but they will notice immediately if your timing is off.

The timing of the notes is what makes the music happy or sad. If we never adjusted the tempo at which we played, every piece of music would sound pretty much the same. Each note has a point where it starts and a point where it ends. As a result, we need to assign values to this length that we are able to count. In this chapter, we are going to learn how to really get the rhythm going and keep it going.

The Beat

When you are listening to music and clapping along or tapping your foot in time with it, the beat is what you are trying to keep up with. The faster the beat, the faster and more energetic the song. The slower the beat, the slower the music is. Getting the tempo, or how fast the beat is, right is extremely important.

Use Tempo to Measure the Beat

When it comes to music, time gets measured in beats. In this case, the number of beats per minute. If you want a piece to sound correct, you need to pay attention to the beat.

Quick Exercise: Get out your smartphone and set the timer for a minute. Every two seconds, tap your foot once. That's a beat. Now, you can speed this up by increasing the number of taps to one per second, or slow it down to one tap every three seconds. That's the tempo.

In the exercise above, the first beat was 30 beats per minute because you tapped your foot 30 times. The second beat was 20 beats per minute because you slowed it down. In both cases, the beat was steady because you were timing your taps to the second.

When reading music, you would refer to the tempo marking to tell you what speed to play the music at. This will either be in the form of either a written word to tell you what pace to use, or a metronome marking that will tell you exactly how many beats per minute.

You can follow the guidelines in the table below to see what the basic readings are in terms of tempo.

Written	Translation	Number of Beats Per Minute
Largo	Very Slow	40 – 60
Adagio	Slow	61 - 72
Andante	Moderate	73 – 96
Allegro	Fast	97 - 132
Vivace	Faster	133 – 168
Presto	Very Fast	169 - 208

Measuring Tempo

When you are playing a piece of music, you won't be able to check your smartphone to see how many seconds have elapsed. A metronome is a handy device that can help you instead. You set it to the rate that you like, and it will tick out the rhythm accordingly.

The Grouping of Beats

Remember how I said earlier that the sheet of music was like a script? Every note is recorded in the order that it is meant to be played in. Unlike a script, however, the stave can be divided up into equal sections of time. These smaller sections make it possible to check the beat and to understand whereabouts you are in the actual composition.

Now, in a slower tempo song, this might not be much of a problem, but when it comes to faster-paced music, you could have a few hundred different beats in just a few minutes. Keeping track of the beat in this manner would mean counting high numbers when you are trying to concentrate on what you are doing.

It would become difficult to do this, so composers have come up with a workaround. Instead, the music is divided up into measures – smaller bits that are easier to keep track of. The number of beats in a measure will normally be decided by the composer, and this can change. They will indicate the end of a measure by drawing a vertical line, or bar line, through all the lines and spaces of the stave. This will look something like:

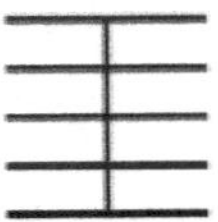

Most compositions, however, will have four beats per measure. This means that you would just have to count to four each time when playing – not too difficult a task. The measures break the music into segments or patterns that we can then use to help determine the time signature of the piece.

The Rhythm of Melody

Without the melody of notes played, the beat wouldn't mean much at all. The different lengths of the notes are what makes the music more interesting. It's like listening to a good public speaker – they change the cadence of their voice and mix up the tones so that it sounds more interesting.

In contrast, if the speaker just spoke in a monotone, without varying the tone or rhythm, it wouldn't be long before everyone became bored with the speech. The same is true of music.

Some music is very distinctive – you can recognize the tune just by hearing the beat. Take "Jingle Bells" for example – you don't have to hear it being played on an instrument to recognize it, you could tap out the beat with your foot, and someone would still recognize it.

We said earlier that you could get away with not having to read all the characters on a standard music sheet. You do, however, need to know exactly how much time every note is meant to last for. At the beginning of the piece, the composer lets you know how many equal pieces to divide each measure into. That means working out fractions but, in this case, it's not hard.

Think of it like cutting up a pizza. You can divide the pizza up into halves, quarters or eighths, or more if you like. When it comes to music, this usually translates into four pieces of "pizza" per measure. Or, more accurately, four quarter notes, or four beats. This is represented by the most common music symbol:

♩♪

You will always know if a note is a quarter note because the head will always be completely black. In our example, you have divided the pizza up into four equal slices and are eating just one, so it is finished faster. In the same way, the notes are played faster and not held for as long.

Quick Exercise: Set your metronome to one beat per second. Every time it clicks, play one-quarter note in whichever key you prefer. Stick to a single note, for now, say for example, "C" so that you can get the hang of playing to the beat. Every time the metronome clicks, hit the "C" key. Get this right before moving on to the next section.

Half Notes

Alternatively, you could choose to divide the pizza into halves and eat one piece again. You will take longer to eat the pizza because there is more of it. By a similar token, half notes are longer than quarter notes, so you would divide the measure up into two instead of four. So, it would now be two beats per measure instead of just one.

This would be represented on the sheet as follows:

Quick Exercise: Set your metronome to one beat per second again, and this time, play a note on every second click. You would hold the key down for the count of these two beats.

Why do the Stems Get Displayed Differently?

You will notice in the examples above, that there are two ways to show the stem of a note – either pointing up or pointing down. Why is that? Any notes that are either on the middle line of the stave or above it, will have their stems underneath the note head and to the right. Any notes that fall below this will have the stems above the note head and to the left.

This helps to make a clearer distinction between the notes on different lines. If all the notes were just circles, it would be a lot harder to keep your place when reading the music quickly.

Whole Notes

A whole note lasts the entire measure for a count of four. So, back to our pizza example, if you ate the whole thing, it would take longer.

It is a simple circle and looks like this:

o

Playing a whole note is pretty simple, just count to four and then play the note. You would just need to make sure that the note lasts for the length of the measure.

Quick Exercise: Set your metronome to one beat per second and again, hold down any key you like. Hold it down for the count of four clicks and then move on to play the next note.

Putting It All Together

Now that you know how the count works, and know how long to hold the keys down for and what the basic note values are, you can start playing around a little and we can move onto the more complex notes.

Again, if you were only to stick to full, half and quarter notes, there would only be so much variation that you would be able to achieve. You can divide it up even more to fit in more notes per measure and increase the tempo.

You don't actually change the speed, but you are holding the notes down for smaller periods at a time. It may take some getting used to so, if you are battling, to keep up, slow things down a bit by slowing the speed of your playing.As you get more used to this rate, and more familiar with the eighth notes, and sixteenth notes, you can start to speed up again.

Eighth Notes

Eighth notes are also known as quavers.This is like your pizza into eight pieces. To eat a piece won't take as long as it would if you were eating half the pizza because you are getting much less pizza. By the same token, you just need to hold the note down for a lot less time, and move faster through the notes in the same measure. Instead of fitting 4-beats into a measure, you need to fit in eight so you will need to speed up your metronome. The symbol for an eighth note is:

If there are two or more of these notes, the flag changes to a solid beam and connects the notes. This helps in making the beat a lot more obvious. It will look something like this:

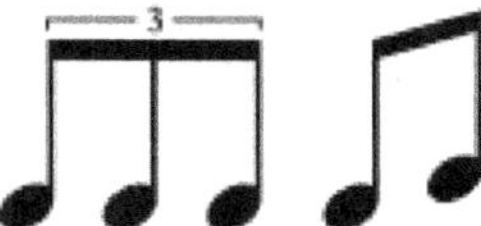

Sixteenth Notes

Sixteenth notes are also known as semi-quavers. The same rule applies to sixteenth notes. Like with eighth notes, when they are by single notes, they are shown with flags – except this time there are two flags.

When there are more than one of these in a row, the flags are changed to beams, as follows:

It is quite common to see four such notes placed together in this way because that represents one beat. You might also find it joined with an eighth note as follows:

Now, if you can slow things down a lot, it is pretty easy to play these notes. However, if you play them at the tempo that they are meant to be played at, it starts getting more complicated. That said, with practice, you will be fine to play these notes as well.

And dividing up the beat doesn't stop at sixteenths, some composers go a step further and halve it again so that it is 32nds, 64ths or 128ths. They show this in the composition by increasing the number of flags. I am not going to go into examples here because these are not as common as the eighth notes and sixteenth notes and should be left until you have had a bit more practice.

Rests

No matter how much practice you have, there is only a certain amount that you will be able to do. Your fingers are going to need a break from time to time and so will your audience. These breaks can be quick or a little longer, but the defining character of them is that you are not playing anything. You continue to count the beat, but you don't actually play or hold any kind of note.

In orchestral compositions, this will often be where the strings take over or someone playing another instrument gets their own solo. All you need to do is to relax your hands and keep them poised over the keys and make sure that you keep up with the count. Just like there are different note lengths, there are different rest periods. Let's have a look at these.

Whole And Half Rests

Let's say that you are playing a whole "C". You press the key and keep it depressed for a count of four beats. When you are playing half note, you keep it down for half as long. Rests will work in a similar fashion – you won't play anymore for the same number of beats.

I like to think of the symbol for the whole rest as a comfortable bed that you can sink into. You would relax for a decent period. It will always be on the fourth line or above so that it is easier to spot. It looks like this:

The half rest is the same symbol, turned upside down. So, still a bed but a little less comfortable. It will always sit on the middle line. It looks like this:

Quarter Rests and Beyond

These are the same as your quarter, eighth and sixteenth notes in terms of timing. Here are the symbols – from left to right, these are the symbols for the quarter, eighth and sixteenth rest respectively.

Time Signatures

In music, a time signature is what you use to find out the meter of the piece. The time signature is split into two numbers; the top number number tells you the meter of the piece you're playing. So, if the number is 4 over 4, that means there are four quarter note beats. If it is 2 over 2, there are two half note beats.

If the composer wants to use more than one type of note, like one-half note and two-quarter notes, that is fine – they could show this as 2 over 4 and 1 over 2. They do need to ensure that the top number adds up to a whole number in the end. So, one-half note and two-quarter notes, if we add them mathematically, would total 4 quarters in total and this makes sense.

If the composer tried to say three-quarter notes and one-half note, you would end up with too many beats, and this would not work. So, you should never see a time signature that is something like 5 over 4.

Common Time

Most composers stick to common time, i.e., 4 over 4. They indicate this by using the letter "C" in place of the standard time signature. It will appear directly after the clef symbol of the stave. This is how this would be displayed within the stave:

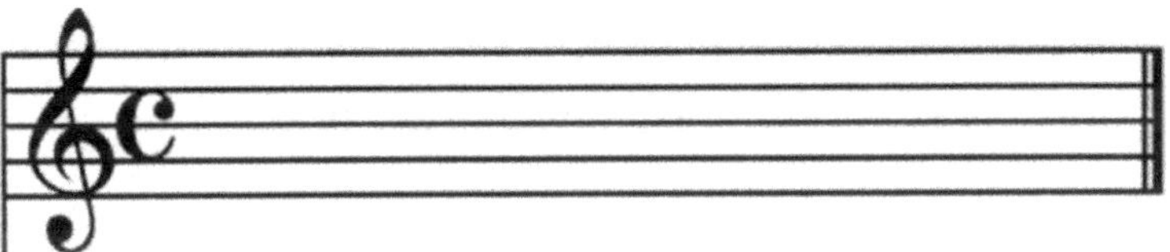

Chapter Summary

- The beat needs to be measured and kept at a steady pace.
- The faster the tempo that the notes are played at, the more energetic the pace of the piece.
- Beats are grouped in measures. These break up the music into equal sections. The composer will decide how many beats to use per measure.
- A whole note will take up a full measure, or four full beats. So, you would hold the note for the full length of that measure and only press the note once during that particular measure.
- A half note is half as long so there will be two beats in one measure.

- The notes can be divided into quarters, eighths and sixteenths as well. Each of these is shorter than the last so there will be more notes to play within each measure. This means that as the tempo increases the smaller the notes get.
- If you are still learning, slow down the tempo until you get used to playing the notes in the right succession. Then you can start worrying about speeding up again.
- The stems of the notes are arbitrary, used more as a way of differentiating the notes than having a very specific meaning.
- Rests are just as important when it comes to playing – they give you time to have a break and also give your audience a little break as well.
- A rest is usually similar in length to the note preceding it. The main thing to remember is to keep track of the beat.
- During a rest, keep your hands relaxed but poised at the ready for the next lot of notes.

Final Words

Well done – you have completed the program. Learning to play the piano can be fun, and it really is not that hard once you know the basics. It's a simple seven-step process:

- Step One: Learn the Keyboard and the keys.
- Step Two: Learn how and when to use the pedals.
- Step Three: Learn something about reading sheet music.
- Step Four: Practice your scales.
- Step Five: Learn about adding chords.
- Step Six: Learn when to use sharps and flats.
- Step Seven: Learn to get the tempo right.

In this book, we have started you off on the basics you need to play your first full composition. You should now be able to play some simple tunes and impress your friends with how fast your learned this skill.

From now forward, all it takes to really master the piano is to practice, and you get to decide how far you want to go. You can choose to practice every day, or trot your skills out on high days and holidays – it really is completely up to you.

Image Credit: Shutterstock.com

300

BOOK 5

HOW TO PLAY UKULELE: IN 1 DAY

The Only 7 Exercises You Need to Learn Ukulele Chords, Ukulele Tabs and Fingerstyle Ukulele Today

Preston Hoffman

Table of Contents

Introduction

Welcome to '*How to Play Ukulele In 1 Day - The Only 7 Exercises You Need to Learn Ukulele Chords, Ukulele Tabs and Fingerstyle Ukulele Today*'! Thank you for purchasing my book. And congratulations! You have just taken the first step in learning how to play the ukulele in one day.

Whether you are learning to read music for the first time or are already a pro musician, this book will provide a collection of useful tips in seven easy-to-follow exercises that will get you playing the ukulele in one day.

The seven exercises cover the basic essentials of ukulele playing from how to buy your first ukulele and read chords to learning to fingerpick and strum your favourite songs.

I've been a musician for many years, playing all kinds of instruments from the guitar and piano to the drum and other percussion instruments. However, I've always had a soft spot for the ukulele. I love its cheerful sound and the diversity of music you can produce with it. When I first started playing it, I spent days of trial and error to get everything right. It wasn't easy, and I would have loved a guide on how to play. That's why I decided to gather my experience and research to present a comprehensive guide to playing the ukulele for anyone starting out.

It's an incredible instrument and it is, in fact, not that difficult to play. That's why I created seven easy steps to learn the ukulele in one day, so you can get the same amount of joy that I get playing it.

Enjoy the book! I hope you get as much pleasure out of reading it as I did writing and researching it.

Chapter One: Buying Your Ukulele

In this chapter, we will look at the main points you should consider before buying your ukulele.

Once you decide to start playing the ukulele, it's important that you invest in a good instrument that will produce a good sound and will last a long time. The first step is knowing your different ukuleles. Here are some points you should know.

➢ Most of the basic music shops will sell the Mahalo. They are a cheap and cheerful type of ukulele and come in every colour imaginable. While they tend to be popular in schools and for beginner ukulele players, they are not the best quality. If you really want to learn the ukulele, it's best to upgrade to something a bit better.

➢ A good quality ukulele is the Kala which isn't too expensive and produces a much better, clearer sound than the Mahalo. See if your local music retailer has Kalas in stock and test out a couple there. Alternatively, you can search online for a decent ukulele. Make sure you search on reputable music retailer websites to get the best quality ukulele you can and ask musicians that you know or even on online forums to get some recommendations for suppliers.

➤   However, there is more to the ukulele than buying the right brand and type. Another important factor is the strings as these are responsible for producing a good – or bad – sound. Good quality strings are not that expensive and are worth paying extra to ensure your ukulele is in the best quality possible. So, how can you be sure you are getting the best type of strings? Aquila is an excellent brand and will produce a nice, crisp sound. It's best to avoid the ukuleles with plastic-looking strings as these not only can break easily but they tend to produce a poor-quality sound.

➤   There are four sizes of ukulele. These are the soprano, concert, tenor, and baritone. The soprano can be considered the traditional ukulele with its classic ukulele sound and its small size of 20 inches. The next size up is the concert ukulele at 23 inches and is a little bit easier to handle than the soprano. A little bigger at 26 inches with a deeper sound is the tenor and is popular among professional ukulele players. Finally, there is the baritone which is the largest ukulele at 30 inches. This last type is probably the least popular among ukulele players who tend to be drawn towards the small size of the ukulele and, as a result, prefer to use smaller types.

Chapter Summary

In this chapter, you learned some tips on what to look out for when buying your first ukulele and some of the differences between the different types.

• When buying a ukulele, it's best to try and get the highest quality possible to make sure your instrument will last a long time and produce a quality sound.

• There are four different common types of ukulele. The soprano is the smallest and the type most associated with the ukulele. The baritone is the largest and the least popular due to its size.

In the next chapter, we will move onto the first lesson on how to learn the ukulele in one day. The first lesson will look at the different parts of the ukulele and how to hold it.

Chapter Two: Lesson One: The Parts of the Ukulele and How to Hold It

In order to learn how to play the ukulele, you first need to know the main parts of the instrument and how to hold it. In this chapter, we will be looking at the basics to get you started.

Why do I Need to Know the Parts of the Ukulele?

You may be keen to dive straight in and start playing, but first you need to learn the names of the parts. Why? Because this will allow you to tune, restring, and essentially take care of ukulele better. This is essential to produce a good quality sound and to make your instrument last longer.

Let's get familiar with the ukulele. Below is a picture of a ukulele.

It is made up of several parts that are essential for making it work and play music. A the very top, we have two important parts – the headstock and the tuners.

Headstock and Tuners

The headstock is also known as the head and is at the top of the ukulele. It needs to be strong to withstand the tension between the tuners and the strings, so it's often made of wood. The head on cheaper ukuleles will probably be made of plastic. The main role of the headstock is to hold the tuners.

The tuners have one of the most important jobs on the ukulele as they are responsible for tuning the strings. Although their most common name is tuners, they are sometimes known as machine heads, tuning pegs, tuning keys, tuning heads, or pegs. Each ukulele has four tuners and, as they are so important, let's look at them in more detail.

The direction that the tuners point in depends entirely on what ukulele you have. Some may point to the side whereas others may point backwards. It doesn't really matter which direction they point to, it's just something to be aware of. The strings of the ukulele are threaded through each tuner. The tuner, depending on the way it is turned, will either tighten the string or loosen it and this is what affects the sound. On the older ukuleles, the tuners depend on friction to turn it although this is an old-fashioned method nowadays. Modern ukuleles have geared tuners which are far easier to turn and if you buy a ukulele now, it's more than likely to have this type of tuner.

The first rule of tuning your ukulele is to gently unwind the tuner first before winding back up to get the right note. This prevents the string from over-stretching and helps avoid the string breaking in the long run. If your strings are made of metal, this rule is especially important.

Nut

Like the nut of the guitar, the nut of the ukulele is the area between the headstock and fretboard (the fretboard we will look at next) that holds the strings. It is a little ridge with small notches where the strings rest on. It helps to keep the strings in place and evenly spaced out. It also keeps the strings lifted off the board below which is essential for when you want to play the strings by pressing down on them.

Fretboard

The neck of the ukulele is what connects the headstock to the body of the instrument. The surface of the neck at the front is known as the fretboard and is the part beneath the strings. When buying an ukulele, you'll probably notice that a lot of the fretboards are black or dark brown. This is purely for aesthetic

reasons and originates from when they used to be made of dark-
coloured woods such as ebony.

Frets

Take a look at the fretboard and you will see the strips
across it. These little bars ae known as frets. They are lifted off
the surface to create a little bump and they get closer together as
they get nearer to the sound hole.

Fret Markers

If you have played the guitar before, you may have noticed
fret markers as well. These are the white indicators – or dots –
that are placed on the fretboard. You may see other shapes or
colours, but they are usually white and circular. They are useful to
help you move up and down the fretboard and find certain notes.

Neck

If you remember, the fretboard is the surface of the neck and
the neck is what supports the fretboard. To facilitate playing, the
neck is curved and is usually made of wood to keep it strong and
supported. It is directly connected to the head of the ukulele.

Body

    The main part of the ukulele is called the body. The shape and size of the body influences the tone as when the strings vibrate, the body amplifies this sound. Ukuleles can have several different shapes and sizes depending on whether it is a more classic or modern type.

The Sound Hole

Like the guitar, the ukulele has a sound hole which, as the name lets on, helps amplify the sound. The sound played will be the loudest over the sound hole whereas higher up the fretboard will have the quietest sounds.

Bridge

The bridge is where the strings are attached, and it is found just under the sound hole. There are two types of bridges. First there is the tie-bar where the strings are threaded through and tied to the bridge. The other is a standard bridge where the string is threaded through a notch at the end of the bridge.

Saddle

The saddle is basically like the nut but at the opposite end of the board. Its role is to lift the strings off the fretboard and works with the nut to keep the strings in place and evenly spread out.

Strings

As we looked at before, it's important to choose your strings carefully. The choice of strings varies depending on the ukulele. For example, on concert and soprano ukuleles, the strings are quite often made of nylon. Other types of ukuleles may have a hybrid of nylon and metal. Some may have just metal strings which tend to produce a full-sounding tone.

Now you know all the parts of the ukulele. The next important part is learning how to hold it. Don't worry, it's pretty easy but you need to get it right from the start as this is what will help you master playing the ukulele in one day. As a note, the instructions below are for right-handed players. If you are left-handed, simply switch it the other way around.

How to Hold the Ukulele

First, prop the body of the ukulele against your chest with the neck supported by your left hand and your right forearm across the body with your strumming finger within easy reach of the strings. If it's a big ukulele, it's totally fine to rest it on one leg whilst your sitting to take the weight off your arms and to stop it from falling.

Your left hand will rest near the near top of the ukulele and keep your thumb behind the neck. It's a good idea to keep your nails short on your fretting hand – that's your left, your right is your strumming hand – as it makes sure that you play with the pad of your finger. Feeling comfortable is key and it may take a little while to get used to holding it in a way that feels natural. Don't worry – this will come.

Chapter Summary

In this chapter, we looked at the basics of the ukulele which are essential to know to get you off to the right start.

- You learnt the different parts of the ukulele including the tuners, the strings, the fretboard, and the bridge.

- You also learnt the best way of holding the ukulele to make sure you stay comfortable and are handling it in the best way to produce the best sound.

In the next chapter, we will look at the chords you should know. This will be the first step to learning how to play.

Chapter Three: Lesson Two: The Chords of The Ukulele

In this chapter, we will look at the chords. They are pretty easy to learn, and will you get you started playing straight away.

As we saw in the last chapter, you hold the neck of the ukulele in your left hand – this is assuming you play right-handed – and you strum with your right hand. In this case, it is your left hand that will form the chords.

To get the chords right, the first thing to know is that the ukulele has four chords. The chord sheets for the ukulele – also known as the Uke chord charts – have four lines, with each line representing one of the four strings.

The order of the chart starts with G, then to C, then to E, and finally to A with G at the left and A on the right. Try to remember them with an acronym, such as, Go Camping Every April, or whatever works best for you!

There are also major chords and minor chords.

> Major chords – make a definite, complete sound

> Minor chords – the sound is softer and almost a little moody.

With these four strings known as G, C, E, and A, you can create several different chords. When reading the chord sheets, there are two things to pay attention to. These are the dots at the top of the chart and the dots on the lines. The white dots at the top of the chart means that those strings don't need to be touched. This is known as an open string and you don't need to do anything about them. The black dot on the vertical line indicates which string you need to play and where, by showing if you should play the G, C, E, or A string and on which fret.

As you can see in the image below, to play this note, you would ignore G, C, and E and just play the A string. You would need to hold it down on the first fret, as the black dot shows. If the black dot was further down, for example by the line marked '3', then you would play string A on the third fret. And that's it! It's that simple to read the chord chart.

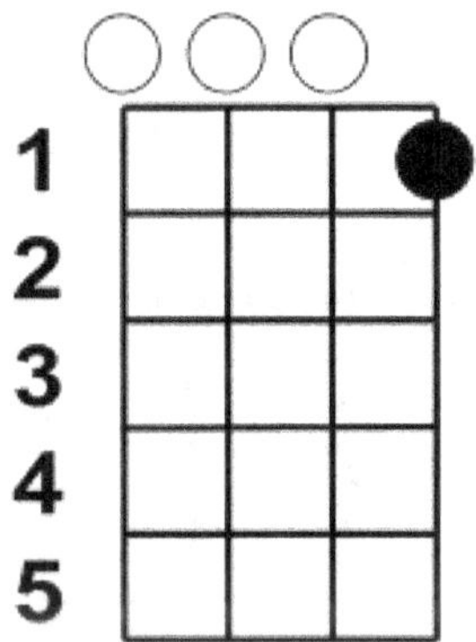

Let's begin with the first and easiest set of chords – the C chords.

C Chords

There are a few types of C chords – the C Major (C), C minor (Cm), and C7. These are the easiest set to play.

The C Major

To create the C major chord, you need to ignore the G, C, and E string and just hold down – or fret – the A string. The black dot for the C chord will always be on the third fret. So, to play the C chord, you need to fret the A string on the third fret.

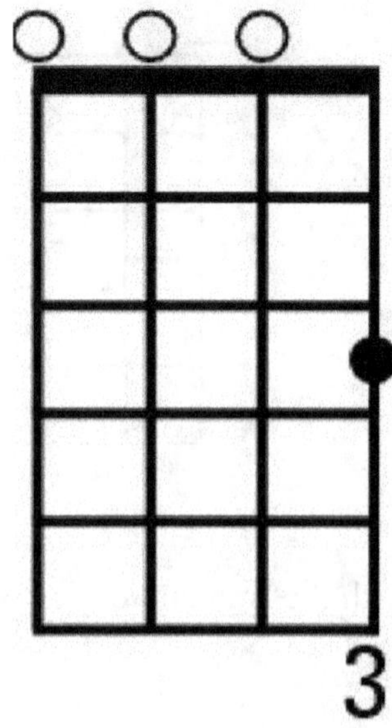

The C Minor

For the C minor, you need to hold down three strings – C, E and A – also on the third fret.

The C7 Chord

For the C7, you need to hold down the A string on the first fret.

The next set of chords we will look at are the A chords. Again, there is A major (A), A minor (Am), and A7.

The A Chords

The A Major

To play the A major, hold the G string on the second fret and the C string on the first fret.

A Minor Chord

Hold the G string on the second fret.

A7 Chord

Hold the C string on the first fret.

The next sets of chords we'll learn are the F, D, and G chords.

F Major Chord (F)

This time, to create the F major, you need to use two fingers. What you will do is ignore the C and A strings and just use the G and E strings. You need to hold down the E string on the first fret and the G string on the second fret. And that's it!

Tip: Using your left hand, place your index finger on the E string and your middle finger on the G string.

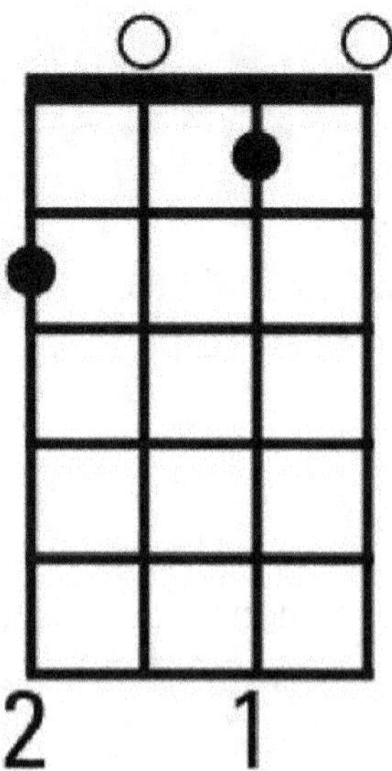

F Minor Chord (Fm)

You need to hold down the G string and the E string on the first fret, and the A string on the third fret.

D Major Chord (D)

You need to hold the G, C, and E string on the second fret.

D Minor Chord (Dm)

Hold down the G and C string on the second fret and the E string on the first fret.

G Major Chord (G)

Hold the C and A string on the second fret and the E string on the third fret.

These are all the most important chords you need to learn in the beginning and they should be easy to learn if you keep alternating between the chords and testing them out until they feel natural. But let's continue by looking at some of the other, slightly trickier chords.

B Chord

The B chord is not used that often in songs but it's worth knowing anyway. It has a complex feature known as the barre chord. The barre chord is when you need to play more than one string at the same time using the same finger.

To play the B chord, hold the G string on the fourth fret, the C string on the third fret, and finally, use your index finger to hold the E and A string together on the second fret. It takes practice but don't worry too much about it for now. You can come back to this chord later.

The B flat chord (Bb) is more common, especially in folk songs. It also has a barre chord.

B Flat

Hold the G string on the third fret, the C string on the second fret, and then you need to play a barre chord on the E and A string on the first fret.

It can be a bit tricky to hold all those strings at once in the beginning, so a good tip is to first master the G7 chord which is similar but a bit easier.

G7 Chord

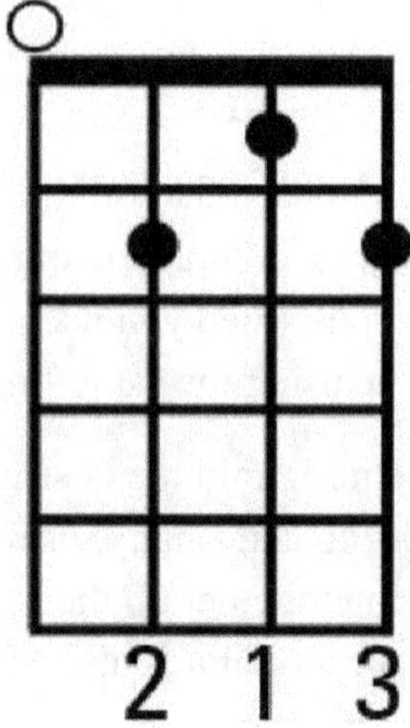

Hold the C chord on the second fret and make a barre chord on the E and A string on the first fret.

Next up is the important E chord. It's a bit more difficult as your fingers will need to stretch a lot which may feel strange in the beginning.

The E Chord

Hold the G string on the first fret, the C string on the fourth fret, and the A string on the second fret.

There is another E chord that you may see. It involves a barre chord on the G, C, and E strings on the fourth fret and holding down the A string on the second fret. Whichever one you choose, learning the E chord is important as it's present in a lot of songs.

Let's look at the other minor chords. These are a little complicated and don't expect to learn them overnight. However, it's fun to test them out anyway for now and learn to master them another day.

B Minor Chord (Bm)

This requires a barre chord on the C, E, and A string on the second fret and holding down the G string on the fourth fret.

E Minor Chord (Em)

Hold the C string on the fourth fret, the E string on the third fret, and the A string on the second fret.

G Minor Chord (Gm)

Hold the C string on the second fret, the E string on the third fret, and the A string on the first fret.

Finally, we have the 7 chords. These are commonly used in blues and jazz and can really add some groove to your music.

B7 Chord

This one is tricky and it's best to know about it now and practice later. You need to use a barre chord on the G, E, and A strings on the second fret and place your finger on the C string on the third fret.

D7 Chord

This one is also a little tricky. Use a barre chord on the G, C and E strings on the second fret and hold the A string on the third fret.

E7 Chord

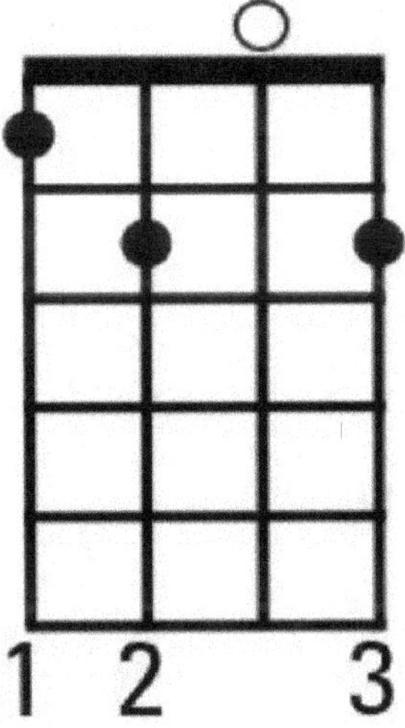

Hold the G string on the first fret, the C string on the second fret, and the A string on the second fret.

F7 Chord

Hold the G string on the second fret, the C string on the third fret, and the E string on the first fret. This is a but tricky in the beginning as it feels your fingers are all over the place! But it will eventually feel more natural.

These are all the chords you need to know in the beginning. Focus on learning the major chords and some of the minors. The chords you can leave for another day at the beginning, but they are worth learning to help you advance onto playing more varied songs quicker.

Chapter Summary

In this chapter, we learned about the different chords of the ukulele.

- The ukulele has four strings – G, C, E, and A.

- The main chords we looked at were the major, the minor, and the 7 chords. Some are easier – such as the C and A chords – than others – such as the E and 7 chords.

- It's worth spending some time practicing each chord individually before trying to transition between the chords. Learn the main chords though and you are good to start playing a wide range of different songs.

In the next chapter, we will learn more about transitioning between chords and chord progression.

Chapter Four: Lesson Three: Chord Transitioning and Chord Progression

In this chapter, we will look at chord transitioning – which is basically just moving from one chord to the next – and chord progression.

The first thing you need to do is to practice memorising the chords from the previous chapter. Don't worry if it doesn't happen overnight – remembering chords can take some time to commit to memory and it is totally fine to keep the chord charts open in front of you. It's better to make sure you are learning everything correctly from the beginning and getting used to where your fingers must go.

Once the chords become more natural, you can start transitioning between the chords.

Chord Transitioning

As mentioned before, chord transitioning is just moving between chords to create a song. Take it slow and steady in the beginning and in time, the flow and pace will quicken.

The easiest step to learning transitioning between the chords is moving between the G chord and the C chord.

To move between them, start with the G chord and place your fingers in the appropriate position. Your ring finger will be on the E string on the third fret. This will then need to be moved over to the A string, also on the third fret. Once it's there, lift the other fingers off the other strings and you are now on the C chord. Practice again a few times before trying to strum each note. It will become smoother and easier with time. That's all it takes to move between the G and C chord.

Next, we will move from the G chord to the F chord.

Put your fingers in the position of a G chord. Then move the index finger to the E string on the first fret and your middle finger to the G string on the second fret. Take the other finger off the other string as you don't need it for the F chord. And that's it!

Keep practising pairs like this to get used to moving between chords. How do you know which are the best chords to practice together though? This is where chord progression can help.

Chord Progression

Chord progression basically shows you the order of chords you need to play. Some chord charts show the chords as letters as we have seen already whereas others show the chords as roman numerals. To keep things simple, we will look at the chords as letters for now.

Music that sounds pleasant to the ear is just a combination of great sounding chords. If you have some experience already playing other musical instruments, you will know that some notes just sound better with some than others. The notes A minor, C major, D minor, and A7 sound nice together, as do A major, D major, and E7. These are some that you can practice together and try making your own tunes.

Here are some easy progressions to start with that will not only get you starting to play some basic songs, but will help you learn the feel of making transitions between chords.

C – F -G

These three chords can be played repeatedly in sequence in major.

Next up is C – Am – F – G

A little more challenging but great practice for getting your fingers used to the movements of the playing the ukulele.

Then try D – G – D -A7

Here are some more easy sequences to practice with:

Am – Dm – Am – E7

Here's one you may recognise from pop tunes.

Dm – A7 – Dm – Gm – A7 – Dm – A7 – Dm

Remember how the minor notes are often softer and quite moody? The sequence above is known as one of the saddest sequences of chords to play on the ukulele. It is used in the song Back to Black by Amy Winehouse, among other songs.

By using these chord progressions, it will help you to get used to changing between chords and start playing some basic tunes. It's the first step towards getting the natural beat of the chords, listening to what sounds good, and becoming more natural with playing.

Chapter Summary

In this chapter, we looked at how to transition between certain chords and how to practice using chord progression.

- An easy beginning is transitioning between the G and C chord then building up from there.

- Some chords naturally sound better together than others and you can make sequences of chords to make a tune. Chord progression is basically the order that you play the chords in. It is good to practice simple sequences in the beginning to get used to changing between chords and to have fun playing your first tunes.

In the next chapter, we will look at how to strum the ukulele.

Chapter Five: Lesson Four: How to Strum the Ukulele

In this chapter, we will look at the art of strumming the ukulele.

There is more to strumming than simply scraping your fingers across the strings over the sound hole. In fact, there is a lot more to it. Luckily, it is not that difficult to learn.

The basic technique is to use your index finger of your right hand with the fingernail facing down. What you are aiming for is to hit the string with your nail as you strum down. When you strum up, you will use the tip of your finger. So, strum down with your nail and strum up with the fleshy tip. It's natural in the beginning to use your whole hand to strum yet you should try just using your wrist to create the movements. This will make sure you don't tire out too quickly.

So now you have the basic technique of strumming, the where to strum part is pretty important too. If you strum too close to the bridge at the bottom, the sound won't be as good and comes out a bit muffled. The best spot can vary from ukulele to ukulele and it takes practice to know what sounds best. However, the best place is usually near to where the neck and the body meet.

To practice this technique, just strum up and down and get used to the rhythm. A great idea for practicing is to put on your favourite music and listen out for the beat. Once you catch it, try moving your hand up and down to match the pace, focusing on keeping the technique right.

Learning to strum shouldn't take too long at all so you will be well on your way to learning to play the ukulele at a strong beginner's level in one day.

Building Your Strumming Skills

The foundations of strumming are the simple up and down technique. Once you have nailed that, you can start experimenting with other tricks and tweaks. For example, you don't always need to just go up and down. You can skip a pattern so that instead of going down-up-down, you try down-up-up by not hitting the strings when you flick your wrist downwards. This helps build up different patterns and rhythms, creating a variety of sounds and beats to allow you to make your own unique music.

Let's look at some other ways you can jazz up your strumming skills.

➢ You can try doing the swing or shuffle strums which is simply when the strum going down is slower than the strum going up. Like the pattern we looked at before where you miss a strum going up or down, the swing strum is simply a way of making the basic up and down strum a bit catchier.

➢ Another way of making the simple up and down strum a bit more exciting is to hit the palm of your hand on the body in between a beat of strumming up and down to get a drum tap as well.

➢ You can also use your fretting hand – your left hand if you are playing right-handed – to influence your strumming. As you strum, it makes the strings of the ukulele vibrate. To create an impact, use your fret hand to hold down the strings at the top to stop the strings making a sound.

Using a Plectrum

There is a bit of a debate about using a plectrum with the ukulele, although it is generally accepted nowadays to use a pick or plectrum.

The ukulele came from Hawaii when instruments left behind by the Portuguese explorers were modified and adjusted to create something distinctly new. In these days, the Hawaiians didn't use picks, simply relying on their hands – in particular, their index finger and thumb – to strum and create music. As a result, the most popular and regular way of playing the ukulele is just with the fingers.

As the ukulele became known worldwide, some people who were used to playing the guitar or other similar instruments, started playing the ukulele with a pick. Nowadays, it is totally fine to use a pick to play the ukulele and some players like to use a mix of both fingers and a plectrum to create a different sound and produce adapted melodies such as rock music.

Some players though, insist that the ukulele can't be played with a pick due to its traditional roots of being played only with the fingers. If you want to follow the older traditions, then playing with the fingers is fine. If you don't mind embracing the modern influences, use a pick too. Some players don't use a pick but grow their fingernails and use that instead! It's all down to personal preference at the end of the day and there is no right or wrong way.

What Kind of Pick?

The type of pick will depend on a couple of factors, one being the size of your ukulele. Th baritone ukulele, for example, uses a long pick that would be tricky to use with smaller ukuleles. Another point to consider is the material of the strings. If the ukulele has nylon strings, a lighter pick will be perfectly fine. Metal strings may need something a little heavier.

How About Using a Guitar Pick with the Ukulele?

A common question when it comes to picks is whether a guitar pick can be used as a ukulele pick. The answer ultimately boils down to personal opinions – some believe that a guitar pick shouldn't be anywhere near a ukulele – but although the size can be a bit different, some guitar picks are fine to use with a ukulele.

A lot of ukulele picks are made from felt or leather so are kinder on the strings. As a guitar pick tends to be harder, there is the worry that it can harm the ukulele strings. However, a harder pick will not cause significantly different damage and strings will always be exposed to general wear and tear and will need replacing eventually anyway. Using a strong fingernail enthusiastically will cause the same damage as a hard guitar pick. This shouldn't be too much of a concern.

An advantage of using a guitar pick is that its allows you to experiment with different sounds and create unique sounding beats. Don't be afraid to test out a guitar pick. You never know, if you really like the sound of it, it can encourage you to produce some fantastic music that is quite unique from anything else!

Will a Pick Damage Your Ukulele?

Not really. If you attack your strings with over-enthusiasm on the pick then you may quicken the rate of general wear and tear. But strings are not built or made for life and eventually you will have to replace them at some point. Using a pick won't have a significant effect on when you need to buy a new set of strings.

So, What's the Conclusion? To Use a Pick or Not?

It's totally up to you. It's worth experimenting with both fingers only and testing out a pick to get an idea for the different sounds. Always remember that you are the musician and you produce your own music so whatever you feel sounds the best, you should stick to. There is no right or wrong way which is why music is so creative.

Overall, a harder pick will help add a bit more volume to your music and protect your fingers a bit. This is especially true if you like playing faster beats. Use a leather or felt pick if you want a softer sound that doesn't produce an after 'clicking' sound that harder picks sometimes make.

As picks generally aren't that expensive, you can buy a few and see which ones you like the most. As you get more experienced, you may find that you lean towards certain picks automatically depending on the sound you want to produce and the music that you are playing.

Chapter Summary

In this chapter, we looked at everything you need to know about strumming.

- The basic technique of strumming is to simply flick the wrist to move the hand up and down over the strings that lie across the sound hole.

- The best place to strum largely depends on your ukulele but generally, the best sound is produced near to where the neck and the body meet.

- You can jazz up basic strumming by missing a strum, using the body to make a percussion sound, or holding the strings on the neck with your fretting hand to get a crisp finish.

- You can use a pick or plectrum if you like. It usually comes down to personal preference.

In the next chapter, we will look at reading tabs.

Chapter Six: Lesson Five: How to Read Tabs

In this chapter, we will look at how to read tabs, an essential skill in learning the ukulele.

The first question is – what is a tab and why do you need to read it?

It's a good question.

A tab is another way of saying music tablature, which is basically a sheet of paper that represents the music that you need to play. It is commonly used among the stringed instruments, such as the ukulele.

The main advantage of a tab is that it isn't that hard to read. It may seem strange in the beginning but it's easy to pick up, especially with practice. It is certainly possible to understand some key parts in one day so that you can start playing some songs on the ukulele almost straight away.

If you have never had formal music training, don't fret. The tab doesn't require it at all. It tells you exactly which string to use to play a certain note and where to play that note on the fretboard. It really makes life easy when it comes to following a particular song.

We will start by reading notes in a tab before later moving onto chords in a tab.

The best way of learning is to see some examples.

```
A --------------------------------------------
E ---------------------------------------------
C -----------------------------------------
G ----------------------------------------
```

This is the general tab table with each horizontal line representing the string of the ukulele and it is labelled accordingly. You may have expected the tab to be the other way around with the top line starting as the G string as when you are playing, the A string is the one that is closest to your body or the floor. If you imagine the head of the ukulele being on the left-hand side of this tab, it can help get some perspective on that.

You will notice on the tab that there are numbers placed on the different strings (or horizontal lines, literally speaking).

```
    A-----2-------------------------------
E----------0---------------------0-----
C---------------0----------0----------
G--------------------0----------------
```

The above is purely an example. The number on each string shows which fret number you need to play. So, the above shows we would play the A string on the third fret, then an open E

347

string, then the open C string, then down to the open G string and continue like that.

· If that's a bit confusing, let's look at this in more details, in particular, for open notes.

Here is another example.

```
        A------------------------------------
E-------1----------------------------
C------------------------------------
G------------------------------------
```

Here, we can see that there is a '1' on the E string. This means that you need to just play this string on the first fret. So, you would hold the E string on the first fret and pluck that with your finger.

Then, we have this example.

```
        A--------------------------------------
E-------0----------------------------
C----------------------------------
G----------------------------------
```

To play this, we would play the E string without fretting. In other words, we would pluck the E string without holding it down.

That is how to play the chords when the numbers are scattered across the tab like we saw above – you pluck the strings. Let's look at something a little different now.

Chords in a Tab

Whereas above we saw how to pluck certain strings, we will now see how to read chords presented on the strings.

Let's take a look at the following:

```
    A--------0-----------
E--------1-----------
C-------0-----------
G--------2-----------
```

As you can see, we have a vertical line of numbers. This represents a chord. So, you would hold down the E string on the first fret and the G string on the second fret. You would leave the other strings untouched and then strum the strings across the sound hole.

This would give you the F chord.

Let's look at another example, but this time a sequence of chords.

```
    A-----2-----3-----0-----0-----3-----2-----
E-----3-----0-----0-----1-----2-----1-----
C-----2-----0-----0-----0-----2-----2-----
G-----0-----0-----2-----2-----2-----0-----
```

This tab shows several chords in a row. In this sequence, we can see that the chords to play are G then C then Am then F then D7 and finally, G7.

This is a really easy way of reading chords and it helps if the chords are written above the vertical lines, as they often are.

The only downside of this style of reading chords is that it is tricky to work out the beat and pace of the song if you don't already know it. The key then is to listen to the song before and get a feel for the beat. Then you can play the chords accordingly.

Sometimes, you may see arrows next to the chords that point up or down. These arrows may be straight or wavy, but they mean the same thing. The arrows simply indicate which way you should strum and it works in a logical order. The arrow pointing up means you should strum up and the arrow pointing down means – you got it – you should strum down.

If you understood all of that, then you are already perfectly capable of reading notes and chords at a great level!

What we will look at now are a couple of slightly more advanced moves. To get the basics of the ukulele in one day, you may not need to utilize the following two concepts immediately, but it's worth knowing what 'hammer-ons' and 'pull-offs' are anyway.

Hammer-Ons

When you come across a tab that looks like this below, it is known as a hammer-on note.

```
      A-----1-------------------
E-----1-------------------
C----------1h2----------
G------------------2-----
```

You can notice the 'h' in between the two notes on the third line. This 'h' represents the 'hammer on'. A hammer on is basically when you pluck a note on the ukulele string and then place a finger on a higher fret to produce a higher-sounding note.

You may see the hammer-on being represented by an arch between the notes, but here we see it as a 'h'. In the above example, the C string is played on the first fret and then your other finger will quickly hold down (hammer-on) the second fret to produce two notes while the string is plucked just once.

The next concept is pull-offs.

Pull Offs

Pull offs are the perfect opposite of hammer-ons. This time, you play a note and produce a second note that is lower than the first one. It can either be represented by a 'p' or by arches in between the two notes. When you see arches on a tab, the way to distinguish whether it is a hammer-on or a pull-off is the sequence of numbers. A pull-off will show numbers that go from higher to lower and a hammer-on will show numbers going from lower to higher.

```
    A-----1------------------
E-----1------------------
C-----------3p2----------
G------------------2-----
```

Here we can see the pull off is on the third line – the C string. What we would do here is play the C string on the third fret and pull off – or hold down – the same string but on the second fret to produce a note without plucking the string again.

Chapter Summary

In this chapter, we learned about how to read tabs. This is important to be able to play songs and music on the ukulele.

• We first looked at how to play notes where you would pluck the strings rather than strum. The tabs show you which note to play and which fret to play it in. Sometimes, you will see a '0' which represents an open string. This means you don't hold the string down and instead just pluck it openly.

• We then looked at reading chords on the tabs where the vertical line of numbers shows the strings you need to play and the frets you need to use to form a particular chord. It's an easy way to read chords – so long as you remember how the chords are made! You may want to jot down the chord letters at the top of the tab.

• Finally, we look at two slightly more advanced parts of the tab which are hammer-ons and pull-offs.

In the next chapter, we will look at lesson six which is all about fingerstyle or fingerpicking as it is also known as.

Chapter Seven: Lesson Six: Getting the Basics of Fingerstyle

In this chapter, we will look at fingerstyle.

First, what is fingerstyle?

Fingerstyle is a style of playing the ukulele with just your fingers and is known as finger picking. If you are used to strumming, especially guitar players, you may find this a bit unnatural in the beginning but as with anything, with practice, it becomes second nature eventually.

There are two ways to fingerpick when playing the ukulele. There may be variations on these, but these are the two most popular and common ways.

➢ One way is to use your thumb, index finger, and your middle finger together. You thumb is in charge of plucking the top two strings – so G and C – then your index finger plucks the next string – the E string – and finally, your middle finger is responsible for plucking the A string.

➢ The other way uses an extra finger – the ring finger. So, your thumb plucks the G string, your index plucks the C string, then your middle finger does the E string and your ring finger plucks the A string.

Which one is the best? Neither is better than the other, it depends on what you feel the most comfortable with. You may actually find yourself using both techniques as you become more advanced, especially as some music patterns you may find easier when you use more fingers. Try practicing with styles to get a feel for which one you like the most.

For the sake of keeping things easy, we will stick to the first technique here and just use three fingers.

Let's begin our practise.

Take a look at the tab below.

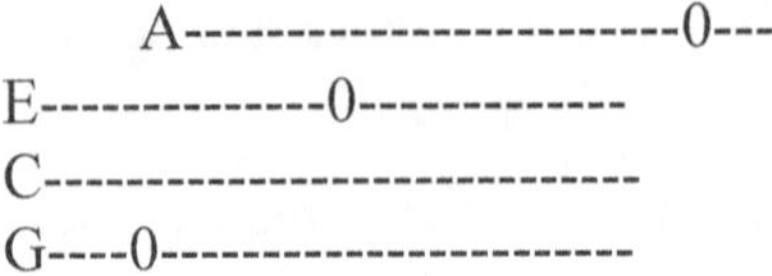

Here, this tab gives you the opportunity to use all fingers required. The G you play with your thumb – the C string you play with your thumb too but in this case, we will skip the C – then the E string you play with your index finger and finally, the A string you play with your middle finger.

Don't worry about the left, fretting hand for now. Simply focus on the right hand and pluck these notes above the sound hole. So, pluck the G first with the thumb, then pluck the E next with the index finger, and then pluck the A to finish with your middle finger.

Keep doing the same sequence several times until you get the rhythm.

At the moment, you are just playing notes and you get that nice, unfinished sound when you pluck the strings. Next, we will add a chord in the mix. Now you must use your left hand to make the chord and your right hand will pluck the strings. It's interesting to hear how the open string makes a different sound to the chord which sounds more closed and tinny when it's played.

Let's look at the following.

```
        A------------------------3--------
E---------------0-----------------
C--------------------------------------
G--------0------------------------
```


Here, we've added in the C chord which you play on the A string on the third fret. So, make the C chord with your left hand. Now, pluck the open G string with your thumb, then the open E string with your index finger, and finally, pluck the A string as it is formed in the C chord.

Keep repeating that pattern to get used to the feel.

Let's add in an A chord now.

```
        A-------------------------0---------
E------------------------------------
C--------------1--------------------
G--------2--------------------------
```


Here, you make the A chord with your left hand by holding the G string on the second fret and the C string on the first fret. Then, you pluck the G string with you thumb, the C string with your thumb again and then pluck the A string on an open string with your middle finger.

Try alternating between the two chords. Play the C chord a couple of times with the open G and E string then play the A chord a couple of times with the open A string to really practice your fingerpicking.

Another easy chord is the F chord. Try fingerpicking several chords instead of strumming to get used to this style of playing.

Here is a short pattern to help you practice. Keep playing this pattern on repeat until you feel you're getting the hang of fingerpicking. A good tip is to keep your hand rested on the body of the ukulele to help keep it steady.

```
A-------3-------------2-------------0---------------2-------
E-----0-----0------3------3-----1-------1--------3------3---
C--0-----------2--------------0------------2--------------
G---------------------------------------------------------
```

Play this slowly and then challenge yourself to try playing it faster. Remember not to strum but to pluck each string.

Chapter Summary

In this chapter, we looked at the art of fingerstyle to play the ukulele.

- Fingerstyle is a way of playing the ukulele. It depends on plucking the stings to play certain notes or chords rather than strumming.

- Start by practicing fingerpicking notes rather than chords. It will help get you used to using you thumb, index finger, and middle finger for playing.

- Once you are comfortable with fingerpicking notes, move onto chords and keep practicing sequences of chords to get used to it.

In the next chapter, we will look at the final lesson which is practicing everything we have learnt and bringing it all together by playing some simple songs.

Chapter Eight: Lesson Seven: Songs to Play

In this chapter, we will look at some simple songs that you can now play on your ukulele.

Over the last six lessons, you have learnt everything you need to know to play the ukulele in one day. You have learnt all about the chords, how to strum, how to fingerpick, how to read notes, and how to read chords. Now, in the final lesson, we will bring all that together for the grand finale – playing songs with the ukulele. This is probably one of the most satisfying parts of the ukulele, coming second only to creating your own music.

Here are some songs for you to play with the chords and the lyrics. You should recognise some but if not, simply search for them online to find out the tune and play along to the rhythm.

How about we start with a Beatles classic? It may seem a bit complicated but it's actually pretty easy to play. You will feel great after playing this after just one day of learning the ukulele!

The Beatles – Let it Be

For this song you need to know four chords – C, G Am, and
F

The intro starts with: C – G – Am – F – C – G – F – C

Verse

      C   G

When I find myself in times of trouble

  Am   F

Mother Mary comes to me

 C   G   F C

Speaking words of wisdom, let it be

   C   G

And in my hour of darkness

    Am   F

She is standing right in front of me

 C   G   F C

Speaking words of wisdom, let it be

Chorus

    Am   G   F   C

Let it be, let it be, let it be, let it be

  Am   G   F C

Whisper words of wisdom, let it be

Verse

    C   G

And when the broken-hearted people

  Am   F

Living in the world agree

  C   G   F

There will be an answer, let it be

  C   G

For though they may be parted

      Am   F

There is still a chance that they will see

  C   G   F C

There will be an answer, let it be

Chorus

    Am   G   F   C

Let it be, let it be, let it be, let it be

            Am   G   F C
Yeah there will be an answer, let it be
        Am   G   F   C
Let it be, let it be, let it be, let it be
        Am   G   F C
Whisper words of wisdom, let it be

F – C – G – F – C – x2

Solo

C – G – Am – F- C- G - F – C – x2

Chorus

          Am   G   F   C
Let it be, let it be, let it be, let it be
        Am   G   F C
Whisper words of wisdom, let it be

Verse

          C   G
And when the night is cloudy
            Am   F
There is still a light that shines in me

                C   G   F C
Shine on until tomorrow, let it be
        C   G
I wake up to the sound of music
      Am   F
Mother Mary comes to me
          C   G   F   C
Speaking words of wisdom, let it be

Chorus
        Am   G   F   C
Let it be, let it be, let it be, let it be
          Am   G   F C
Yeah there will be an answer, let it be
         Am   G   F   C
Let it be, let it be, let it be, let it be
        Am   G   F   C
Whisper words of wisdom, let it be

Adele – Someone Like You

The next song is a quite well-known pop song. It's 'Someone Like You' by Adele

Like the Beatles song above, you just need to know G, C, Am, and F chords. Just with four chords, you will be able to play two great songs!

Verse

```
  C         C
```
I heard that you're settled down
```
      Am
```
That you found a girl
```
        F
```
And you're married now
```
  C         C
```
I heard that your dreams came true
```
        Am
```
Guess she gave you things
```
        F
```
I didn't give to you
```
  C         C
```
Old friend why are you so shy
```
        Am
```

It ain't like you to hold back

  F

Or hide from life

  G   Am   F

I hate to turn up out of the blue uninvited but

     F

I couldn't stay away I couldn't fight it

   G

I'd hoped you'd see my face

  Am   F

And that you'd be reminded that for me it isn't over

Chorus

C   G   Am F

Never mind, I'll find someone like you

    C   G   Am F

I wish nothing but the best for you too

    C   G   Am   F

Don't forget me I beg I re-member you said

      C   G   Am F

Sometimes it lasts in love but sometimes it hurts in-stead

      C   G   Am F

Sometimes it lasts in love but sometimes it hurts instead, yeah

Verse

C   C

 You'd know how time flies

  Am

Only yesterday

    F

was the time of our lives

    C

We were born and raised

   C

In a summer haze

  Am   F

Bound by the surprise of our glory days

  G   Am   F

I hate to turn up out of the blue uninvited but

F

I couldn't stay away I couldn't fight it

  G

I'd hoped you'd see my face

  Am   F   F

And that you'd be reminded that for me it isn't over

Chorus

C   G   Am F

Never mind, I'll find someone like you

    C   G   Am F

I wish nothing but the best for you too

    C   G   Am   F

Don't forget me I beg I remember you said

      C   G   Am   F

Sometimes it lasts in love but sometimes it hurts in-stead, yeah

G

Nothing compares no worries or cares

Am

Regrets and mistakes their memories make

F

 Who would have known how

   Dm Em   F

Bitter-sweet this would taste

Chorus

C   G   Am F

Never mind I'll find someone like you

     C   G   Am F
I wish nothing but the best for you too

    C   G   Am   F
Don't forget me I beg I re-member you said

        C   G   Am   F
Sometimes it lasts in love but sometimes it hurts in-stead

Chorus

C   G   Am F
Never mind I'll find someone like you

    C   G   Am F
I wish nothing but the best for you too

    C   G   Am   F
Don't forget me I beg I re-member you said

        C   G   Am   F
Sometimes it lasts in love but sometimes it hurts in-stead

        C   G   Am   F
Sometimes it lasts in love but sometimes it hurts in-stead

        C   G   Am   F
Sometimes it lasts in love but sometimes it hurts instead

Leonard Cohen – Hallelujah

This song requires an extra chord compared to the others, so it gives you a bit more of a challenge. For this song, you need to know G, C, F, Am, and Em.

Verse

```
      C                 Am
I've heard there was a secret chord
      C                   Am
That David played, and it pleased the Lord
      F          G          C   G
But you don't really care for music, do you?
```

Chorus

```
      C          F          G
It goes like this, the fourth and the fifth
   Am            F
The minor fall, the major lift
      G          Em    Am
The baffled king composing hallelujah
```

Chorus

     F   Am

Hallelujah, hallelujah

     F   C-G-C-C

Hallelujah, hallelujah

Verse

      C   Am

Your faith was strong, but you needed proof

      C   Am

You saw her bathing on the roof

      F   G   C   G

Her beauty in the moonlight overthrew you

      C

She tied you

      F   G

to a kitchen chair

     Am

She broke your throne

     F

She cut your hair

     G   Em   Am

And from your lips she drew the Hallelujah

Chorus

    F   Am

Hallelujah, hallelujah

    F   C-G-C-C

Hallelujah, hallelujah

Verse

 C   Am

Maybe I've been here before

  C   Am

I know this room, I've walked this floor

   F   G   C   G

I used to live alone before I knew you

Pre-chorus

    C   F   G

I've seen your flag on the marble arch

 Am   F

Love is not a victory march

   G   Em   Am

It's a cold and it's a broken hallelujah

Chorus

    F   Am

Hallelujah, hallelujah

F   C-G-C-C

Hallelujah, hallelujah

Verse

        C   Am

There was a time you'd let me know

  C   Am

What's real and going on below

      F   G   C   G

But now you never show it to me, do you?

Pre-chorus

        C   F   G

Remember when I moved in with you?

      Am   F

The holy dark was moving too

    G   Em   Am

And every breath we drew was hallelujah

Chorus

    F   Am

Hallelujah, hallelujah

    F   C-G-C-C

Hallelujah, hallelujah

Verse

    C   Am

Maybe there's a God above

    C   Am

And all I ever learned from love

    F   G   C   G

Was how to shoot at someone who outdrew you

Pre-chorus

    C   F   G

It's not a cry you can hear at night

    Am   F

It's not somebody who's seen the light

    GE   Em   Am

It's a cold and it's a broken hallelujah

Chorus

    F   Am

Hallelujah, hallelujah

    F   C-G

Hallelujah, hallelujah

    F   Am

Hallelujah, hallelujah

    F   C-G-C

Hallelujah, hallelujah

Chapter Summary

In this chapter, we looked at three songs that will help you learn to play music on the ukulele in one day.

- We looked at three songs – The Beatles, Let it Be; Adele, Someone Like You; and Leonard Cohen, Hallelujah.

- These songs only need knowledge of five chords so if you learn those, you will quickly be playing the ukulele.

Final Words

Congratulations! You have reached the end of 'How to Play Ukulele: In 1 Day - The Only 7 Exercises You Need to Learn Ukulele Chords, Ukulele Tabs and Fingerstyle Ukulele Today.'

By now, you should have a good foundation of knowledge to be able to play the ukulele and even play a couple of songs. You should be able to read chords and know how to both strum and fingerpick to music.

I hope my book has encouraged you to keep learning and building your skills, so you can become a successful and experienced ukulele player. It's a great instrument – have fun playing it!

HOW TO PLAY
CHORDS
IN 1 DAY
The Only 7 Exercises You
Need to Learn Guitar Chords, Piano
Chords and Ukulele Chords Today
PRESTON HOFFMAN

BOOK 6

HOW TO PLAY CHORDS: IN 1 DAY

The Only 7 Exercises You Need to Learn Guitar Chords, Piano Chords and Ukulele Chords Today

Preston Hoffman

Table of Contents

Chapter One: Know Your Instruments

Welcome to your handy-dandy guide to learning how to play chords on the guitar, ukulele, and piano! It may come as a surprise—or it may not—to learn that all three of these instruments are quite easy to learn and you can quickly play thousands of songs on them just by following a few simple exercises and learning about the basic chords. But first, we need to break down the differences between these three instruments, since playing them will be slightly different for the chords and for your hands.

The Guitar

The guitar is the world's most popular instrument, and for good reason. It's versatile, easily portable, works well with other instruments, and is easy to learn—as you're about to find out. It has a wide range and is great for people who also enjoy singing, since you can easily play the guitar while you sing and it accompanies voices well.

There are many different types of guitars, the two main categories being acoustic and electric. It's recommended that you start with an acoustic guitar.

This here is an acoustic guitar:

And this is an electric guitar:

But there are variations within that, as well, like nylon
versus steel strings, for example. Nylon strings are more mellow

and easier on your fingers, while steel strings produce a bright tone and are louder. They're also harder on your fingers.

These here are nylon strings:

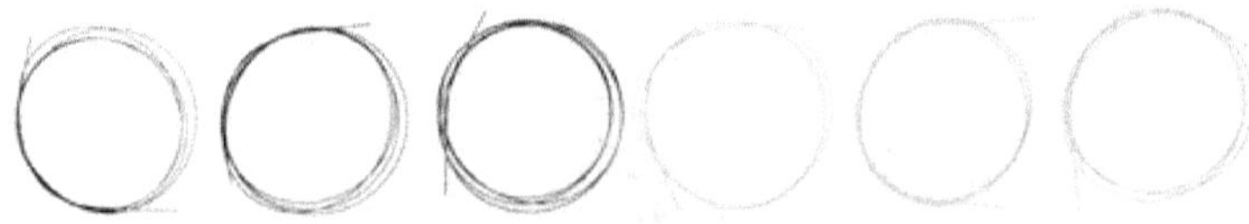

And these here are steel strings:

If those two images don't look too different to you, it's because the nylon is wrapped in either bronze-plated copper or in silver wire. If you're just looking at strings on a guitar, you might not be able to tell the difference at first. But you'll feel the difference in your fingers when you play them.

The best type of guitar for a beginner is a steel-strung guitar with round holes in the sideboards. They're the best for playing most of the songs you'll come across, including all of the songs in this book, and they create a good sound for accompanying singers and other instruments.

Another type of guitar is the Jumbo Guitar. It has an extra-large body, which means that it produces a better bass sound. If you're a bass player in a band, this might be the type of guitar you'd go for. This is a great guitar but with twelve strings and a larger body, it's not good for beginners:

384

It can be hard to see in this image, but where on a regular acoustic guitar like the one above each of the notches only has one string, these have two. Definitely not easy on your hands and the added musical value won't be of use to you until much later when you're further down the line in your understanding of music and can start to play around with the melodies of your songs instead of just focusing on the chords, which is what we're doing in this book.

Flamenco and Classical Guitars are strung with nylon and are used specifically for flamenco and classical music, respectively. They're good guitars and easy to learn on as a beginner but since they're for specialized music, you won't want to use them unless you're planning on playing mainly classical music.

There might not seem to be much of a difference in these guitars when you look at them, but it's all in the tuning. Flamenco guitars are designed to have a higher note register and the strings are therefore slightly different to accommodate this. Regular acoustic guitars have a lower register.

A classical guitar, on the other hand, will have a wider fret board, which can make it difficult for newer players to reach all of the strings, and they don't always have fret markers to help you out. Classical guitars just aren't designed for modern-day pop songs. Trying to play a Beatles song, for example, or that guitar classic "Wonderwall" on a classic guitar would just make it sound weird. So for our purposes, unless you want to play more classical music or more folk-sounding music, stick to regular acoustic.

Note: "Wonderwall" is considered one of the most overplayed songs on guitar, so it's best to avoid playing it.

Finally, electric guitars are the kind of guitars that can only be played when you plug them into an amplifier. You can attach pedals and other instruments to help play around with the sound of them. They're great for jazz and rock, but they might not be a good bet for a beginner. If you know your way around a guitar and want to start picking up some fancy tricks, new ways to play with sound, or you're joining a band and want to be able to be heard, then you can get an electric guitar.

Be sure to take good care of your guitar! Buy a sturdy case for it and store it in there. Hang onto the receipt after you buy it in case you're traveling with it and need to show the receipt to customs. Never let your guitar lie in the grass or dirt and be careful with it around moisture.

The Ukulele

There are, as you can tell just by looking at them, a lot of similarities between a ukulele and a guitar. However, there are also some differences to keep in mind.

First, there are the four types of ukulele: soprano, alto, tenor, and baritone—yes, just like singing voices. The soprano is the smallest, and the easiest to start out with as a beginner, since it has only four strings. The baritone is the largest and most expensive, and personally, if you're looking at a baritone then at that point you might just want to get a guitar instead.

Here is a soprano ukulele:

Here is an alto ukulele:

This is a tenor ukulele:

And finally, a baritone ukulele:

The ukulele will always sound a bit higher than the guitar, so it's natural when you're learning a song on the ukulele versus guitar for it to sound a bit higher—but the notes should still sound *right*. You'll find that it's easy for your ear to pick up the difference between notes played correctly at a higher pitch and notes that are played incorrectly. Fortunately, it's actually simpler to play chords on a ukulele than a guitar, so now that we've got you on the guitar, you'll find the transition to ukulele is pretty easy.

The most notable difference in a ukulele versus a guitar will be the strings. The tuning for a ukulele is usually GCEA:

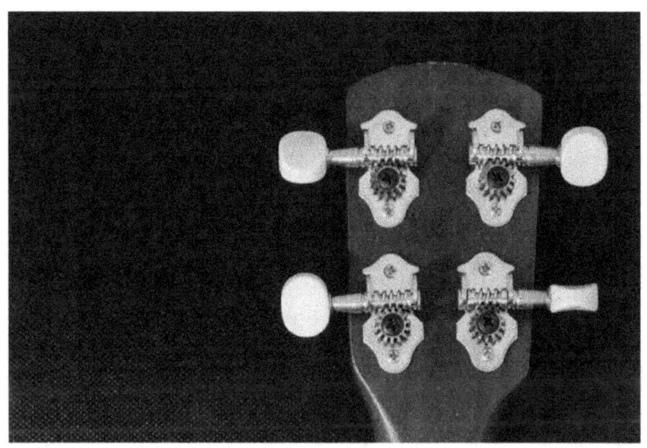

To compare this to a guitar, put a capo on the 5th fret of a guitar. A "capo" is a bar that you can buy that will hold down all of the strings on a particular fret for you. This will come in handy when you've progressed further and are performing songs where you're doing chords but can't have a finger free to hold down all the strings. With the capo on the 5th fret, play the four highest strings on your guitar. That's what it's like to play a ukulele, except that the G string on the ukulele is an octave higher even than that.

Baritone ukuleles, however, are exactly the same as the four highest strings on the guitar, no capo needed. This is why it's probably best not to buy a baritone ukulele—any song that you'd play on there you can just play on the guitar by ignoring the two lowest strings.

The Piano

The piano is probably the best known, and most beloved, of all musical instruments. Many composers started composing their pieces on piano to start with, before adding in the other instruments, and it's a versatile instrument that can handle pretty much any song that you throw at it.

A piano is, technically, a string instrument. When you press down on a key, you're actually starting up a mechanism that causes the string or strings to be plucked, causing the sound. It's also one of the most complicated instruments in the world, with 2,500 parts, and it's easily broken. The many parts of a piano include the soundboard, ribs, bridges, keys, pedals, hammers, the strings, and the cast iron plate.

Yes, a cast iron plate. It's put in over the soundboard of the piano and anchors the strings and keeps them tense so that they will vibrate properly when plucked by the hammer, which is caused by pressing on a key. The largest kind of piano is the grand piano:

These are also known as winged pianos and are the largest in size. You would need a rather large home to fit one of these.

The next smallest is the baby grand piano, structured in every way like a grand piano, only with smaller dimensions:

The other kind of piano, and the one that most people can afford both economically and size-wise, is an upright piano:

And finally, we have the electric keyboard, the least expensive and most convenient for when you're living in a small house:

Unless you're living in an area where you have access to a grand or a baby grand, you don't need to worry about practicing on one. Practicing on a keyboard or upright piano will give you the same kind of understanding and practice, and if you're looking to perform, those are the two kinds of pianos that you'll most likely be performing on when the time comes.

Now that you understand your instruments, it's time to learn how to play them!

Chapter Two: What are Chords?

Chords are the basis for an entire song or piece of music. Without chords, you don't have a song, which is why if you know the chords of a song, you can play those same four or so notes over and over again in the rhythm of the song without learning the rest, and the audience will still recognize said song. By learning the chords through the exercises this book will teach, you'll be able to play thousands of songs. But what exactly are chords and how do they work?

What Is a Chord?

A chord is a combination of three or more notes. They're built off of a single note, known as the 'root note.' The root note will always be the first note in the chord sequence. So if you see the chord sequence C-E-G, that's a C chord. Those three notes together create a harmonious, blended sound, called the chord. When you're playing chords, whether it's guitar or piano or ukulele, you create the song by keeping your fingers in the same position, just moving them slightly up or down—so you're always playing the same notes, just as a higher or lower pitch.

How to Read Guitar and Ukulele Chords

Reading guitar and ukulele music is a bit different than reading piano music. Piano tends to use sheet music—which is important to know as a guitarist, because you'll have to read sheet music a lot of the time. Sheet music is the foundation on which all music is written, even if that music is later translated into another form, like guitar tabs.

Guitar tabs function for guitar and ukulele the way sheet music does for a piano. In fact, you can read the tabs without actually having to learn sheet music. This is part of why it's so easy to learn guitar and ukulele (and you can transfer this knowledge to the piano, as we'll discuss shortly).

Tabs are, essentially, a visual representation of where the notes are on the guitar or ukulele that you should be playing:

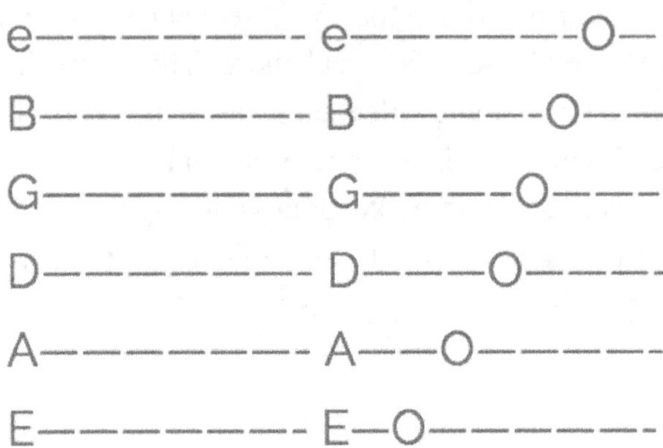

The strings on the guitar (if this was a ukulele, there would only be four strings) have the thickest, the E string, at the bottom, and the thinnest, the e string, at the top. If there is a number next to the letter, say, a 5 next to the D, that means you're placing your finger on the 5th fret of the D string. If there's a zero, that means the string is being played 'open' with no frets pressed down.

Look at that graphic again. A helpful way to remember the notes is to make an acronym for them. The one I learned was Every August Dogs Go Biting Elvis. E-A-D-G-B-E.

This is another diagram of how guitar chords might be written. The three black dots on the diagram show you which strings to press down—in this case, strings D, G, and B—and you will press down on them on the second fret. The E and A strings we're going to play open, without any frets pressed down, and the High E, or e, we're not going to play at all.

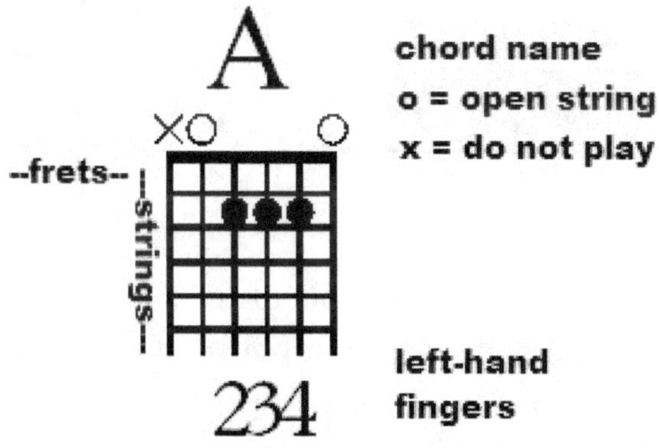

The numbers at the bottom of this chart are telling you which fingers to use to hold down the strings. Your index finger is number one, and your pinkie is number four. So for this, you'll use your middle, ring, and pinkie finger, and leave your index finger free. Keep in mind that your thumb doesn't come into play with the guitar. You use your thumb to brace against the back of the guitar so that it holds still while you move your other fingers. Here's an example of proper finger positioning:

Notice how the thumb is out of sight, bracing on the back of the guitar. The wrist is pushed forward which makes for an angle that will take some getting used to. The fingers, as you can see, are in position, so your index finger (number one) is stretching up to hit the top string.

Let's go back to that chart. So you'd put your middle finger, the 2 finger, on the D string, your ring finger, or 3 finger, on the

G string, and your pinkie or 4 finger on the B string, all on the second fret. Use the tips of your fingers only! Otherwise you'll press down on other strings and the sound will come out muffled. Then strum with your other hand. Ta-da! You're now able to read a ukulele or guitar chart and figure out what to play.

The only difference in reading between a ukulele and a guitar is that there are only four strings on a ukulele, so there's just two fewer strings to worry about. But the finger positioning and how you read the chart is all the same.

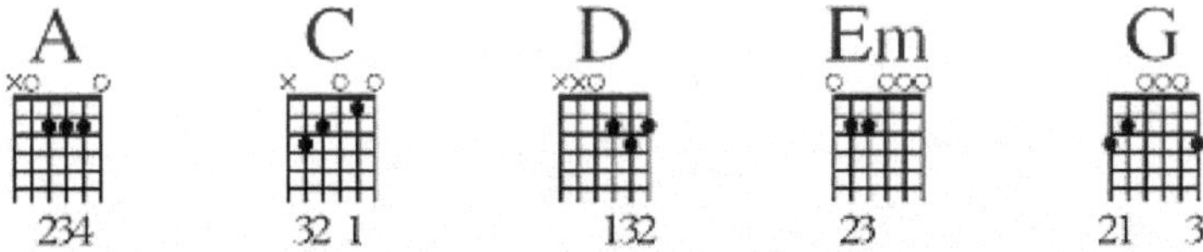

Take a look at these. We have the first one, the A chord, and now the C, D, Em, and G chords. Take a moment and figure out where your fingers go to practice reading it.

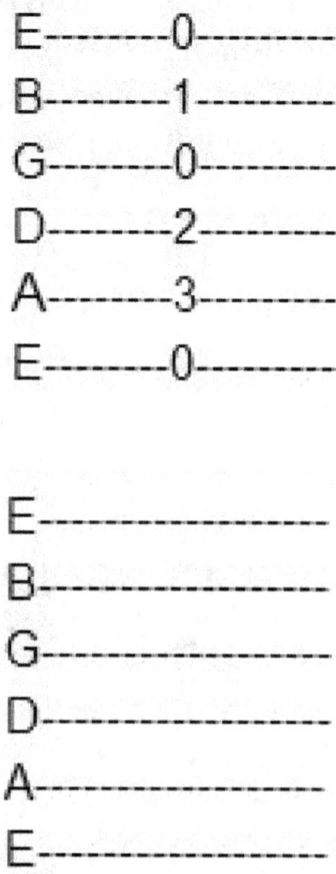

Now, look at the tabs again. The one on the right has no numbering. The one on the left has the numbering showing the fret you want to put your finger on. Unlike the previous chart, it doesn't tell you which finger—so we go with the basic principle of highest string goes to the index finger, second highest to the middle finger, and so on. For this one, you'd have your middle finger on the first fret of the B string, your ring finger on the second fret of the D string, and your pinkie on the third fret of the A string.

It's important to know these tabs because they'll help you for reading sheet music, and moving your chord exercises from guitar to the piano.

Piano Versus Guitar Chords

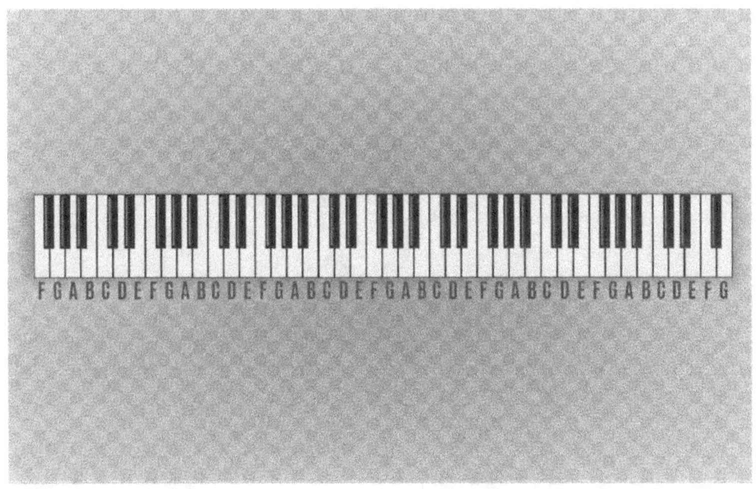

Ah, pianos. You've got a lot more room to work with than guitars, which is both a blessing and a curse when you're a beginner. Take a look at the image up above. Right away you'll notice that it has all of the notes laid out for you. Unlike a guitar, where you create the higher and lower notes by pressing down on the frets, the piano does that for you already. This means that you can play more complicated songs on the piano but it also means your fingers are going to be exhausted.

The key with playing the piano is to stretch your fingers and to keep your wrist light. This is very different from a guitar. In a guitar, if I were to grab your wrist and tug, your wrist shouldn't move. It should be firm to support the guitar neck and your fingers. A piano is the opposite—your wrist should be completely loose and relaxed to allow your fingers the most freedom of movement. If I were to press down on your wrist while you were playing piano, it should collapse.

Keep in mind as well that with both guitar and piano, each finger must move simultaneously. You will be fighting against instinct here. We have trained ourselves to treat our fingers as one unit, to pick things up, to throw things, and so on. Typing is arguably the only thing where our fingers move independently of one another. But look at this picture below:

Note how the thumb is down on the keyboard but the other fingers are not. The thumb is moving independently of the others. If you move one finger on a piano or guitar, the other fingers shouldn't move at all.

Take a look at this picture:

Notice how the hands seem to dip down a little from the wrist, and the fingers are slightly curled. Like with guitar, you want your fingertips to be the ones making the notes, not your whole hand. See how relaxed the wrist is to allow the hand to droop like that? With the guitar, it's all about wrist strength. With piano, it's about wrist relaxation. But with both, remember, you need fingertips and finger flexibility.

Now, like guitar, a piano chord is any set of three or more notes played simultaneously. Note the image below:

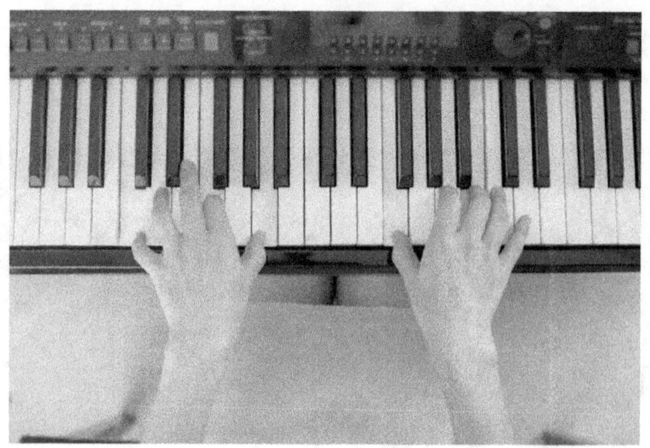

The person's fingers are pressing down on keys while there is are white keys in between them. The thumb, middle finger, and pinkie of the person's right hand are pressing down on the white keys. This creates a chord the same way you do on a guitar. Most piano chords, and certainly these basic ones, will be made with your thumb, middle finger, and pinkie.

The person's left hand is doing the same thing—here is where you can get in some variation. In a guitar, for example, when you're playing the four or five notes with just your one hand, using all of your fingers. As you can see from the image above, those same four or five notes are played with both of your hands. Pressing down on the notes with both hands will create the chord for a piano, while strumming with one hand while the other holds down the strings creates the chord for a guitar or ukulele.

Now, fingers are numbered when you play piano, just like with the guitar. The only difference is that the thumb is included with piano, so instead of the index finger being number one, the thumb is number one, and you go on with the pinkie being number five. So most chords are 1-3-5 chords, using your thumb, middle finger, and pinkie, on three alternating notes.

Alternating is something you're going to come up against in both piano and guitar/ukulele. Now, there are half-steps and full-steps in notes. In a piano, a half-step is when you go from a white key to a black key, or vice versa. You're going from one note to the one directly above or below it. So if you're on the white key C, then go up to the nearest black key, C#, that's a half step. A full-step is where you go up two notes, or one 'full note.' You're not going up from a C to a C sharp or down to a C flat. It's just a full note, so from C to D—which is the next white key.

The only exception? When you're going from white key E. The F key is the same thing as an E#.

All you need to worry about, though, is that when making your chords go from guitar to piano, you put your thumb, or 1 finger, on the root note. Let's say it's C. You would then count up two full-steps. So you'd count up: C#, then D, then D#, then E. So you put your middle finger on E. Then count up two more full-steps: E, F/E#, then F#, to put your pinkie on G.

Now you have the C chord, C-E-G. This is called a major chord, by the way. A minor chord is the opposite. You would put your thumb on C, then go up only one full-step and one half-step, so you wouldn't go all the way up to E—you'd stop at D#. Then you'd put your pinkie on the same place, G. An easy way to remember this? Just put your fingers in position for the chord, then move your middle finger up one half-step.

This is an easy way to have fun with songs, by the way. Play any chord song, but move your middle finger up so that it's now in minor key. It'll sound cool and unusual and completely change how the song sounds.

Another way to help with figuring out the differences in your hands on the piano versus your one hand on the guitar is to imagine the three lowest guitar strings as what you play with your left hand on the piano, and the three highest strings as what you play with your right hand. So let's say you've got your five fingers on five strings on the guitar. Your left hand would take some of those notes, while your right hand would take the others, on the piano. You're just dividing up the notes in a different way, but you still play them all at the same time. A good rule of thumb is that your left hand on the piano plays the root note (so C, for C-E-G), and your right hand plays the others.

But what about sheet music?

That right there probably looks very intimidating. Never fear, though, you won't be learning any of that here—in fact, you won't have to. If you want to play more complicated, classical pieces, then you can learn those once you've mastered these basics, but we're here to learn chords that will allow you to sit down and play the songs that come on the radio. This will, in turn, give you the basic understanding that you'll need if you want to play these more complicated pieces but in the meantime, you'll make a killing serving as the human jukebox for your friends. So, sheet music!

This is a piece of blank sheet music. The first thing you should notice should already be familiar to you—the lines are just like the guitar strings on the guitar tabs we just learned. These lines are called the staff or staves, by the way. This is where you'll see the notes, rather like where you'll see the notations on the tab for which fret to hold down. However, unlike the tabs, which just tell you which fret, notes will tell you how long to hold the note for, so you can look at the sheet music and learn the rhythm even if you don't previously know the song.

This symbol here on the left is called a clef. This indicates the pitch of the notes that you're playing. F, C, and G are the usual types of clef. This here is a G clef, the one you'll probably recognize the most easily.

This here is an F clef.

And this:

Is a C clef. The G clef is the one that you'll come across the most often. You probably haven't even seen a C clef before. As you noticed in the image of the blank sheet music, there's a G and an F clef. A G clef is also known as a treble clef, and indicates higher notes, which is why it's higher on the lines. The F clef is also known as a bass clef and means lower notes. You won't often have to deal with such lower notes on your chords, not unless you choose to make your song lower in pitch.

But what are those symbols next to that image of the G clef? Those are 'key signatures.' They indicate how many sharps and flats are in a piece. You won't often need these but they can be helpful when you're going to play a chord to remember this when you're trying to remember which note is which that you're playing.

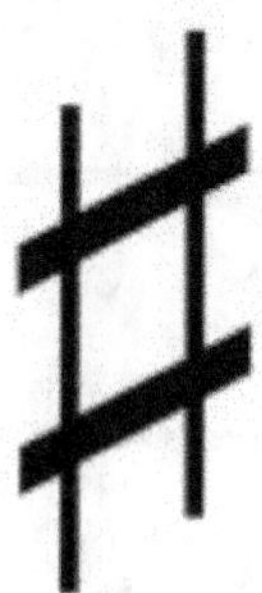

This symbol here is a sharp.

And this symbol is a flat.

Note that you'll run into sharps more than you'll run into flats. So if you're playing and you see a letter with one of these symbols after it, it will tell you to place your finger on the white key, and then either move it up a half-step to the nearest black key (a sharp) or down a half-step to the nearest black key (a flat).

The number of sharps and flats next to a clef will tell you what key the piece of music is in. The position of the flats and sharps tells you whether it's an F sharp or a G sharp or so on, and judging by how many there are and what position they're in you'll be able to know what key signature this is in.

This is helpful to keep in the back of your mind for playing classical pieces, but again, it's not necessary for knowing how to play the chords for songs.

Go back and look at the image of the blank sheet music again. You'll see that it ends at the edge of a page. This is called a bar. It will tell you that the measure, or period of time for this part of the music, is over. The number of beats per measure can vary, but there will be however many notes on the sheet music as there are beats, and then at the end there will be the bar. So if you're trying to figure out how many notes are in a measure, count the notations, and when you've reached the bar, you know how many there are—if you counted eight, then there are eight, and so on. The more notes, the faster the piece.

Unlike a guitar or ukulele, where you have to know the song to know how the rhythm goes, the piano music will tell you.

This is a whole note. You hold it four a count of four:

This is a half note. You hold it for a count of two:

This is an ordinary note. Technically it's a quarter note, but it's the most common note that you'll find. You hold it for a single beat:

Sometimes you'll run into these notes:

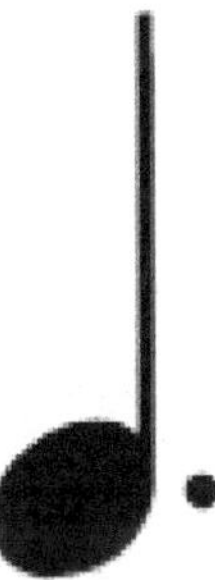

This dot serves as a half beat. Normally, you're multiplying and dividing by two—a quarter note is one beat, a half note is two beats, and a whole note is four beats. When you see a dot next to this, it means add half of the note's value. So this dot is next to a quarter note, meaning you add half a beat. If it were next to a half note, you'd add one beat, making the entire note three beats long.

This is an eighth note:

As you can imagine, eighth notes are very short, half a beat. They are always half a beat, unlike dots, which can change in value based on the note they're next to. A dot is half the value of the note it's next to, so the value of the dot changes depending on whether it's accompanying a quarter or whole or half note. An eighth note is always half a beat, no matter what other note it's with.

If you ever see a symbol like this:

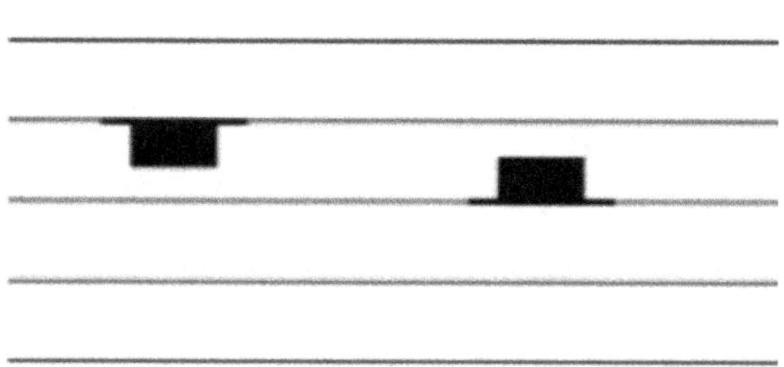

Whether it's facing up or down, that means it's a rest.
Facing down, it's a whole rest, so four beats. Facing up, it's a half
rest, or two beats.

These indicate shorter rests:

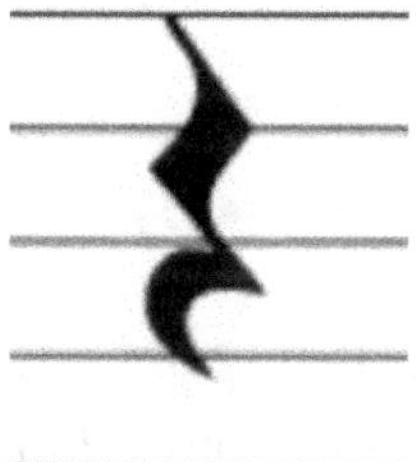

This is a quarter rest.

And this is an eighth rest. You count them just like you count the musical notes, but you don't play anything. These symbols stand for silence, and once again they indicate to you the rhythm of a piece.

Learning these basics of piano sheet music are helpful because while you can learn a song using guitar tabs for the guitar and ukulele, if you're ever unsure about the rhythm of a piece, you can look it up on sheet music and see how long each note is and figure out the rhthym.

Vocabulary

Here are some terms that you'll need to be familiar with, especially for piano, for when you pick up sheet music or if you are performing with others.

- Playing in Different Keys: This means that the position of your finger stays the same but the root note changes. For example, "I'm playing in F major instead of C major." Same chord position, but different notes, because you moved your fingers higher or lower on the guitar or piano.

- Arrangement: This is for if you're playing with a group. The arrangement decides who is playing what notes on the chord, which tempos, and when.
- Chord Extensions: This means adding alterations to a chord, which can make it sound completely different even if the basic notes are the same.
- Rhythm: This is how many pop songs can sound different even though they are all using the same chord. The rhythm is one of the first things that people notice when listening to a song, so changing it up can change the song almost completely.
- Melody: These are the varying notes that you play over the base chord—again, a way to take the same chord and make it sound different.
- Lyrics: You probably know this one already, but lyrics are the words that someone sings in time to the music.
- Adagio: This means to go slowly.
- Allegro: This means to play quickly.
- Beat: This is another word for rhythm.
- Leggiero: This is used mostly in piano, and means to play 'lightly' without putting too much force on the keys.
- Time Signature: How many beats are in each bar of music. So if there are eight beats, then the time signature is eight. The more beats, the faster you play.

- Bridge: A transitional passage. The repeated lyrics that a singer sings just before the chorus is the bridge—it literally 'bridges' the versus to the chorus.
- Chorus: The repeated phrase of the song, the heart of the song's meaning and music.
- Measure: One complete cycle of the time signature.
- Meter: This is the pattern of the rhythm. Think of it as the pauses in between the beats.
- Forte: To play strong and powerfully.
- Piano: This isn't the instrument—if someone says to play piano, it means to play it gently.
- Tempo: This is the overall speed of the piece. The meter and beat and rhythm make up the tempo.
- Rest Signs: This indicates when you stop playing your instrument and let it 'rest' for a period of time. This is usually done when you're playing with other instruments, so you all get your turn in the spotlight.
- Notes: The indication of what string or key you should be playing and for how long. Depending on the shape or shading of the note, it'll tell you how long to hold it for.

Chapter Three: The Seven Exercises

Now that you understand what your instruments are, how they work, how to read and understand music and bar chords, you're fully equipped to sally forth and play these instruments like a pro. Here are the seven basic exercises that will help you to play pretty much any song in the world.

Exercise One:

We're going to start with a C Major chord. This is the easiest chord to learn. Lots of songs, including "Are We Out of the Woods" by Taylor Swift and "Stay with Me" by Sam Smith use this key.

So, if you're on a guitar or ukulele, put your index finger on the first fret of the second string (B string). Then put your middle finger on the fourth string, on the second fret (this is the D string). Your ring finger goes on the third fret of the fifth string, or A string, and that's it! You don't play the sixth string, E, and the other two strings, e and G, are played open, so no fingers on those frets. Here's a picture of what that looks like on a guitar:

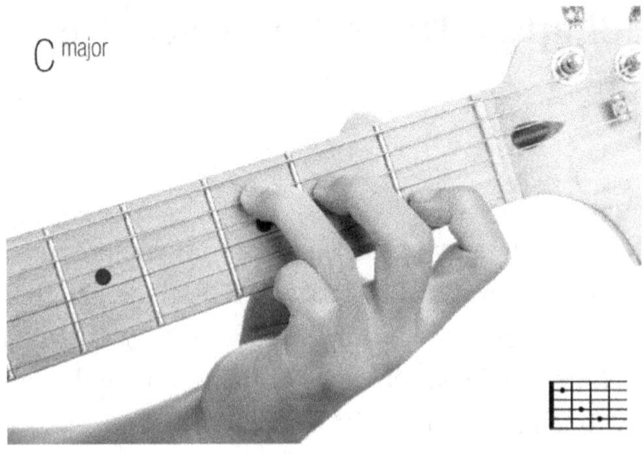

To play this on piano, you want to do these three keys that are in red:

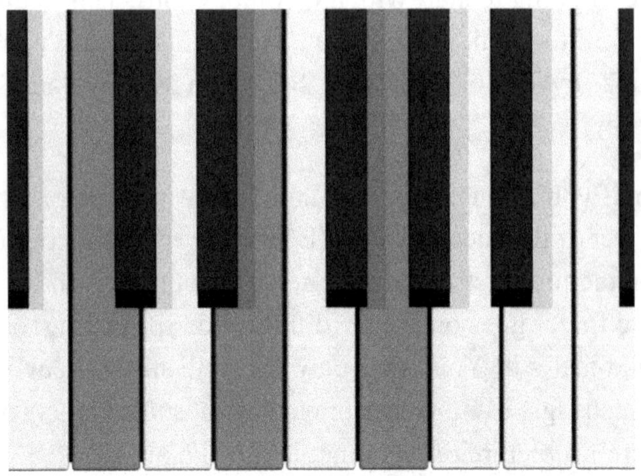

You can play them in any part of the piano, it's still the same chord. Practice doing it on the piano and on the guitar—

remember to only strum five of the strings, not the E string—and on the ukulele, until you can do it in a steady rhythm of one, two, three, four.

To get an idea of how rhythm can completely change this song, do this chord while singing "Are We Out of the Woods" by Taylor Swift. You can play the song itself to accompany you if you feel more comfortable with that. Feel how fast that chord is. Then play "Stay with Me" by Sam Smith. This is very slow, with the chord playing, and then a long rest. That change in rhythm completely changes how the song feels.

Exercise Two:

Next exercise is the G major chord! "You Shook Me All Night Long" by AC/DC and "Heart of Gold" by Birdy are two G major chord songs, and again, very different in sound because of the rhythm.

Put your index finger on second fret of the fifth string, or A string. Then put your middle finger on the third fret of the bottom string, the E string. Your ring finger goes on the third fret of the e string, the first string, and your pinkie doesn't have to do anything. Keep in mind that your index and middle fingers have to be arched up so they don't accidentally brush other strings. This is where using your fingertips is important.

Here's an image of what your hand should look like:

Here is that same chord on the piano:

The red are the ones you want to be hitting. Use your fingertips on your thumb, middle finger, and pinkie, so that you don't hit any other keys while you're playing this. Again, practice just doing this on your guitar and piano and ukulele as just a one, two, three, four beat rhythm. Don't try to rush things. Try out the two songs, by Birdy and AC/DC, just to feel the difference the rhythm and the melody of the singer can do to change a song that has the same chords.

Exercise Three:

Next we're doing the D chord. This is an important chord on guitar for pop songs, so while you wouldn't normally learn it as quickly if you were studying piano for classical music, you're going to learn it here so that you can play all those songs on piano and guitar easily. Songs that use the D Major Chord include "Send My Love (to Your New Lover)" by Adele and "The Boys are Back in Town" by Thin Lizzy.

Put your index finger on the second fret of the fourth string, or G string. Then put your middle finger on the second fret of the sixth string, the e string, and then put your ring finger on the third fret of the fifth or B string.

If this chord seems a little more difficult for your fingers to handle on the guitar, that's how it should be. Some other very common chords that we're going to learn next are going to have four notes in them instead of just three, so this D major chord will help you, especially so that you can learn the F Major chord for the next exercise.

This is what this chord looks like on the guitar:

And this is what it looks like on piano:

Notice that for this you're using one black key on the piano. Practice strumming on guitar or ukulele and getting the rhythm on the piano, using the two songs as accompaniment to help you if you feel you need it. Having a song in mind as your goal can be helpful as it helps you to integrate the idea of a rhythm into your playing.

Exercise Four:

Now we're getting into that F Major Chord that we mentioned. "Still Into You" by Paramore, "What's My Age Again?" by Blink-182, and "Ain't No Rest for the Wicked" by Cage the Elephant are all in this key. It's a popular one.

This is the first chord that uses four fingers on the guitar, and it's difficult because it's a bar chord. This means you have to take your index finger and put it down across the first fret on all of the strings. Yup, all of them. This will take some getting used to because your finger needs to build up the strength to hold all six strings (or four strings, for the ukulele) down at the same time.

Keep in mind that your finger shouldn't be directly on the fret. Rather, it should be directly behind the fret. So when you put your finger on, say, the second fret of the D string, your fingertip should actually be right before the line of the fret. This actually gives you less work to do as the fret can then do its job to hold the string in place and help it resonate. If you ever pluck a guitar string and it doesn't have a clear, resonating sound, it's probably because your finger is on the fret rather than behind it.

So, put your index finger across all the strings on the first fret. Then put your middle finger on the second fret of the third or G string, your ring finger on the third fret of the fifth or A string, and your pinkie on the third fret of the fourth or D string. This is how it should look on guitar:

Notice how the index finger looks curved? You're going to have to do that in order to cover all of the frets while giving your other fingers the room to press on their strings.

On piano, however, this is one of the easiest chords. It looks like this:

You don't even have to stretch your fingers. Practice with this chord as well and get the feel for it.

Exercise Five:

We're going to get really fancy now. This exercise, you're going to practice doing a chord progression.

Songs progress from one chord to another, generally in four sets. So you'll have four sets of three or four notes that you repeat, over and over again. Take the F Major Chord that we just used. You won't keep your fingers on the same fret the entire song, but you will keep them in the same position. You just slide your hand up or down to hit different notes. Same with a piano.

To play the full song, you keep your fingers in the same position and just move your and up or down the keyboard or neck of your guitar and ukulele.

For example, for "Ain't No Rest for the Wicked" by Cage the Elephant, you get your hands into the F major position. You start on the third fret. Then move your hand until the index finger is on the fifth fret. Now move it so your index finger is on the eighth fret. Now move your index finger to the first fret. Now back down to the third fret.

You've now just played the entirety of the song, all without moving your fingers, just sliding your hand up and down and strumming to the beat. Do that with all of the songs on guitar and piano and ukulele: find the notes on the sheet music and move your hands up and down until you've got it all down.

Exercise Six:

So, our next mission: practicing those chord progressions. Let's take a look at this handy dandy chart:

See how you can look at the notes both on piano sheet music, on the charts, and on guitar tabs? Chord progressions are often written in roman numerals. So G major is I, and C major is IV.

The list of progressions at the bottom is what you need to practice. You switch your fingers from chord to chord. Start just with the four that you know. The I-V-vi-IV chord progression, or

435

G-D-em-C, is one of the most common in pop music. The only difference is the rhythm and which one of these four you start on, but it's the same order. So if you start on C, the next three notes are G, D, and em, then back to C again. If you start on D, then it's em, C, and then G before back to D. If you just practice going through these four, going slowly, then you can find you're playing pretty much every pop song that you know.

What's a metronome, you ask? This handy-dandy little thing:

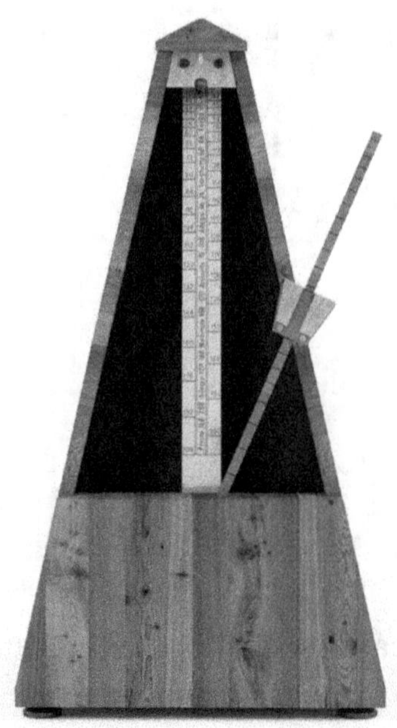

You can get a version on your phone or computer if you don't want to buy one. It keeps time for you. Put it on a slow setting and try to strum, or if you're on piano press down, in time with the metronome. This will help you improve your sense of rhythm while you do these chord progressions.

It's okay if you can't get all of these chord progressions right away. But by now your fingers will have gotten used to the positions on the piano and on the guitar, and you can always go back to the earlier exercises if you need. Just keep following these chord progressions until you're able to move back and forth smoothly between them.

Exercise Seven:

Here are some more chord progressions, this time in E major! What is E major for guitar and piano? It's a little more difficult, so here are some visuals:

You want your index finger on the fourth string on the first fret, your middle finger on the second string on the second fret, and your ring finger on the third string, also in the second fret—which is where it gets tricky, since you're having two fingers share that same space and need to press down on both strings in the same place. Your pinkie can stay out of the way. "Back in Black" by AC/DC and "Pour Some Sugar on Me" by Def Leppard are two songs in the key of E Major.

Here's what it looks like on piano:

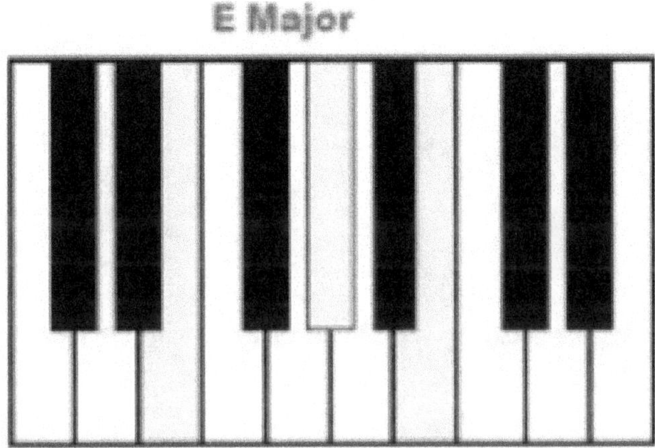

Again, much easier on piano than on guitar. You'll find that most of these chord progressions are easier to do on the piano rather than on guitar or ukulele, whereas reading sheet music for piano is harder than reading tabs and charts for guitar. It's a give and take, but both instruments are easily translatable into the other.

Here are the chord progressions for E Major:

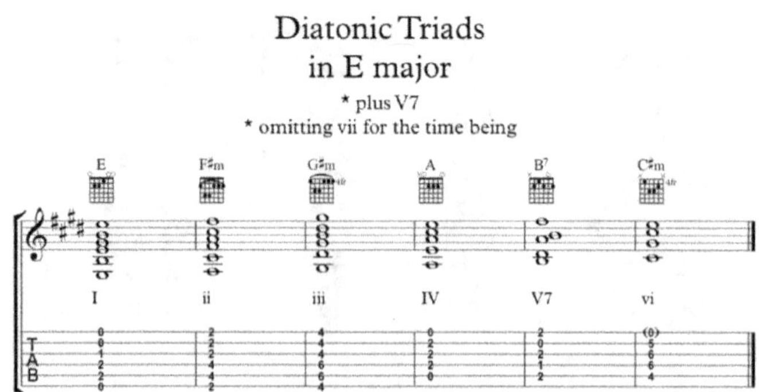

Look at it as a chart, as a tab, as sheet music, and as roman numerals. The more you practice, the more you'll be able to just look at any one of these and understand. Go through the chord progressions on this sheet, and the previous one, and you'll know pretty much everything there is to know about playing basic songs by the time that you're through.

It's almost unbelievable how easy it is to pick all of this up—constant practice is the key, but with these fundamentals, you'll be wowing your friends and family in no time. In the next chapter, we'll explore some tips to keep in mind not just as you do these exercises but as you progress further.

Chapter Four: Tips for Practicing

So now we're going to go over some random tips that'll help you out as you're practicing. Keep in mind that everyone learns just a little bit differently, so what might work for one person won't work for you. But these are all things to keep in mind as you practice the seven exercises:

Tip #1:

Practice doing your chord shapes one finger at a time, if you're having trouble remember where to keep all of your fingers. Starting with just one finger at a time can help take the pressure off and keep you from getting confused. There's no harm in starting slow.

Tip #2:

Practice the chord shapes without strumming. Again, no harm in starting slow if that's what you need. The key here is to get those chords memorized so that you can play any song that you want, so don't rush forward if you don't have those.

Tip #3:

Pay attention to the chord changes. Transitions are the hardest thing to get down, so you'll want to practice those a lot. It'll seem hard at first, switching the positions of your fingers, more so on guitar than on piano since you're bending your wrist into an odd shape. With piano, the struggle will be teaching your fingers how to stretch out. But don't get discouraged! Practice transitions.

Tip #4:

Keep your metronome slow. I know, you want to go fast! And you'll be surprised by how fast even the slower songs feel once you start playing them. Getting these exercises down is what matters, not the speed.

Tip #5:

Make a practice plan and stick to it. This can go both ways—don't overbook yourself, but don't sell yourself short, either. Plan for a good amount of time that works easily with your schedule. Otherwise you'll find yourself making excuses. Say, for example, you've planned to practice for an hour every day. But when you get home from work, you find that the idea of practicing for a whole hour is just too draining. So you make excuses to not do it, thinking you'll make up the time later. Or, conversely, say you've promised yourself that you'll practice for ten minutes a day—and then get frustrated when you're not making a lot of progress. Find a time that isn't too ambitious but still gives you a good solid bit to practice your exercises.

Tip #6:

Find a chord dictionary so that when you've progressed beyond the more basic chords of these songs you can learn new ones and keep in practice. It's amazing the amount of chords and chord variations that are out there, and once you've mastered these, you can get really fancy and wow everyone. This is especially true of piano—once you've mastered these exercises and chords, go ahead and get a beginner's piano book with some classical pieces in it. You'll be surprised at how many you'll be able to play!

Tip #7:

It's important to keep your fingers and wrists healthy. Remember that with piano, your wrist is supposed to be completely relaxed, and your fingertips have to do a lot of stretching but remain light. With guitar and ukulele, your wrist has to be strong and in position, and your fingertips have to be strong to put the right amount of pressure on the strings. It can be easy for you to hurt your fingers and wrists over time if you don't do proper exercises. Take time to bend your wrists, rotate them, clench and unclench your fist (a small exercise ball is good for this) and practice lifting and extending your fingers and holding the position. It might seem silly, but doing these exercises before you play will help to prevent hand cramps and wrist pain later on. Below is an example of some wrist exercises that you can to do help keep your wrists flexible, strong, and healthy. A ten-minute warm up for your fingers and wrists might very well seem silly, but carpel tunnel syndrome and other health hazards have seriously affected the performance of guitarists and pianists for years, including famous ones. It's better to do some warming up than to spend months in pain and unable to practice.

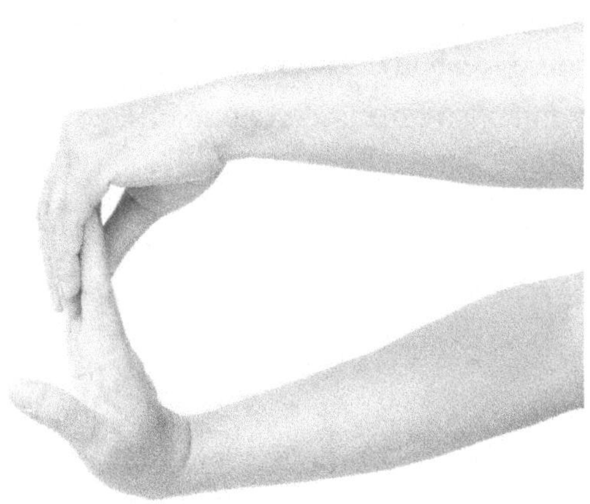

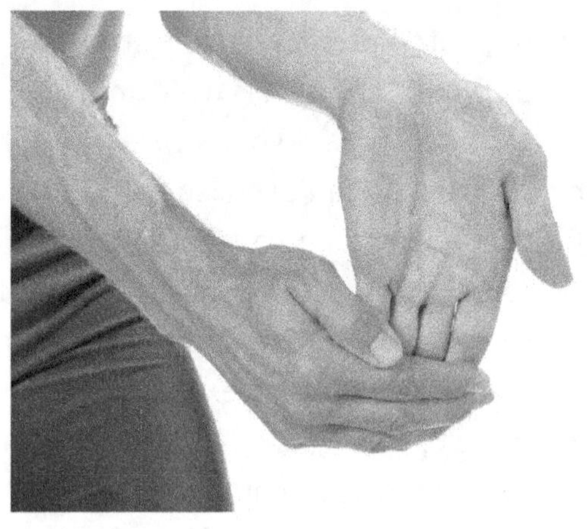

Tip #8:

If you find yourself getting frustrated or tired, or like you want to smash your piano to bits, then take a break. Walk away and get some fresh air. You won't learn if you find yourself hating practice, so go easy on yourself!

Tip #9:

Regular practice is better than how much you practice. Practicing for twenty minutes a day is better than practicing for two hours once a week. You want the repetition to get into your fingers.

Tip #10:

Count out loud as you practice your rhythms when you're doing these chords. It might sound silly, but it helps you to integrate the rhythm into your head. Some prefer, for example, to count using numbers. Others use phrases corresponding to the notes on the sheet music: "whole note hold it," for a whole note, or "quarter dot" for a quarter note with a dot on it. Whatever you use doesn't matter so long as you say it out loud to practice.

Tip #11:

Explore and have fun! Go onto the internet and find videos that show you how to play new songs. Go to a local jam session or open mike night at a café and perform for some people. Try writing your own songs or playing around with chord combinations. You learned these instruments because you wanted to, so don't lose sight of that. Do this for your own enjoyment.

Chapter Five: Moving Beyond the Basics

Ideas to keep in mind as you progress to more complicated chords, especially on the piano, and the idea of songwriting, and how these instruments can all play together at the same time.

Keep in mind chord changes and how they affect the song. You want your transitions to be smooth, for the sound to be clear and to resonate, and for you to get good at knowing where to place your fingers without having to pause and look.

Piano and guitar, and even ukulele, are great instruments for accompanying singers. You're going to get a lot of requests to accompany people when they want to sing a song, and you're probably going to want to sing a song yourself while providing your own accompaniment. As you gain confidence, you'll be tempted to really let your playing skills shine. Don't! The melody, and therefore the singer, is the star of the show. Practice playing at the right volume without too much energy so that you don't drown out the singer and steal the show, even if it's from yourself. After all, your chords are great but what if no one can hear what you're singing?

You're going to sometimes run into a problem where you have a piece on guitar tabs that you want to translate to piano sheet music, and vice versa. Doing this should wait until you've gotten comfortable with chord progressions and the exercises listed previously. You'll be able to figure out dozens of songs just by doing the chord progressions using different rhythms and accompanying a recording of a song (it can help to get an instrumental copy of said song, so the singer doesn't distract you with her melody). But when the time comes, here's a good example using the classic "Stairway to Heaven":

Tabs and sheet music are, fortunately, both on lines. So you would start by looking at what line the first note is on. It should say 7 and be on the third line from the bottom: the seventh fret of the D string. Now, you count backwards seven frets until you get to the open string—and count backwards on the piano at the same time. D, D#, E, F, F#, G, G#, and then ending on A. So the first note you'd play for this on the piano is A.

You just keep transcribing that way, counting backwards on the piano from how many frets there are on the guitar, to find each note. It's time consuming, but once you've moved past the beginning stages and want to learn more complicated songs like "Stairway to Heaven," you'll find yourself in this position a lot.

Piano can be especially difficult to learn as you progress further in your understanding of music. With the guitar, you'll want to start to simply incorporate the melody—this means plucking individual strings in between the strumming of the chords. But integrating the piano melody can take a lot of practice as you're moving both hands in different ways simultaneously. This is where fundamentals are important. Return to your chords when you feel frustrated and keep practicing those. Work on tapping each individual key out to improve your fingers' ability to move independently. And do the fundamentals like learn your scales. They're not necessary to learn for these chord songs, but if you want to move beyond that into more classical pieces, then you'll have to start learning them.

As you progress, you'll start to develop your own personal style. You might add a little flair to your version of "Don't Stop

Believing" by Journey, or perhaps you moved your middle finger up to switch to a minor key for when you play "Hey, Jude" by the Beatles on the piano. That is totally right and natural to do. Embrace your personal style and as you grow in confidence, experiment. Experimenting on already-existing chords and chord songs is how new chord songs are made, so have at it.

If you want to start getting into songwriting, there are tons of ways that you can go about it. Tom Waits, a singer-songwriter, would play multiple radios at once to find where the songs overlapped in their chords. You might find that the chords of one song would match the riff of another, and combining them makes your own song.

Another way to do it is don't give yourself time to second-guess anything. Set a timer for fifteen minutes. You now have to get your song written in that time. Ready, set, go! This eliminates your ability to second-guess yourself and agonize over a particular chord. You never know what you'll find when you're racing against the clock.

And sometimes, just stop listening to music. Stare out the window for a while. Revel in the silence. Spend a day not talking, just listening to everything around you. Shutting off one of your sensory inputs or outputs, whether it's forcing yourself to just stare out of your skylight, promising yourself not to talk, or not listening to anything. Removing one sense can heighten the others and give your brain a chance to rest and see things in a new way that might give you the inspiration that you need.

If you've moved past the chord progressions and have learned the songs in this book and still want to go further, remember, you can always get yourself a teacher. Even if that 'teacher' is someone on the internet who posts videos about their work on ukulele or piano or whatnot, they can be a source of inspiration and added learning for you as you move farther along in your study of music. There's only so much that you can learn on your own without someone helping to walk you through the more complicated parts, so if you find yourself moving past the chord songs and want to challenge yourself, a teacher can be someone to help walk you through that.

Similarly to that, join in the conversation in the music world! Look up what musicians are saying about their work, listen to new songs, join a band, go listen to an open mike night. You can't operate in a vacuum and collaborating with others, even if that collaboration is just you sitting and listening, is an important part of the artistic process. Find a group of people that you can share ideas with and who you can learn from. You'd be surprised at how it helps improve not only your playing but your understanding of music in general.

Chapter Six: Chord Songs

Here is a list of different songs that you can play using the basic chords. Most of them use the most popular "pop music" chord that we previously discussed, but others use some of the six other chords. Now that you know the basic chords you can play any of these songs with ease—you just have to learn the tempo. One of my personal favorites, and the song that I started learning when I was a beginner, is "Ain't No Rest for the Wicked" by Cage the Elephant. If you're a little amazed by how many songs are on here, just think of how your friends will feel when you sit down at a piano or whip out your guitar or ukulele and find that you've turned into a musical genius. It's all in those basic chords.

Something to keep in mind is that the melody will vary from song to song. That's not actually what matters when playing the song, though. If you play the right chord, in the right rhythm, you'll actually be fine. In fact in a lot of bands, one guitar plays just the chords while the other plays the melody. If you have the chords down, the audience will know the song—especially if you're singing, because your voice then carries the melody so you don't have to worry about actually doing it with your guitar. Helpful, right?

I-V-vi-IV Songs:

The following songs are songs that are done using the most common chord, I-V-vi-IV. Many people have pointed out the use of this chord in pop songs, and while some would argue it's overused, this is good news for you because with this chord you can play hundreds of different songs using this one chord. Songs that use this chord include:

Don't Stop Believing by Journey

You're Beautiful by James Blunt

Forever Young by Alphaville

I'm Yours by Jason Mraz

Hey Soul Sister by Train

Wherever You Will Go by The Calling

Can You Feel the Love Tonight by Elton John (from The Lion King)

Take Me Home, Country Roads by John Denver

She Will Be Loved by Maroon Five

Let it Be by The Beatles

When I Come Around by Green Day

Save Tonight by Eagle Eye Cherry

Africa by Toto

Behind These Hazel Eyes by Kelly Clarkson

One of Us by Joan Osborne

Complicated by Avril Lavigne

Apologize by OneRepublic

Otherside by Red Hot Chili Peppers

Kids by MGMT

Superman by Five for Fighting

Going by Key:

Another way that you can look up songs is to look them up by the major chord. The following are songs divided by the chords that we learned in our exercises.

C Major Songs:

Happier by Ed Sheeran

Heaven by Bryan Adams

How Does it Feel by Avril Lavigne

Sweetest Devotion by Adele

When My Heart Beats Like a Hammer by B.B. King

Bang Bang by Ariana Grande

Stay with Me by Sam Smith

Are We Out of the Woods by Taylor Swift

Minority by Green Day

Stockholm Syndrome by Muse

Use Somebody by Kings of Leon

Wanted (Dead or Alive) by Bon Jovi

Stay by Rihanna featuring Mikky Echo

G Major Songs:

Under the Tide by Chvrches

Make You Feel Better by Red Hot Chili Peppers

Wake by Linkin Park

You Shook Me All Night Long by AC/DC

How Do We (Party) by Rita Ora

Shake it Off by Taylor Swift

Welcome to New York by Taylor Swift

Heart of Gold by Birdy

Been a Son by Nirvana

Whiskey in the Jar by Thin Lizzy

She's a Rebel by Green Day

Here I Go Again by White Snake

Little Wing by Jimi Hendrix

Sweet Home Alabama by Lynyrd Skynyrd

Wonderful Tonight by Eric Clapton

Call Me Maybe by Carly Rae Jepsen

I Gotta Feeling by The Black-Eyed Peas

Swing Swing by All-American Rejects

Good Riddance (Time of Your Life) by Green Day

Wake Me Up When September Ends by Green Day

D Major Songs:

Send My Love (To Your New Lover) by Adele

We Sink by Chvrches

Castle on the Hill by Ed Sheeran

Align by Nina Nesbitt

All is Now Harmed by Ben Howard

Lithium by Nirvana

Settle Down by The 1975

Home by Gabrielle Aplin

Grow Up by Paramore

Wake Up by Rage Against the Machine

Hysteria by Muse

Under the Bridge by Red Hot Chili Peppers

Times Like These by The Foo Fighters

Only Girl (In the World) by Rihanna

Love Story by Taylor Swift

Summer of '69 by Bryan Adams

Hey There Delilah by The Plain White Ts

E Major Songs:

Break My Heart by Hey Violet

Don't Tell Me by Avril Lavigne

All I Ask by Adele

Piano by Ariana Grande

Ain't it Fun by Paramore

Basket Case by Green Day

Buck Rogers by Feeder

Back in Black by AC/DC

Sex on Fire by Kings of Leon

Pour Some Sugar on Me by Def Leppard

Midnight Memories by One Direction

Fat Lip by Sum 41

I Believe in a Thing Called Love by The Darkness

F Major Songs:

Ain't No Rest for the Wicked by Cage the Elephant

I'm Not the Only One by Sam Smith

Blank Space by Taylor Swift

What's My Age Again by Blink-182

Party in the U.S.A. by Miley Cyrus

Still into You by Paramore

The Wind Cries Mary by Jimi Hendrix

The House of the Rising Sun by The Animals

Bed of Roses by Bon Jovi

Scar Tissue by Red Hot Chili Peppers

Just the Way You Are by Bruno Mars

HOW TO PLAY
SCALES
IN 1 DAY

The Only 7 Exercises You Need to Learn
Guitar Scales, Piano Scales and
Ukulele Scales Today

PRESTON HOFFMAN

BOOK 7

HOW TO PLAY SCALES: IN 1 DAY

The Only 7 Exercises You Need to Learn Guitar Scales, Piano Scales and Ukulele Scales Today

Preston Hoffman

Table of Contents

Introduction

Congratulations on purchasing *How to Play Scales* and thank you for doing so.

The following chapters will discuss how to play scales on piano and stringed instruments. It will explain the utility of scales as well as the underlying theory. More than that, it will teach you all of the scales that you need to know to be an improvisational master or to have a firm handle on your next composition.

If you're wanting to become an incredible musician, then this book is the place to start. If you practice the techniques in this book, then you can start from square one and make massive progress in as little as one day. The knowledge in this book is invaluable - I've attained all of it over years and years of musicianship. Now, I get to impart all of that wisdom that I've gained to you. My goal is to do so as efficiently as I possibly can while not compromising the educational worthiness of the book.

No matter whether you want to play piano, guitar, or learn the theory behind major scales so that you can apply them to any given instrument out there, this is the book for you. So read on to become a much better musician in absolutely no time flat.

There are plenty of books on this subject on the market, thanks again for choosing this one! Every effort was made to ensure it is full of as much useful information as possible, please enjoy!

Chapter 1: Exercise 1 - Understand the Theory

As somebody who wants to start learning the art of playing scales and improvising and having a greater musical knowledge in general, it's very possible that you have a misconception about how things exactly work in these contexts. Indeed, it's really easy for people who aren't as familiar with the fluidity of improvisation and musicality to really not have so much of a grasp on the reality of these things.

People who aren't as accustomed to music beyond simple chords or potentially even what they've heard on the radio tend to think that improvisation and mastering scales is very difficult. This isn't quite the case. It's a combination of two things: *feel* and *practice*. Feel is the big part. Over time, as you work more and more with your scales and learning your influences, you're going to gain a greater and greater appreciation for how things *should* sound.

This chapter isn't about the *feel*, though; this chapter is about the structure. The key to playing scales is to understanding the underlying musicality. The purpose of this chapter is to teach you several different things about music theory. There's a very good reason for this chapter: I'm a long-time music teacher, specializing in guitar. In my years teaching the guitar, I've had many people who come to me knowing a basic amount of the instrument, but when push comes to shove, they have little to no understanding of what everything they're doing actually amounts to. They can play chords, but they don't really know how chords *work* or why they're named like they are. If I ask them to tell me the practical difference between the A major and A minor chords, for example, they may go as far as to tell me that the chords are related but different, or they may just relate the two chords as "happy and sad", but sometimes they'll have no clue that the two chords are even related at all.

Would this stems from is a fundamental misunderstanding of music in general. There is nothing spontaneous in music. The spontaneity - and therefore the art - of music comes from the person creating it, but music itself is actually quite structured.

All of music can be broken down into sequences of notes. Notes are just a way of breaking sound down into chunks. To have a better understanding of what exactly I mean here, think of a siren going from a high note to a low note and back - although it may cycle through many different tones on the way up and down, it's actually just going through a sonic spectrum and manipulating soundwaves to produce different tones. Giving notes names is just a way of solidifying, identifying, partitioning, and breaking these sonic identities down into smaller chunks.

In the Western musical tradition, music is broken down into 8 distinct chunks which repeat themselves over and over: A, B, C, D, E, F, and G. Once you reach G, the cycle starts over again with A. This space between these two 8 notes is referred to as an *octave*.

If you were to look at a piano, you would see that there are black keys and white keys. These notes represent the white keys. If you look at a full 88 key piano, the lowest note on it is an A.

However, music is usually broken up with the C chromatic scale. I'll explain what this means in a second.

In the Western musical tradition, there is often a midpoint between two notes. These midpoints exist between the notes C and D, D and E, F and G, and A and B. If you will the midpoint *above* a note, you are playing the note's *sharp* variant. If you will the midpoint *below* a note, you are playing the note's *flat* variant. Flat means that a note is lower in tone than normal; sharp means that the note is higher in tone than normal. Flats are represented in music with a *b*, where sharps are represented in music with a #.

E and F, as well as B and C, do not have these steps between them. This is because the difference between these two notes is the same as the difference between A and A# or between F and F#. The difference between the two is really just a historical codification more than any meaningful musical differentiation.

The best explanation for the reason that things are this way is that most instruments in an orchestra will tune to the note C and for much of musical history, a large amount of music was written in C. The white keys on the piano represent the *natural C major scale*. So, in a manner of speaking, this all cropped up out of simple ease of writing and use.

The piano, and indeed most musical instruments in the Western tradition, are based off of the chromatic scale. What the chromatic scale is is the combination of all the primary divisions as well as the midway points between them. The chromatic scale in the Western tradition can be written out like so:

C, C#/Db, D, D#/Eb, E, F, F#/Gb, G, G#/Ab, A, A#/Bb, C

You'll notice that C#/Db, D#/Eb, and so forth are all the same notes. This is musically significant and something worth paying attention to. It's going to play a role in the rest of this book and the rest of your musical career as a whole.

The musical division between all of these notes is equivalent and is referred to as a half-step. If you were to first play a C then play a C#, the difference between those notes would be a half-step; the same applies for G# to A, for F to F#, and for B to C, as well as any other side-by-side set of notes in the chromatic scale just listed off.

If you're playing guitar, then the neck is divided into half-step frets. The same is true for ukeleles and pianos as well, though on pianos the half-steps are denoted by different keys.

Don't be confused, notes can be broken into smaller chunks - they could technically be broken down into millionth-step variations, though that would be long before there was any sort of discernible tonal difference between the notes. In the Western musical tradition, the most notes will ever be broken down is generally into quarter-tones, and even then, this is extremely, extremely rare; these pieces are generally very rarely performed and are equally rarely composed for the reason that it's just impractical for the vast majority of instruments (it requires special guitars and pianos, for instance), or takes an extreme amount of ear training and vigilance on others (violins and violas can play quarter tones with ease, but the difference is difficult to discern, often.)

A difference of two half-steps is referred to as a *whole* step. Whole steps are the difference between any two white keys separated by a black key on a piano, or two frets on a guitar. It's also the difference from Bb to C or Eb to F on a piano.

The chords you play are based upon combinations of notes. These notes are based upon intervals built upon those that we've already discussed. They can take several different forms.

If you're a pianist, then you already understand this in a basic way; however, this may improve your understanding of the underlying concept, or perhaps even cement what is *actually* going on from a theoretical standpoint.

Every chord has a root. This goes without saying. This root is called such because it's what every other interval built into the chord is built off of.

The chords, from the root, will then form different shapes based off of exactly what you're trying to do or convey. The neat thing is that a lot of the time, these musical concepts will stack on top of one another.

These shapes are like so:

Major chords, which are traditionally "happy" chords. These chords are the ones that you play when you want to impart a *positive* emotion. However, in other contexts, they can create a bittersweet feeling or, with the right lyrical setting, even create an eerie feeling.

Minor chords, which are traditionally "sad" chords. However, due to the prevalent of folk music, minor chords have started to take a more ambivalent nature and be useful in other contexts. This is another case where lyrical content and delivery can make a huge difference in the overall tone of the song.

Diminished chords, which are "spooky" chords. These chords in more mature contexts aren't used in a spooky way, though; instead, they're usually used to bridge two other chords.

Augmented chords, which are "spacious" chords. Augmented chords have a very ethereal feel and have been traditionally used as a means of conveying a sense of space; they're frequently used as a bridge to other chords and are increasingly rare.

Suspended chords, which are "glorious" chords. These chords are typically used in conjunction with their major or minor origin chord as a compelling intracordal melodic line.

Starting with these chords, we're going to build up an understanding of the workings and theory of chord voicings before moving onto other chord forms. Let's start with a major chord.

All major chords are formed in the same exact manner. First, you take the root. From there, you build the chord. All chords are composed in this manner, actually. The chord is built from corresponding interval chords. The major chord, in particular, is built off of the *root*, the *third*, and the *fifth*. The *third* is the note two whole tones away from the root note, and the *fifth* is the note four whole tones away from the root note.

Let's take the chord C major, for example. First, think about it in terms of a chromatic scale.

C, C#/Db, D, D#/Eb, E, F, F#/Gb, G, G#/Ab, A, A#/Bb, B, C

The root will be C. Now, from C count up two whole tones:

C, C#/Db, D, D#/Eb, *E*

.5   1   1.5   2

This tells us that *E* is the third interval of C. It is actually referred to as the tonic *perfect third*. The perfect third refers always to an interval of two whole tones.

We could repeat the process from E, counting two more whole tones, or count four whole tones from C to find that the tonic *perfect fifth* of C is G.

The major chord is composed of the *root*, the *perfect third*, and the *perfect fifth*. Taking all of this into account, we can say that C major is definitively C, E, and G.

This holds true regardless of what instrument you play it on. On pianos, you play a C by playing C, E, and G, regardless of what order these notes are put together in on the keyboard. (This leads to the musical concept of inversions, which is a little beyond the scope of this book.)

On guitars, if you were to look at the exact notes played when you play an open C chord, you would say that they were C, E, G, C, and E again.

On ukuleles, the same applies.

To form minor chords, you took the root, the third, and the perfect fifth. However, instead of playing the *perfect* third, you play the *flat* third. This means the interval of 1 and a half whole tones from C. This is the flat version of the perfect fifth. So instead of being C, E, and G, the notes would be C, Eb, and G. This would explain why on guitar, it's hard to play a C minor in open position - the open *E* string would clash with the Eb, creating a chord without a resolute center.

On diminished chords, you use a flat fifth as well as a flat third. On augmented chords, you use a perfect third and a raised (sharp) fifth. On suspended chords, you either raise the third or lower the third by a whole step.

There are also other chords which are additions to these chords, like seventh, ninth, and eleventh chords. To form these chords, all that you do is add the note of the corresponding interval. For example, for a seventh chord, you would add the perfect seventh - which, following the pattern, is the chord which is six whole tones from the root note. For C7, that would be the corresponding Bb.

The major seventh is the chord which uses a raised seventh, so something like C, E, G, and B.

The trend would continue for 9th chords, 11th chords, and so on.

The logic of chords is relatively simple, but it's paramount to understanding what happens within the next chapter.

Chapter 2: Exercise 2 - "Playing" within Chords - Your First Scale

This chapter is based on the idea of playing within chords. When you play with scales, whether there is a background for the melody or not, you still are playing within chords *tonally*. Chords provide the central basis and foundation for everything else that you'll be doing in music.

Every song has a key. The key is the center around which the rest of the song is based. For example, a song with the chords C, F, and G would be based around C. This creates a chord progression. Chord progressions are based on the major scale and are the corresponding tonalities.

Major chords have corresponding *relative minors*. Relative minors are minor chords which have a different root but incorporate the root and perfect third of the major chord as the flat third and perfect fifth of the minor chord. For example, take C major again. C, E, and G are the chord's notes. A minor would be the relative minor of C major because it uses the root and the third of C major in the construction of the minor chord.

In this specific chapter, we're going to be discussing the *pentatonic scale*. The pentatonic scale is so named primarily because it only has 5 different notes - therefore, *penta* (5) *tonic* (tones).

The pentatonic scale is based around the relative minor of a given major chord or can be played in exact key of any given minor chord.

If a song is in A minor, for example, you can play the pentatonic scale in the key of A, and it will work out fine. If it is in A *major*, however, you will need to find the relative minor to play the scale to the key.

On the guitar, this will be essential to building an understanding of basic scale structure as well as the way that scales "flow." On the piano, this will be essential to building a sense of memory in terms of what keys are played in what musical keys. It is equally important to learn on piano as it is on guitar or any other stringed instrument because, while the piano is more "connected," and scales flow more naturally and intuitively on the piano (especially when practicing proper piano technique, since scales on piano tend to happen within the context of complimentary melody lines, arpeggiated chords, and so forth), you won't have nearly as much of a bearing on what to play and when if you don't try to pin down what to do with your hands. Doing pentatonic runs on the piano is a fantastic way to grasp the shell of the chord. Additionally, you can do pentatonic runs on the first five notes of the natural scale - we'll go over this in the chapter on modes.

The important thing to remember when playing scales on a stringed instrument is that your hands generally will take a certain position. For example, on the guitar, most scales will be played with your hand in the general area of the scale (in the proper key) and won't move much at all. What I mean by this is that if you're playing a Dorian in A, your hand will be at the fifth fret, finding its home there - generally, at least for simple scale runs, you aren't going to be moving your hand up and down the neck to reach new notes. The only exception comes for when a note is one fret behind the root fret. In this case, it is acceptable to shift the hand down one fret to hit the necessary notes, then shift back to your home position.

This isn't a stagnant rule, of course; the purpose of this book, as you'll learn later, is to teach you to allow music to flow. Getting stuck within rigidities of scales is a good way to halt your ability to grow musically. If you listen to great musicians like Steve Vai or the flowing compositions of Debussy, you'll notice that they don't stay in one position the entire time. Rather, they let their compositions flow all over the available range of the instrument. This is a skill that will come with time, experience, and experimentation. Don't get into the habit of letting yourself be stagnant. Even when you're doing scale runs, do what you can to train yourself to let it flow. Notes shouldn't escape rigidly from your fingers. They should be spoken through them - with intention, tenderness, and above all, honesty.

Music, once you allow it to speak through you, escalates from something standard and inhibitory to something intuitive and expressive. This, too, is the honest truth of playing scales on the guitar and piano. Scale runs go a long way as far as learning the structure of the scales and music itself goes, but music is a very fluid language, and it's through scales that you learn this fluidity. That will become clearer later on in the book, but I digress. The key point is that your hand, at first, will be in position to play at the given key.

So now that we've said all of that - what exactly *is* the pentatonic scale? Well, the primary variation of the pentatonic scale is like so: you start off with the root note. From here, you go up three half steps. For example, this would be the distance from A to C. From here, you go up a whole step, from C to D. Then another whole step from D to E. Then, you go up another three half-steps from E to G. Lastly, you hit the A again, another whole step, before coming back down. The sequence on the A minor pentatonic would be like so: A, C, D, E, G, A, G, E, D, C, A.

This translates to any minor chord. You'll just have to do the necessary changes, remembering to follow 3 half steps, whole step, whole step, half step, whole step, then the return.

This is often extended into another octave. This is especially common on guitars. On the guitar, the A minor pentatonic run is seen as A, C, D, E, G, A, C, D, E, G, A, C - then the return. This is played on the following frets:

```
e  |   -5-8-

B  |   -5-8-

G  |   -5-7-

D  |   -5-7-

A  |   -5-7-

E  |   -5-8-
```

If, instead, you were trying to play the *C minor* pentatonic scale, you would follow the same pattern but shift everything up 3 half-steps so that the root was C rather than A. On the guitar, this would imply playing on the 8th fret.

This should also solidify what I said earlier about the hand position on the guitar being relatively stable. Later in the book, when exact scale tabs aren't given (this isn't entirely a guitar scale book, after all), this lesson should remain intact. If you ever have to move your hand more than a fret to reach a note, reconsider the way that you're playing the scale and see if you're missing an equivalent but an easier way to play it. This is quite easy to do when you're just working with theoretical notation. However, at the same time, it's also an important lesson on the levity of playing. A note in one position is, on stringed instruments, a note in another. This means that it's really easy to create long and flowing melodic lines that sound much like something you would hear from a piano. This sort of concept is what allowed things like *Cliffs of Dover* by Eric Johnson to exist - not just an awareness of the fact that a note in one position is a note in another, nor the fact that he had spent a vast amount of his life up until the initial recording practicing scales, but rather the synthesis of these two things in addition to the fact that he's *aware* of how to manipulate these factors to create sprawling sonic landscapes. While a large part of the ability to do such a thing comes through in talent, an even larger part comes through internalization of the fact that music is as music is, and you are enabled through your knowledge to access the sonic springboard of the guitar and propel it forward.

In other words, this is only the beginning. Here, you need to work on the concept of understanding the concept of relative minors and how to find them. You also need to be working on the pentatonic scale. Also, the largest part of getting something useful out of scales - beyond just playing them and practicing them as they are, which is also important - is to flex your creative muscles and attempt to do something with the scales in question. It is through creating things that you'll really be able to cement the concepts that you're working with. It also will allow you to emulate some of the things you'll be working on in the next chapter. Don't worry - I know it seems like you still haven't learned much, but we're teaching heavy concepts in these initial chapters to get all of the heavy liftings out of the way for the later chapters.

In the following chapter, we're going to discuss that essential idea of internalizing the music and becoming a creative musician. This is yet another extremely important lesson to learn that is simple enough in concept but surprisingly difficult to make happen.

Chapter 3: Exercise 3 - Having a Feeling for the Music

This chapter is relatively simple in essence, but it's of the utmost importance to really start to grasp. Indeed, developing a feel for the music is emblematic of everything that this book stands for. The most important thing that you're going to need to do musically is to develop a real and honest understanding of not necessarily how things *should* sound, but rather how to get the sound in your head out of your fingers and into the world.

This is one of the hardest skills to develop musically. Every time that you play a song, you do so with some idea of how you're wanting it to sound. Musicians are innately creative people, and the ability to create a melody out of thin air is the hallmark of truly creative people - natural musicians if you will. The type of people who would pick up this book, generally, are of that same class of people: the natural musicians who are interested in learning how to produce the sounds that they're hearing internally.

To be honest, while memorizing scales is extremely important, there are underlying concepts to scales that you'll be carrying with you through all of them, regarding tonality and musical "movement." These are things that you're simply going to be internalizing through time, practice, and work.

For example, on the guitar, there's a movement pattern that happens on the neck which is extremely difficult to *explain* and can vary depending upon the needs of the song, but it's certainly there. It's something along the lines of:

2-4-5-7-9-10-12

With those being the given frets. However, those can be a little bit more difficult to pinpoint - for example, in a song in Eb, everything would be shifted up one fret. If the song were in G, you could play it exactly as is, as well as if the song were in B minor, but if the song were in A minor, you'd have to make small changes like 2-3-5 instead of 2-4-5.

This is, of course, not the end all be all of the musicality. There's a lot more to music than just this simple axiom, and there are even ways to build upon this. In fact, this is just a smaller part of another scale. However, the key lesson is that over time you build up an intuitive feeling for what you *should* play and what you *want* to play based on a combination of the scales that you've studied and the work that you'd done with other songs.

So how do you build up this sense? It's relatively simple. The first way to build up this sense is by finding songs with guitar parts that you *want* to play. This can vary depending upon your musical taste, but it's almost certain that there's at least one artist that you like who has a confident guitarist (or *is* a guitarist) who will create intuitive guitar lines.

With piano parts and ukulele parts, you can do much the same - however, with ukulele, you may have to do a musical note-for-note conversion of other melodies that you've heard. The key and crux here is that you don't rely on chords so much and begin to rely on melody in addition to chords. This concept of

incorporating melodies with chords will come especially useful
when you start to work with jazz music because jazz music very
much incorporates both chords and melody extremely
intrinsically.

The entire point of all of these exercises is to help you to
develop an idea of what you *should be playing*. This sense
doesn't come naturally to everybody. Even natural musicians
need to train their ear. This exercise will teach you to listen to
melodies and make sense of them musically by playing along.
You'll subconsciously learn how to do the things that other
people are doing if you listen to the melodies that they're making
and you make them for yourself.

Chapter 4: Exercise 4 - Practicing Improv with the Blues

In the last chapter, we spent a bit discussing the importance of being able to "feel" the music and play along with what you're hearing and feeling. There is no genre of music where this is more important than the blues, and there is no style of music that will better solidify all of the many different concepts that we've worked with so far than the blues, likewise.

However, there's an even bigger reason that this is an important exercise and will remain important as the book goes on. While blues is, sure, somewhat of a guitar-centric improvisational genre, blues improvisation is enough of a wide gamut that many different instruments can hold their own while soloing. Additionally, there is no other genre that will allow you to so seamlessly combine all of the elements we'll be working on in this book, either; in other words, while there are many different genres where you can center yourself upon a certain sound, there are few genres that - going forward, at least - will allow you to use all of the different influences that we're going to talk about in this book with so little genre clashing.

More than anything else, though, it's really difficult to pinpoint how much practical skill you gain while practicing to blues tracks; you get their opportunity to really work on your technique and experiment with different solo structures, as well as learn what sounds good and what doesn't.

Moreover, if your goal, in the end, is to learn some scales, then there is no better way to do so than by drilling them over and over by practicing them through improvisation.

In this chapter, we're going to discuss one small change to the pentatonic scale - which will ultimately serve more as an addition to it than a change per se - which will take the important pentatonic scale that you've already learned and give it a different bent that allows you to do a little bit more with it.

If you look back at the pentatonic scale, you'll remember that it followed a pattern - root, then flat third, then perfect fourth, then perfect fifth, then perfect seventh, then the octave. The standard pentatonic blues scale takes this same exact pattern but adds in the flat fourth. This, in essence, makes it hexatonic. I digress, though.

The example of the A minor pentatonic blues scale on a guitar would be like so:

```
e  |  -5-8---

B  |  -5-8---

G  |  -5-7-8-

D  |  -5-7---

A  |  -5-6-7-

E  |  -5-8---
```

On a piano, you would simply add a D# in between the D and E. And just like any other scale, this is movable, and you can play it anywhere on the neck with zero issues.

So, what exactly does this teach us about scales and music? The biggest thing is that musical standards are created reactively - not the other way around. This change between the pentatonic scale and the pentatonic blues scale didn't occur as a result of somebody saying "this is the way that we're going to play this scale in blues music" - it happened as the result of the natural evolution of the pentatonic scale and the way to make it fit within blues music. They made the scale fit the music, rather than the other way around. This became so ubiquitous that it now is considered the standard blues scale.

However, this also teaches us something else: you are allowed to add flavor to the music, and you are allowed to make it your own. For example, it was not heard of for Stevie Ray

Vaughan to include the perfect second alongside the rest of the scale, like so:

```
e  |  -5-7-8-

B  |  -5-8---

G  |  -5-7-8-

D  |  -5-7---

A  |  -5-6-7-

E  |  -5-7-8-
```

By now, we have a very distended version of the pentatonic scale that we were working on. The key to understanding this, though, is understanding that what is going on with the scale is indeed reflective of that lesson I was trying to communicate earlier: music is simply music. Notes are as they are, and there is little rigidness to it. Look at the underlying notes in the above scale: A, B, C, D, Eb, E, G, A.

Also look at the context of the scale. This is the A minor pentatonic scale. So what notes are in the A minor chord? A, C, and E - there's a basic starting point. However, we can also use other pleasant harmonies, such as those of seventh, ninth, and eleventh chords to give us a greater texture. If you take this into account, then Am7 would have the notes A, C, E, and G. Am9 would have the notes A, C, E, and high B. You could also form the suspended fourth version of A minor with the notes A, C, D, and E. Meanwhile, you could do the suspended second version by voicing the B - yielding A, B, C, and E.

This yields us A, B, C, D, E, and G for voicings which are all yielding valid chord voicings when taken in tandem with the A minor. This also matches up to our scale - all except for Eb. So what is Eb doing? Well, The flat fifth in the pentatonic blues scale is typically treated as a bridge note. What this means is that the note is hardly ever played on its own. Rather, it's treated as a means to give color to the licks which are played and used to connect two other notes.

Ultimately, there is a simple lesson to be taken away from this: scales are malleable. However, they are also very important to practice. You can't bend the rules that you don't know.

Another lesson to take away from all of this is the way that scales and the notes of chords work together. If we go back to the Stevie Ray Vaughan reference, remember what I was saying about him sometimes adding in the perfect second before the flat third?

It also wouldn't have been unreasonable for him to do a continuation of the scale like so:

```
e  |  -5-8-10-12-

B  |  -5-8--------

G  |  -5-7-8------

D  |  -5-7--------

A  |  -5-6-7------

E  |  -0-3-5-8----
```

Why is this? What makes this allowable?

Well, the answer to this is simple. When you're playing piano, it's obvious, but on other instruments, it isn't always so simple or apparent. The simple answer is this: scales don't stand for a single place to play chords. They simply mean that these notes will work in *this* context for *this* sound. Because this is the implication of scales in general, we aren't stranded between our fifth and eighth frets when we are playing in the key of A minor. Since the scale has the notes E and G as well, it's totally reasonable to drop below the lowest note of the fifth fret pentatonic scale and hit the third-fret G and the open E string.

In other words: every chord has notes, and every scale uses some of these notes (as well as others, often, as you'll learn in the next chapter) to give a musical playground, and this playground will span as far as the notes do - and notes span far much more than an octave. One of the most important lessons that you can learn is looking at the chords that you're working with and working within the framework of those chords to pick the right scales, intuitively know what notes to play, and also develop a fine sense of how scales complement chords.

So how can you solidify all of the stuff that you've worked on in this chapter? The best way is to go to YouTube and look up blues backing tracks. There is a huge number available for you to play on there. They will have the key in the name of the title, generally. Just turn on a backing track and start improvising on it. This is the best way to memorize your scales, on top of rote memorization and scale runs.

Chapter 5: Exercise 5 - Learning Modes (Exotic, Classical, and Metal)

In this chapter, we're going to start the process of learning all about modes. Modes are one of the greatest ways to add a new dimension of color and beauty to your playing. We'll start this chapter by discussing what exactly a mode is.

There are many ways in which a mode is no different from a scale. Actually, a mode is just a relation of different notes that can be moved up and down the neck. There are many different kinds of modes - after all, modes just refer to the specific idea of movable scalar phrasings. However, at the same time, when one refers to modes, they are generally referring to the modes of the natural major scale.

This lesson won't apply so much on piano where the scales are innately movable. However, on stringed instruments such as the guitar and ukulele, learning modes is of paramount importance. The biggest reason to learn modes is that they're innately interconnected. When you learn to play modes, as well as become practice with them enough so that you can move them all over the neck and play them in any position, as well as make essential connections between them through things such as glissandos, hammer-ons, and other clever ways of transition to different places on the neck, you gain a special ability: the ability to play stringed instruments like a piano.

I'm sure that at some point, you've heard some absolutely insane guitarist play notes all over the neck as though they were just spreading glitter all over the guitar. Believe it or not, what they're doing isn't very *difficult* in reality. It's more of an issue of a long time of careful practice and reinforcing essential concepts. However, musical notes are musical notes, and there is most definitely a way to get a similar amount of melodic flexibility out of a guitar or ukulele that you could out of a piano, and perhaps even greater at times.

Playing modes on a ukulele can be a little difficult because the ukulele has a bizarre tuning that, frankly, isn't meant for playing scales. However, you can pretty easily learn the underlying concepts, at least, and attempt to transfer those to your ukulele playing.

The important thing to remember is that the natural modes are just variations on the same exact notes. What essentially happens with every mode is that the root note of the mood is shifted. When this happens, the rest of the notes must shift as well to compensate, of course. What this means is that you can find a place to play the same set of notes anywhere on the neck in a systematic manner rather than slowing yourself down by thinking about which notes are in the scale you're playing and what note you're playing on the neck, as well as what note you want to play next.

Additionally, on a personal level, I've often found - at least for myself - that modes have a really unique sound, all of them. Every different modes will have different sounds. For example, the Mixolydian mode and the Dorian mode, despite being in the same key, will have diametrically different sounds. The

Mixolydian mode sounds a fair bit brighter than the Dorian does, where the Dorian mode sounds more stately and reserved.

Modes work in a somewhat similar way to factorial math functions. What happens between modes is that you take your initial scale. Every subsequent progression of the mode will use the second note of the preceding mode as the root note of that specific mode progression's root note.

Take, for example, the natural C major scale: C, D, E, F, G, A, B, C.

The first degree of the mode, mode I (C Ionian) is the progression of these notes, plain and simple. However, the second degree of the mode would start off with the note D - D, E, F, G, A, B, C, D. The third degree of the mode would start off with E - E, F, G, A, B, C, D, E.

To start understanding modes, we need to start with a new sort of notation that we haven't really covered in this book. This will allow us to speak about scales in a more abstract manner for this chapter and the next, where things can start to be a little strange and scary (especially in the jazz scales chapter.)

Essentially, every scale is just a collection of notes and their respective intervals. This allows you to think of scales in a bit of a different way than you likely have been already. Where the pentatonic scales had only 5 notes and had too large of intervals for this method to be practical, most other scales move in smaller intervals. It's for this reason that scales will now be notated based upon the order of these intervals. This will also make it easier for you to translate to you respective instrument.

The way that this will work is that, for any given scale, the root note will be implied - from the root, you will take the next stated interval (either a half-step or whole step).

On guitars, take the path of least resistance. What I mean by this is that if you have to significantly move your hand from a given fret position, then you likely aren't playing the scale sequence correctly. For modes, there should generally not ever be more than 3 notes per string. To help you understand modes better, I'll show depictions of the way that the scale is played on guitar. For piano, just follow the mode line through each version until you need it - it would not be doable to have every single mode in every key in this book.

Allow me to explain this a bit better - I'm going to go over the Ionian mode using this notation method. Take the Ionian mode and assume it's in the key of C. Your root, therefore, would be C. The next note would be D - this is a whole step. This would be notated as *whole*. The next note is E. This, too, is a whole step, so this would also be notated as *whole*. The following note is F, and the difference between E and F is a half-step, so this would be a half-step. Therefore, this would be notated as *half*. This would carry on until the end of the scale.

Ionian: root, whole, whole, half, whole, whole, whole, half

This would work out to C, D, E, F, G, A, B, and C again, respectively.

Remember that mode degrees shift up. So for a song in the key of C, the next degree after the Ionian mode would have its root in D, even though the song is in C.

Here are the natural modes:

Ionian - root, whole, whole, half, whole, whole, whole, half

Dorian (second mode) - root, whole, half, whole, whole, whole, half, whole

Phrygian (third mode) - root, half, whole, whole, whole, half, whole, whole

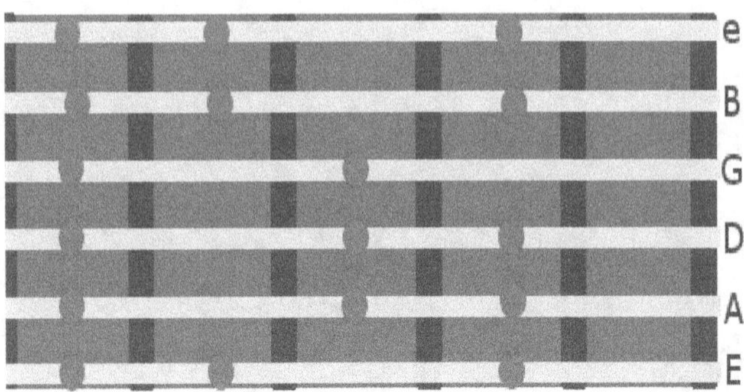

Lydian (fourth mode) - root, whole, whole, whole, half, whole, whole, half

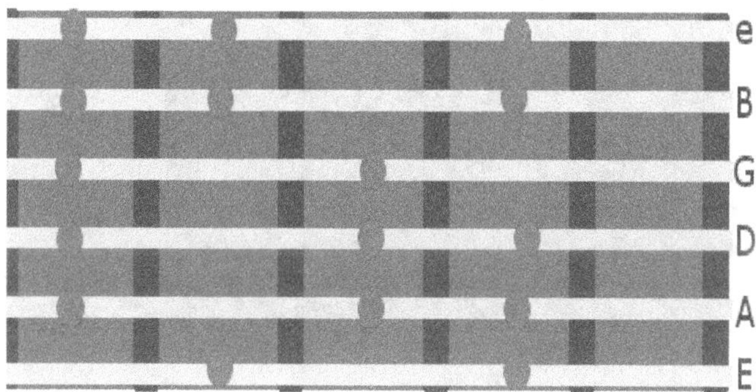

Mixolydian (fifth mode) - root, whole, whole, half, whole, whole, half, whole

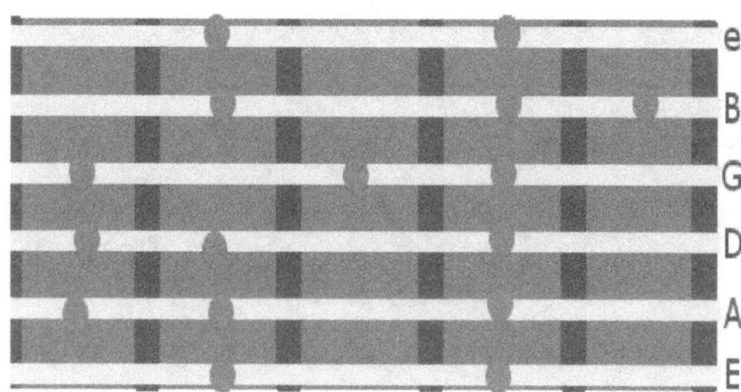

Aeolian (sixth mode) - root, whole, half, whole, whole, half, whole, whole

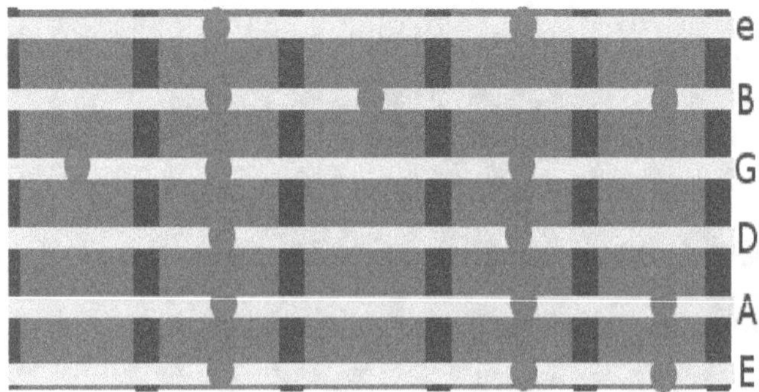

Locrian (seventh mode) - root, half, whole, whole, half, whole, whole, whole

Memorization of these modes is essential if you'd like to progress as a player of whatever your instrument may be. They will open up your playing by leaps and bounds. As you go further, you'll start to see how they all connect and link together.

Chapter 6: Learning Jazz Scales (and Why Jazz is Hard)

This is the most intimidating chapter to tackle in this entire book and is likewise one of the most difficult things that you'll be tackling as somebody trying to grasp scales. Throughout this whole book, I've been saying over and over that one of the most important things that you can do for yourself is try to internalize chords and music and the way that scales work off of chords. There's no genre for which this is truer than jazz.

Jazz is one of the easiest genres to improvise to, and one of the hardest - if not the hardest - to improvise too intelligently. There's an old joke among musicians that improvising to jazz is easy because if you miss a note, you can just hit it a few more times to make it sound intentional. This is only a joke, of course - if you actually try to do this, your fellow jazz musicians won't take you seriously. However, at the same time, the joke itself is based upon the notion that jazz scales and jazz improvisation can be a bit arbitrary.

And the fact is that there's a little bit of truth to this statement. Of course, you should never intentionally try to shoot for this (unless it's the vogue of what you're doing, like if you're playing free jazz.) However, it does unintentionally happen sometimes. Why is this?

The simple fact is that jazz is just incredibly and unbelievably musically complex. It's musically complex to the point that it's hard to really ascertain how complex it really is without a firm grasp on music in the first place.

The point of jazz music is for it to flow naturally and rhythmically. This means that chords, often, are a flurry of notes rather than concrete structures. Instead of crisp major chords, there are often floaty major 7th chords or sharp m7b11 chords. Chords are used as individual voicings instead of broad phrasings. It is, in this capacity, a furthering of classical composition in the modern area - though its heavy use of motif betrays it to modernity, the lasting impression of diverse composition stays intact. Jazz has an incredible amount of musical rigor behind it.

Since chords are used as broad-stroked voicings and as flowy musical statements rather than as simple boxes that everything else fits within, very, very complex chord voicings are often formed. These voicings are much harder to play within than, say, a chord progression of Am, C, G, D. This is because where these voicings have a relatively finite structure to them, jazz chords are *not* finite. That's not to say they're infinite - rather that they use notes and chord voicings in ways that other kinds of music simply don't.

This creates a strange situation where a lot of the times where something that would sound good in a simpler context - for example, a pentatonic blues scale against a normal C minor (Cm) would sound fantastic, but when you change the voicing drastically so that it's a Cm7b5#11 will cause the pentatonic scale to now sound horrible, or at the very least, it will drastically increase the odds of you playing a "wrong" note, which can throw the entire solo off kilter.

So what can you do to alleviate this situation? Well, there are two things that you have to do. The first is to simply practice, try and fail, and overall immerse yourself. If you There is no way to really get better and to start to adjust to the intensity and difficulty of jazz improvisation without really spending a lot of time doing it.

However, the other thing that you have to do is to really take a bit to try to learn what situations that you should play certain scales over. As you work more and more with jazz improvisation and jazz scales in general, this will make more sense.

So, the first situation to discuss is with scales we've already talked about. First and foremost, the modes. There's an entire subgenre of jazz dedicated to modal improvisation known as modal jazz. The modes are also the typical scales used to improvise over any other form of jazz. Just like with anything else, their use will be situational. Refer back to the former chapter if you're confused as to when to use something. With these scales, you should play them with the root of the given mode matching the chord. For example, if the chord is Am7, since the Dorian mode fits well over minor seventh chords, you can play the Dorian mode with the root on A. (Meaning on the fifth fret, if you're playing guitar.)

First off, you should use the Ionian mode when you're playing major sevenths.

You can play the Lydian mode over major seventh chords as well, in addition to any other voicings of major sevenths.

The Mixolydian mode will fit well over dominant seventh chords.

If you'll recall, the difference between dominant seventh chords and major seventh chords is that the dominant seventh chord utilizes a flat seventh while the major seventh utilizes a perfect seventh.

Lastly, the Locrian will fit well over chords with a flat fifth and a flat third. Namely, minor seventh chords with a flat fifth.

Additionally, you'll find great use of the pentatonic scales we covered in the last chapter, too. You can use it, of course, of normal minor and major chords, but you can also use it to outline things like major sevenths and dominant sevenths.

If the music that you're playing has augmented chords, then you can bring out the tones in these by using the whole tone scale. This is exactly what it sounds like. It starts at the root and then is simply whole tones all the way up.

One new scale that we need to cover in this chapter is the half diminished scale. You can use this scale over half diminished chords, much like the Locrian mode. The half diminished scale is like so: whole, half, whole, half, whole, whole, whole.

Finally, the last scale that we need to cover in this chapter is the melodic minor scale. This differs from the normal minor scale in that it could be seen as the *minor scale of jazz*. In fact, this is what it's generally called. A lot of the time, when jazz music is played in a minor key, they'll opt for this over a traditional minor scale. You'll find that this plays rather similarly to the Dorian mode; however, the primary difference is that it's written as a major seventh as opposed to a minor seventh. This one is yet another really important one.

The piano progression would be like so:
Root, whole, half, whole, whole, whole, whole

And here is the guitar chord which corresponds to it:

Because of all the nuances and the different chords, a different mode or scale is probably going to sound better or worse from chord change to chord change. This can be frustrating to deal with. On the other hand, since these usually are intended to bring out the colors in the chord voicings, if you have a decent handle on the underlying chords, then you should have very little difficulty at all trying to play over the chords.

Really, the biggest thing that will catch you in jazz improvisation and jazz scales, in general, is the fact that sometimes, you're not 100% sure what the chords you're playing to are. This is where you really need to develop a sense for your instrument and how to get the sounds that you're wanting out. Don't worry, though - if you practice everything in this book, you'll get to that point with no problems.

Chapter 7: Exercise 7 - Putting It Together

This chapter is about synthesizing all of the things that we've talked about before to develop a really unique and personalized style of playing. It can be pretty difficult to do at first. But that's okay! You aren't trying to do it, at first. At first, you're only trying to make something coherent.

So when I say synthesizing everything that we've covered, what exactly do I mean? I mean that we've covered a lot of different things in this book. At the very least, we've discussed different scales and how you can use them - pentatonic scales and modes will end up being of the utmost importance as you carry on, regardless of whether all of the jazz scales we talked about come in handy or not. If you're trying to learn scales, it's because you understand that there's something truly essential about them as a musician, and that's the truth. There *is* something essential. So what is that something?

That something is the underlying knowledge that learning scales gives you. If you're coming into this book as a pianist, you have a very different road ahead of you than somebody who plays a string instrument. For example, as a pianist, you have the task of memorizing which notes make up which scales. (Though, hopefully, the things we've discussed already will do an able job of explaining all of that.) As a string instrumentalist, you only have to memorize the general shape of the scales and then transpose them to whatever instrument you're trying to play. This is a very different experience, but they both have a commonality:

the fact that making use of these things requires a basic knowledge of music theory and why things work the way they do in music.

It's not magic that certain scales sound good over certain chords - that's just the science of music. It's exactly how it should be!

So what can you do going forward? The first thing that you need to be doing is *applying* all of this. Firstly, try playing other people's music. As long as it has your respective instrument in it, you're fine. Pay close attention to when people are trying to utilize the various things that you've learned in this book. You should have an easier time picking certain scales out of a line-up, now, for certain.

And then there's the second thing: practice the scales in this book. Practice them every day until you know them by memory. It shouldn't take that long to have them all fully memorized. You can go through this entire book in one day and learn everything that's inside with minimal difficulty. After that, it's just about remembering everything that you learned. Therefore, just like anything else, the best way to remember what you've learned is by reinforcing it through use.

That brings me to my third point: a bit earlier in the book, I mentioned that you should find blues backing tracks on YouTube and play along with them. You should just start doing that in general, at this point, though. Jump from genre to genre and try to play along with the songs in question by improvising to solidify everything that you've learned.

The hardest thing is to realize that although there is often a simple answer in the name of a scale, what it all comes back to is what music *sounds* good. This means that after a while of creating melodies, you're

Over time, what you will find is that you come up with your own manner of mixing all of these influences that you've developed over the course of your life on top of all of the things that you've learned while playing other people's songs. What this will result in is you naturally developing your own method of playing your respective instrument.

Getting to this point will take a while, though. Just relax and settle in for the ride and enjoy it.

Another thing that you'll notice, if you haven't already from playing other people's songs, is that it's quite rare that scales just exist on their own, especially when it comes to the piano or stringed instruments. Sure, occasionally people will do single-note runs on their respective instrument (namely jazz guitarists, whose entire part in a song may consist of a single note compliment), but the vast majority of the time, people are interspersing their knowledge of scales with other things like chords.

In other words, there are a lot of different techniques and nuances that come into play that will exceed just knowing and using scales. This book's goal has been to teach you the scales, but it will be up to you to put in the practice to make something cool and meaningful with them.

The thing to take home from all of this if you're playing piano is that a lot of it comes down to the fact that, well, *notes are notes*. There will be a lot of overlap between these scales, and it won't always be clear which one you should be playing either. Let me be frank: the point of scales is not to give you a framework to work within. Rather, the point of scales is to give you the tools to make the sound in your head come out. As long as the scales help you to do such, then the overlap shouldn't be an issue at all.

If you're learning guitar or another stringed instrument, you should work on linking your scales. For example, in most situations where you will play a minor pentatonic, you can also add a splash of the Dorian mode and have it work out perfectly. Don't be afraid to slide and move around the neck, either - remember, the instrument is your playground.

Conclusion

Thank you for making it through to the end of *How to Play Scales*, let's hope it was informative and able to provide you with all of the tools you need to achieve your goals whatever it may be.

The next step is to do everything that I've said, practice, and create.

Creating is the biggest step of all. Whether you're trying to improvise to other music or just have a better idea of what you're doing when you're making music, everything in this book becomes practically useless if you aren't using it to create. Just like when you're learning a language, you have to speak to remember what you're doing, you must do the same in music. Scales are their own sort of language. If you don't use them, you will forget them. Don't worry; as I said in the last chapter, eventually you will develop your own style, and it will come naturally to you. However, you absolutely have to put in the work to get to that point.

Let me be clear - music is not easy to make for ninety-nine percent of people. Everything in this book will take work; there is no "easy" way to learn scales and modes. With that said, if you take the time to practice them every day and learn more music and identify what you learned while learning, in addition to taking time to improvise and create your own compositions, then you can make a ton of progress. You can work your way through all of the scales in this book and have an extremely solid foundation in music theory in just one day. What you do after that is up to you. It will take time and dedication to not only be able to play the scales but to use them properly and effectively.

At the start of the book, I said that I wanted to impart some of the knowledge that I've gained in my time as a musician to you. I sincerely hope that I've succeeded in accomplishing this goal. If you found that this book helped you to understand this otherwise-intimidating topic, then I'd really appreciate it if you left me a review and rating. Feedback helps me to produce quality content.

I'd like to wish you the best of luck one last time on your musical adventure. Thank you for reading this book.

More by Preston Hoffman

Discover all books from the Music Best Seller Series by Preston Hoffman at:

bit.ly/preston-hoffman

Book 1: *Music Theory*

Book 2: *How to Read Music*

Book 3: *How to Play Guitar*

Book 4: *How to Play Ukulele*

Book 5: *How to Play Piano*

Book 6: *How to Play Chords*

Book 7: *How to Play Scales*

Themed book bundles available at discounted prices:

bit.ly/preston-hoffman